W9-BCS-487

The FUTURE Is OURS

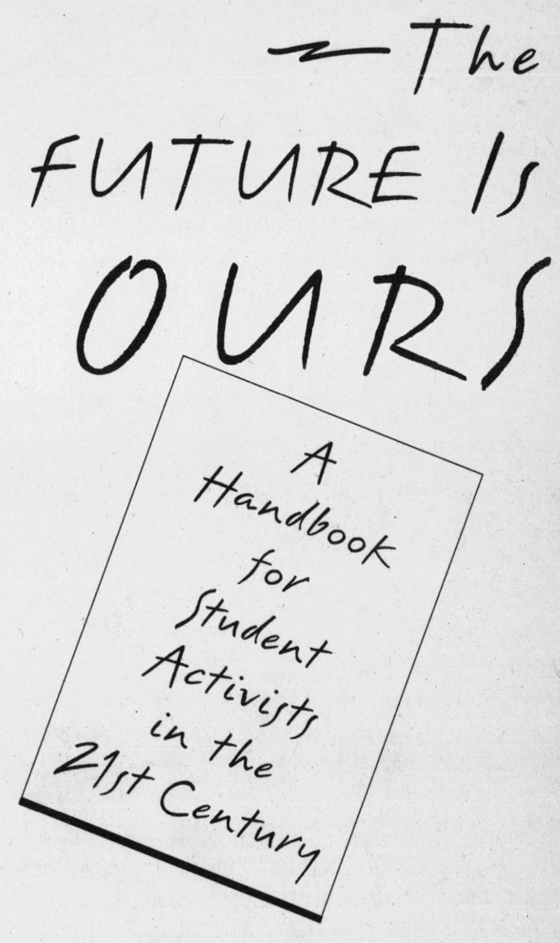

Edited by John W. Bartlett

An Owl Book

Henry Holt and Company / New York

The publisher gratefully acknowledges permission to reprint the following excerpts:

Excerpt from *Silent Spring* by Rachel Carson. Copyright © 1962 by Rachel L. Carson, renewed 1990 by Roger Christie. Reprinted by permission of Houghton Mifflin Company. All rights reserved.

Excerpt from "Declaration of Independence from the War in Vietnam" by Martin Luther King, Jr. Reprinted by arrangement with The Heirs to the Estate of Martin Luther King, Jr., c/o Writers House, Inc., as agent for the proprietor. Copyright © 1967 Martin Luther King.

Excerpt from "Reveille for Radicals" by Saul Alinsky. Copyright © 1974 by Saul D. Alinsky, renewed by Irene M. Alinsky. Reprinted by permission of Random House, Inc.

Excerpt from *Earth in the Balance* by Al Gore. Copyright © 1992 by Senator Al Gore. Reprinted by permission of Houghton Mifflin Company. All rights reserved.

Henry Holt and Company, Inc. / *Publishers since 1866*
115 West 18th Street / New York, New York 10011

Henry Holt® is a registered trademark
of Henry Holt and Company, Inc.

Published in Canada by Fitzhenry & Whiteside Ltd.,
195 Allstate Parkway, Markham, Ontario L3R 4T8.

Library of Congress Cataloging-in-Publication Data
The future is ours: a handbook for student activists in
the 21st century / edited by John W. Bartlett.
p. cm.
Includes index.
1. College students—United States—Political activity—Handbooks, manuals, etc. 2. Student movements—United States—Handbooks, manuals, etc. I. Bartlett, John W.
LB3610.F88 1996 96-22616
378.1'981—dc20 CIP

ISBN 0-8050-4787-5
Henry Holt books are available for special promotions and premiums. For details contact: Director, Special Markets.
First edition—1996
Designed by Victoria Hartman
Printed in the United States of America
All first editions are printed on acid-free paper. ∞
10 9 8 7 6 5 4 3 2 1

Contents

Acknowledgments

I always thought the acknowledgments were the most pompous part of any book. They seemed to me to smack of an Academy Awards acceptance speech thanking all the "little people." I vowed I would never be caught dead sounding like that. But now I've finished my first book, and I've realized the truth about acknowledgments: They can never convey the debts an editor owes, and the people listed below are not little. They're huge, and this book is as much a credit to them as to me.

My highest gratitude goes to all the talented individuals who contributed chapters to this volume. It is said that "if you need something done, give it to the busiest person you know"—and there are few people busier than those whose work appears in this book. That's why it's so good. I especially thank Mark Fraioli for his early faith in the project and for writing the chapter that got the ball rolling way back in 1994.

Many thanks also to all the individuals whose work is featured here as "Success Stories" and in the sample materials accompanying Part One. You, friends, are the kind of activists I hope this book will nurture.

I would be remiss if I failed to give all due credit to my agent, Andy Zack, and to Alison Juram and Darcy Tromanhauser, my editors at Henry Holt and Company, for their expertise and commitment in guiding me through the new territory of publishing.

For twenty-four years of guidance and support, a horizon-wide thank you to my parents, Glen and Carole Bartlett. For additional inspiration, heartfelt thanks go out to Natasha Franceschi and

Zornitsa Ivanova, whose correspondence was a reminder of the simple truths that sometimes get lost in the minutiae. For a very different sort of inspiration—the caffeine-generated variety—my blood pressure thanks the nighttime wait staff at Dempsey's Restaurant in Hummelstown, Pennsylvania.

For their counsel and feedback on the ideas in this book and the process that brought it to fruition, thanks are due to Benjamin Goodrich, Mary Grenadier, Celeste Katz, Amir and Orna Medovoi, Justin Pritchard, Ashley Rogers, Peter Schurman, Jonathan Strout, James Todd, Emogene Trexel, Maryam Zarnegar, and many others. I owe a particular debt of gratitude to Beth Berlin, Khyati Joshi, and David Morenoff, whose advice and support in frazzled, panicked moments were the salvation of my sanity.

"And of course," he said, finishing with a smile, "all errors and shortcomings are strictly my own."

Introduction

> This world demands the qualities of youth; not a time of life but a state of mind, a temper of the will, a quality of the imagination, a predominance of courage over timidity, of the appetite for adventure over the love of ease. . . . It is young people who must take the lead.

Robert F. Kennedy spoke these words in 1968, in the middle of an era that shapes our perceptions even today. The 1960s in America were indeed a moment for youth. Those formative years for the "boomers"—our parents' generation—saw the most profound successes in extending civil rights to all Americans, the birth of the modern feminist and gay rights movements, and the advent of an environmental movement with the realization that "progress" is not always a good thing for the planet. Thousands of students organized voter registration drives in the South, sought ways to live in closer harmony with the natural world, and stood up against a war that was claiming tens of thousands of lives in Southeast Asia.

But the promise of that era soured, falling victim to a national malaise brought on by the assassinations of President John F. Kennedy and the Reverend Martin Luther King, Jr., and the political and financial crises that shook the country in the late 60s and early 70s. Moral, spiritual, and economic self-centeredness experienced a horrifying resurgence as our parents dropped the ball and picked up that good old 80s greed.

Today, the wheel has turned around again. Young people all over the world are taking the lead in seeking environmental protection and social justice in their own communities and beyond. The technological advances of the last decade have given us access to information and resources previously unimaginable. We are, on the whole, more familiar with the questions and debates affecting policy decisions and more able to use that information quickly and efficiently to advance the causes that will shape our own futures. We are also living those issues "on the ground" every day. Perhaps most important, we are less isolated from one another than ever before.

We do not suffer the pie-eyed idealism that led our parents to despair when they failed at creating the perfect world. Our idealism is just as real and just as hopeful, but it is tempered with images of the harsh reality around us: environmental disasters in our backyards and across the globe, ethnic and religious oppression from East Timor to the American Southwest, spiraling violence at all levels of global society, the purchase of "public opinion" by moneyed interests, an economic downturn that raises questions about our own futures, and the ongoing scourge of AIDS.

At the same time we have been labeled by others before we have had the chance to define ourselves. We are "Generation X," lost, frustrated, and apathetic. We are either spoiled brats or violent dropouts—subtle code words for racial and class divisions that seem ever more pronounced. But do we actually believe in these labels? No. Because they never seem to fit *us*.

So who are we? Our detractors and our allies alike have focused on what we have come after: We are the "post-partisan" inheritors of a post-industrial world in the post–Cold War era. We are post-*Roe* and post–Reagan era—young adults at the close of the twentieth century. It's time for us to look ahead with conviction, to define the present and future in our own terms.

This book is not about endings but about new beginnings. The advances that have brought us to this point enable us to shape the new millennium beginning today. The needs of the world and its peoples, and the ability of each of us to play a major role in achieving them, are a call to action. "Think globally, act locally." Forget for a moment the huge world and focus on what is right in front of you. Clean up your patch of the planet first; this alone will take a lot of work. Then keep the movement alive by growing and changing—seeking new people, new issues, and new ideas.

But most important, *act*. Seize your responsibility to the future—ours and the planet's. Be proactive: Visualize a better place and work to bring it here.

This book doesn't seek to tell you what issues to address; it is designed to help you in addressing the problems and divisions that are *your* priority. It is a set of strategies, to which you and those around you must supply the content and conviction.

You will find that taking part in shaping the future of your community and of the world is one of the most rewarding things you can do. Not just rewarding in the tangible ways that immediately spring to mind—yes, experiences of "real world" activism look great on a college or job application—but also in the spiritual sense. The people you will encounter and the sense of accomplishment you'll feel as you touch the future are the real rewards.

Be innovative. If you don't see your concern or strategy in this book, that doesn't mean it isn't viable. This guidebook is just that: some ideas about the "lay of the land" as mapped by young people who have made the voyage of activism. Each of us will—and should—seek his or her own path, because that is part of the excitement of doing what you are doing. What you don't have to do is make the same mistakes that those before you did. (Rest assured, you'll make plenty of your own.) This book is meant to provide a framework to help you through the process of addressing your concerns, and to share with you the experiences of young activists in a variety of fields.

Most of all, you should feel good about yourself. Anyone with the discipline and compassion to sit down and read about organizing is going places. Reach out, seek help, focus on the positive, and learn from your mistakes. Don't fall prey to vague "save the world" sentiments but focus on concrete action—achievable projects, specific time frames, real results. Learn the facts, understand your opponents, and give everything you've got to what matters most:

Our future.

Part One

A Step-by-Step Guide to Effecting Change

1

Getting Started

If you've picked up this book, you may already have found the issue or problem that you are most concerned about—or it may have found you. Or if you're like many young people today, you may have a broad sense that "something needs to be done" about the world, the environment, or a certain situation in your community. If you fit into the latter group, this chapter will give you some idea on how to find and define an issue to confront; if you fit more into the first, this chapter should help you narrow your focus and figure out where you're starting from.

Finding an issue is as easy as looking around you and as hard as defining your personal priorities. The place to begin is in your own community. Even if you have grand visions of snatching the whole planet from the jaws of destruction, it's your own corner that you're most familiar with. It's where you have the resources to begin the process. As with any endeavor, you'll be more effective in the long run if you start on a small scale, at the community level. Vast changes are needed in this world, and numerous opportunities exist to make a difference by thinking big. Beginning in your own community and learning the ropes as an effective activist there will give you the knowledge and network to do even more as you broaden your scope of influence.

The first step is to become aware of what's happening around you. Read local and national newspapers; talk to your parents, teachers, and others in the community; learn what issues your friends and classmates are concerned about. Think about what matters to you, and realize that if it matters to you, it must matter to dozens of other people around you. You may not know who they are right now, but that will change as you begin the process. Seek out organizations that are addressing various needs in the community or that are active on legislative issues. These may include local service clubs or chapters of national organizations like the League of Women Voters and the Sierra Club. Your goals and visions may lead you to decide against working with these groups (that's a question we'll address later), but you will find them to be a good source of information.

Even more than basic library research, the resources most useful to you will be your parents, teachers, friends, and community leaders. Approach these people with questions like, "Which organizations are working on this issue?" and "Do you know where I can get up-to-date information on this topic?" When you go to the library, ask the reference librarian to help you get started. See the Resource Directory at the end of this book for a list of pertinent books and periodicals.

As you begin to focus and define your priorities, start asking some more pointed questions: What's the nature of the problem? How is it affecting different parts of the community? How are—or aren't—they reacting? Think in both the short and the long term, taking into account how conflicting interests might play out over time. Learn to read between the lines and realize that what's left unsaid is often as important as what is said. (An industrial project trumpeting "rapid economic gains" won't tell you about the long-term environmental costs, but you can be sure they're there.)

Access the resources of local colleges and universities. Many schools now have specialized departments such as environmental studies and public policy. With a little diligence you may be able to find a faculty member who is not only knowledgeable about your issue but actively involved in the subject as well. Colleges are also a good place to get hold of specialized research in academic journals; also, they are usually hooked up to the Internet, a huge and invaluable source of information.

Perhaps the most important thing to do as you begin planning your action is to find out what's already happening on the issue. Existing groups may be working on some aspect of the issue. If it's a question of public policy or regulations, you may even find that

WORDS OF WISDOM
The Road Ahead

If we do not change our direction, we are likely to end up where we are headed.

—Ancient Chinese proverb

there's already legislation "in the pipeline." Learn about what's happening and about who's making it happen. You may be able to start out "ahead of the game" through pre-existing groups with their own resources; or you may decide you want to adopt a different focus or agenda.

Put quite simply: Don't reinvent the wheel if you don't have to. There's no rule that says to be an environmental or social activist you have to start from scratch. Know the facts and learn from those who have worked toward similar goals so that you can start off with as much in your favor as possible. Knowing your facts and being prepared will earn you the respect of both allies and opponents, epecially those in positions of authority.

Even if no one has tried what you're trying to do, talk to others about what they've done and think about how their strategies can be integrated into your own. Maximize the value of your time and energy by coordinating your efforts with other individuals and groups on issues of common concern.

As you start to define your goals, go back and have further discussions with people knowledgeable and influential on the issue. Seek published material and other information specific to your topic and your "angle."

Stay organized. Have a file folder, a notebook, or a desk drawer where you keep your information. Keep track of what you have, and of people you have spoken to and when you did so. It's tough to plan or take any action when you're surrounded by hundreds of scraps of paper or have to arrive at a meeting with a story like "the dog ate my agenda."

Once you have a good idea of where things stand, figure out where you want to be and start to think about the best ways to get there. Visualize the ideal solution to your problem in realistic and more specific terms (for example, "world peace" and "environmental harmony" are not valid); then consider what solutions can be achieved in the short term. Realize now that you may not get everything you want, and you'll eventually need to find an acceptable compromise with people on the other side of the issue. Figure out what some alternatives are and jot down your ideas on their relative advantages and disadvantages.

The final word on research: Keep it direct, to the point, and rapidly paced. Before delving into a book or sending away for a report, ask yourself, "How relevant is this to the issue at hand?" Skim long works and avoid going off on tangents—as interesting as they may seem—unless they can lead to a more important or motivating action opportunity. Retain your focus and remember that your goal is *action.* It's easy to slip into a pattern of constantly looking for one more journal article, sending away for one more publication, or waiting for some "crucial" person to return your call. Set a time limit for each endeavor—a month or less is reasonable for most research—and stick to it.

2

Traveling Companions: Joining a Group or Forming Your Own

> One person working alone is a martyr. A group of committed people working together is a movement. Start a movement.
>
> —Adam Werbach,
> founder, Sierra Student Coalition

In this deceptively simple statement lies a message you'll probably have to keep telling yourself: Don't work alone. If you're like me, you may have a tendency to try to do it all. There's a certain comfort in doing that, because you always know what's happening and who's in control. But there are better ways to organize, and you'll be much more effective and much happier if you organize a group to work on your issue. Also, it's a lot more fun that way: Activism becomes a social experience, and everyone gets to grow and gain from it.

One of the first dilemmas you will likely face is whether to work with an established group or start a new one. Each option has its advantages and disadvantages, and the best choice depends on your situation. You might even switch back and forth between the two options as the issues and challenges change.

Joining an Established Group

Working with local organizations can be a good way to get started. Such groups usually have an established network in your area, and if they've been around for a while or include influential members of the community, they'll probably have legitimacy and name recognition. They're also likely to have materials and research on the issues and access to small-scale funding.

The flip side of the legitimacy issue is that the group may be unpopular in the community because of a history of difficult relations with local government or other organizations, or because of a reputation as extremist or combative. The group may have become stagnant due to losing members, trying to do too much, or becoming lost in the minutiae of language and logistics. It may also be dealing with internal strife—a sure way to turn even the most well-intentioned group into a pit of social and organizational power games.

You won't know any of these things until you've given the group a try. Attend a meeting or two, talk to members, and see what opportunities are available to become active in the organization. Find out what they've done; most groups have an "accomplishment list" or collection of press clippings. While you're at it, talk to other knowledgeable people in the community about their impressions of the group.

The appearance of stagnancy may not mean that a group is "beyond repair" for your purposes. You may be the individual whose energy and enthusiasm can revitalize a struggling group by reminding them of their initial goals. If it becomes apparent that this is not the case, there's plenty of time to get out and start your own group. Beware of becoming the "new kid"—which could mean being marginalized or ignored but could also mean having all the work dumped on you by longtime members looking for an out.

Working with national organizations—often by forming a chapter or affiliate in your community—also has its advantages and disadvantages. On the up side, these groups will usually have established name recognition, which can give you a good deal of clout when you're trying to get the attention of the powers-that-be. They will also have a broad network of other chapters, will usually have a library of materials for your use, and may have access to "big names" that could help you out as guest speakers at events. Most hold annual conferences, which are an unbeatable opportu-

SUCCESS STORY

"Heal Sofia": A Community Cleans Up

Zornitsa Ivanova, fifteen, and her friends were frustrated by the litter that is part of daily life in Sofia, Bulgaria, a city of over one million people. They wanted to encourage citizens to cut down on their littering and to fill the gap left by inadequate social services in the fledgling Balkan democracy. An alumna of the *Peace Child* International theater exchange program (see the Resource Directory), which brings together young people from regions in conflict to write their own piece of musical theater about the issues that matter most to them, Zornitsa decided to organize a concert to raise public awareness on the issue.

With the help of two adults at the National Palace of Children, a hub of youth-oriented projects in Bulgaria, she began planning the concert and contacted a new environmental organization called Don't Pollute. Don't Pollute was largely inactive and unknown, but its leadership had something that Zornitsa's Heal Sofia lacked: access to financial backing. Heal Sofia—a name inspired by Michael Jackson's song "Heal the World"—became the public face of Don't Pollute. Zornitsa and her friends gave interviews on radio and television, and created an ad that ran in a popular Bulgarian music magazine. The concert was a success, drawing media attention from across Bulgaria and leading to a continuing interest in the youths' efforts.

On the day of the first cleaning effort, Zornitsa and her friends swept and picked up garbage around the Children's Palace as radio journalists broadcast news of their work. From across Sofia, people began calling the radio stations to say that they were also cleaning their own neighborhoods. "The cleaning happened in many places," said Zornitsa with a smile, "but not everywhere. We'll do a better job next time."

---

nity to learn and make connections within the movement. There's a chance that such groups will have funds available for your use, but this is unlikely for two reasons: Most national organizations are also strapped for cash, and usually face large operating expenses; and they will often be reluctant to direct their very limited funding to someone new and unproved.

On the down side, working with national organizations may make you feel like a "small fish in a big pond." Their agendas are usually of national scope, meaning that their ability to help you address the nuances of your community could be limited. Also, they tend to be very busy and understaffed—a chronic problem with large non-profit organizations—which can make it difficult for them to give you the attention you need or respond to your requests in a timely manner. Whichever is the case, you may find national organizations more trouble than they're worth but, again, give them a try, at least during your early research and networking efforts.

Finally, remember that organizations are ideas. People are real. As you contact organizations, remember that the person-to-person connections are the important ones. The person on the other end of the line is an ally; treat him that way. Get his name and ask if he knows anybody else you should connect with.

Starting Your Own Group

When it comes time to start organizing a group of your own, you'll want to have a fairly specific idea of what you want to do and how you want to do it. Don't be so specific that other people feel you're just looking for helpers as opposed to coworkers and co-organizers. (As you'll read in the next section, the first step of your first meeting will be to turn "my idea" into "our idea.") For now, sketch out a tentative outline to show people what you want to do. Use the old who-what-when-where-why-how questions: What are you concerned about? What type of program might you use to address it? Who should be involved? Why is the project important? When will you be ready to do it? How do you want to carry it out?

Avoid vague, overly broad terms: Stick to tangible projects. Instead of "educating everyone about the environment," try "hosting a speaker series on local environmental issues." Instead of "doing fund-raisers," try "hosting a charity dance for the homeless." Instead of "publicizing an issue," try "holding a letter-writing drive for the Endangered Species Act."

Write a short list of students at your school who might be concerned about the same issues you are. In school the next day, describe to them the project you are considering and tell them why it means so much to you. Ask them to be part of the task force—everybody loves that phrase—that designs and carries out this project.

At the same time, if you feel you are ready to open this up to the whole campus or community—and you should soon—make up a simple poster explaining what you're trying to do and place copies of it in visible locations in the area. High-traffic areas such as the campus post office, gym, cafeteria, and student union are good bets for maximum visibility. So are the offices of relevant departments, such as environmental studies, where you're likely to reach knowledgeable individuals, including faculty.

You may decide it's better to start off with a meeting of the "core group" of people whom you feel will be most active. This is fine, too, but make every effort to expand your group soon. This will avoid appearances of elitism and keep you from missing out on the contributions of great people you don't even know yet.

It may be to your advantage to have a faculty advisor, particularly in middle school and high school. Many schools require them, and schools often have a whole set of arcane rules about what kinds of groups can identify themselves with the school or use its building for meetings. Sit down with your advisor and learn the rules; get them in writing if you can. Even if it's not required, having a faculty member formally affiliated with your group can make a lot of things much easier, such as reserving space for meetings and events, and keeping abreast of what's going on in the school administration. Don't make your advisor feel like a pawn by going to her only when you need something—unless that's the kind of relationship she suggests—but don't feel you must seek approval for every action you undertake unless it involves use of facilities or other activities that fall under your school's rules for student organizations.

If you're working in a community outside your school, there may be some influential individuals who can support you in a similar way—the owner of the local youth center or theater, for example—as well as give you added legitimacy with others in the community.

Now that you have a mission and have something down on paper, you may be inclined to go straight to the local media and proclaim your new role. Resist this temptation. You may have only one chance to get coverage from the fickle media, particularly in larger papers and on television; you shouldn't squander it in saying, "Look, we exist." Wait until you've taken some action and have an event or some success to claim. This will get you more useful coverage in the long run and will introduce you to the community as an effective, active group. The risk is always there, as we'll talk about later, of being treated as a "poster child" for environmentalism or whatever your issue is. This is particularly likely to occur if you go to the press now and get the "look what the kids are doing today" treatment.

Make a timetable for action and keep to it. You can be a little more flexible at this stage, since the process of "talking it up" and getting support will depend on others' availability, but try not to let things drag on. To a great extent the time you take in organizing will depend on the issue: If you're reacting to, say, a sexual assault on campus or some other emotionally charged event, you'll need to move very quickly to capitalize on public sentiment and media attention. If, on the other hand, you are starting a recycling effort or planning a peer mediation program, your time frame is your own and you'll be able to move at a somewhat slower pace.

Too Many Groups? As you grow more familiar with other efforts in your field, you may actually find yourself surprised by the number of small and large organizations addressing different parts of the problem. Perhaps the world needs the Earth Action Group, Earth Action International, Earth Awareness Foundation, Earthcare Network, Earth Child, the Earth Corps, Earth Ecology Foundation, Earth First!, Earth Force, the Earth Island Institute, EarthMind, EarthPulse, Earthrise, the Earth Regeneration Society, Earth-Spirit, the Earthspirit Community, Earth Save, the Earth Stewards Network, EarthVote, and EarthWatch. But this laundry list illustrates another point: There are many organizations out there working separately, often toward very similar goals. Each day they are missing opportunities to gain strength by collaboration, and each day this weakens the overall effect that a movement can have on policy and action.

Many action guides begin this discussion by warning about the "dangers" of working with other organizations—the risks it could present to your group's viability and autonomy. I choose to begin by encouraging you to collaborate with other groups. There is strength in numbers, and members of the environmental and social justice movements don't have the resources to work separately or at cross-purposes. Working with other organizations will usually strengthen yours and can magnify the effect you have on policy and public opinion.

Having said that, I will add a few words of caution. As when joining an existing group, be wary of having a disproportionate amount of the work dumped on you and your group. The basis of cooperation should be an equitable sharing of responsibility and credit for your efforts. Beware of situations where you find yourself fund-raising for another organization instead of your own, or not getting equal mention in the press. Likewise, be sure the other group doesn't start to feel that way about you; work to avoid being the one at fault when cooperation breaks down.

When you join a coalition—a "group of groups" working together on a specific action, piece of legislation, or other goal—be sure you know and agree with everything that coalition stands for. Don't be afraid to leave a coalition, even in a very public way, if you feel you cannot support what they stand for or if you find your group's name being used inappropriately.

We all have our own precise vision of what we are after. In forming a group, you will face the challenge of making personal compromises in order to find a common issue that all members can support. Intergroup coalitions multiply this challenge, as groups with different goals and understandings attempt to mass their influence behind a common goal. There is great strength to be found when this occurs successfully.

3

Getting Organized: Meetings

Drawing People In

The first challenge in organizing a meeting is getting people to attend. Your first official meeting will set the tone for how your group interacts, so it's important to bring a lot of people into the process at this point. The guidelines in this chapter apply to any meetings you and your core group may have but are specifically relevant to your first and subsequent general meetings.

Think about the posters that advertise your meeting: They should be eye-catching and explain the relevance of your issue briefly and succinctly. Don't be afraid to use "fighting words," but consider how your statements will be perceived by those reading them. Also remember the limits of appropriateness to your community and audience: Explaining that your town's air quality is "under siege" by automobiles may not go over very well if you live in a steel town. No matter how long your group has been meeting or how consistent your attendance, never advertise your meetings as occurring at "the usual time and place," and avoid using inside jokes that may make your group seem cliquish. You don't want to exclude other people who may be interested in getting involved.

By far the best way to get a large number of people to attend your first meeting can be summed up in two words: FREE FOOD. (Pizza is a perennial favorite.) Advertise it. This may sound like baiting your potential audience, and to some extent it is. Don't be surprised if attendance drops sharply when the eating stops and the working begins. Still, having a social or food element at your first meeting will draw a large number of people to hear your pitch, and this may leave you with a larger pool of genuinely interested people to work with. If you can get the food donated or convince your school to underwrite the cost, this is ideal. Even if you have to foot the bill yourself, it is usually worth the investment. Of course, you can ask at the end of the meeting for people to contribute a buck or two to cover expenses.

Preparation

As you read through this chapter, think about what you will need at the meeting in order to make it as productive as possible. This may include gathering highlights of your research into an information packet for attendees or having a sign-up sheet to circulate when the meeting begins. In all cases you'll want to get permission to use your meeting space well in advance, and be sure you know the rules about using it.

If you're a new organization at your school, particularly at the college level, find out how to become an officially sanctioned student group and discuss appropriate steps at the first meeting. Unless you have a particular interest in remaining "unofficial"—because of manipulation of constituted student groups by the student union or because the stance your group is taking is in such opposition to the school that you want to avoid affiliation—this should be an early priority, especially if it gives you access to facilities and funding from the school.

Demonstrating preparedness is a big part of showing people at the meeting that you are serious about the issue and ready to work in an organized manner. Plan to arrive a few minutes early so people don't wonder if they've made a mistake about time and place. Arrange the room properly, erase the blackboard, and do whatever else it takes to turn the room into *your meeting space.*

Sit down the night before the meeting and prepare an agenda in outline form; make a note on it of approximately how much time you want to spend on each item. Keep it simple by not trying to deal with too many issues at any one meeting. Include time for introductions and/or an activity at the beginning of the meeting, discussion of current projects, introduction of new ideas, and reports from committees and the treasurer. If there's time, include some kind of activity—a schoolyard cleanup or writing letters to your representatives in Congress on a bill currently under consideration—to keep everyone focused on actions and outcomes.

Make a schedule and stick to it. This will keep things moving and prevent discussions from running in circles. It will keep people engaged and minimize their frustration—voiced over and over about many groups—that "we just talk and talk." Staying on a schedule also adds a certain sense of urgency to each meeting, as long as it doesn't make participants feel rushed or force you to omit important parts of planning and discussion. Announce at the beginning of each agenda item how much time you're going to spend on it, and watch for that point in the discussion where people start repeating thoughts or fidgeting. Have someone else checking the clock as well, in case you're the person who tends to get carried away in discussion.

Keep discussions moving toward decision and action. Don't ever leave an agenda item without having made the necessary decisions and dividing responsibility for carrying them out. Take a look at the "meeting log" worksheet (see example) to give yourself a better idea of how to organize the decision-making process for each agenda item. Make copies of this page and fill it out (or have someone do so) during the course of the meeting. Keep these together in a binder, along with your research, the group phone list, and other project-related materials. Use whatever system works for you—separate folders for every issue, one binder with everything in its own pocket, a section of your school notebook—to keep these materials organized. Having the facts and a record of group discussions and responsibilities at your fingertips is a must whether this is your first project or your twentieth.

Breaking the Ice

Depending on how well attendees already know one another, you may want to start off with an icebreaker. You know these from summer camp or youth groups—name games or the always popular "If you were a fruit, what fruit would you be?" kind of thing. A friend

Meeting Log

Date ____________________

Time ____________________ Place ____________________

Facilitator ____________________

Members Present ____________________

____

Topic	Who	When
Decision/Action:		

Topic	Who	When
Decision/Action:		

Topic	Who	When
Decision/Action:		

Other good ideas introduced today ____________________

____

Next week's facilitator ____________________

of mine swears by the activity of drawing an abstract image on the blackboard and then talking about what each person sees in it. This stuff may feel a little dumb, but it will loosen people up, help new members learn one another's names, and make them more likely to speak during the meeting.

Getting people introduced is an important step toward getting them to feel they have a personal investment in the group and what is going on. To put it more simply, people who know more about each other are more interesting to talk to. It also adds a social aspect to your group that is too easy to lose in an intense, action-oriented situation.

Getting Started

Begin the meeting by introducing yourself and explaining your reason for calling people together. Define the situation or problem in concrete terms and explain why this problem is so important to you and to the other people in the room. Imagine that each member of your audience is wondering, "Why does this matter to me?" Your ability to answer that question will determine your ability to maintain their interest and get them involved in your project. It's not as intimidating as it may sound; a discussion will ensue, and others at the meeting will pick up the ball and run with it. Your job is to get the ball rolling and then to steer the discussion as it develops.

As you make your opening remarks, be sure to demonstrate through your words and inflection that you are committed to seeing changes made, but also make it clear that this is to be a group project. Once you've made your point and advanced whatever suggestions you have for possible group action, open the floor to organized discussion of the issue. Demonstrate genuine interest in what others have to say, keeping in mind how these different ideas and approaches to the problem can be incorporated into a single effort. Don't be afraid to let the conversation touch on related issues, but beware of wandering off on tangents or descending into bickering or joking around. If you feel this is starting to happen, quietly remind the group to stay on the topic or ask a leading

WORDS OF WISDOM

People Power: Deciding the Details

The phrase "people's program" has become well worn with lip service, but whether such a program exists in practice is something else again. The words have become like "democracy," a common carrier of so many different meanings that they are meaningless.

Under such circumstances it behooves us to raise the simple question, "What is a people's program?" The question itself leads to the obvious and true answer that a people's program is whatever program the people themselves decide. . . .

This does not mean that the organizer cannot state certain general principles during the initial stages of organization. . . . But the objective of securing a people's program absolutely precludes the organizer's going beyond these broad general principles into a detailed blueprint for the future. That kind of program can only come from the people themselves. The actual projection of a completely particularized program by a few persons is a highly dictatorial action. It is not a democratic program but a monumental testament to lack of faith in the ability and intelligence of the masses of people to think their way through to the successful solution of their problems. It is not a people's program, and the people will have little to do with it.

—Saul D. Alinsky,
Reveille for Radicals

---

question like: "So what should we consider as our highest priorities on the issue at hand?"

Group Memory

If you have access to a blackboard or can hang some big sheets of paper on the wall in your meeting space, keep a "group memory" as discussion goes on. Try using three columns: Issues/Problems,

Possible Solutions, and Action that will be required to make those solutions happen. Start by brainstorming a list under your first column, then move on to talking about possible solutions for column two. The Action column will take you into another type of discussion, which I'll address below and in the next chapter.

Your "group memory" is a rough draft for organizing your ideas and planning action, and it will help ensure that all good ideas brought up in discussion are covered. It also has the positive effect of making participants see their ideas as important parts of the process. All people like to have their ideas written up for everyone to see.

Convey Ownership

As soon as the meeting convenes, "my" idea becomes "our" idea and "my" plans become "ours." This is vitally important: People want to be members, not helpers. The onus is on you as the facilitator to convey that everyone has a part to play.

There are some guidelines that everyone in the meeting, especially the facilitator, should follow: Be responsive in your words and body language. Praise good ideas and avoid reacting to bad ones in a purely negative way. Don't just say no to an idea, because that shuts down the discussion and will probably make the speaker feel dumb. Instead, look for the germ of an idea that can be turned into something worthwhile. Respond to a not-so-good strategy idea, for example, with a nod and say, "Or maybe we could accomplish the same goal by using *this* strategy." Seemingly minor turns of phrase—describing a good project as "more useful right now" rather than calling a bad one "less important"—define the character of your meeting in a positive way. Keep this in mind as you lead group discussions.

To increase everyone's sense of participation and lighten your own load, consider having someone different facilitate each meeting. One popular scheme that works well is to have one facilitator and one assistant for each meeting. At the end of the meeting, the assistant selects someone else to be her assistant at the following meeting, which she facilitates. This approach develops leadership skills in each member of the group and helps everyone appreciate the challenges of running the show. It also allows group leaders to focus on projects rather than getting tied up with the details of each meeting. Just be sure that there's always someone who knows what's going on and who is responsible for the next meeting. Make this information part of your meeting log.

Go out of your way to make newcomers feel welcome by explaining issues and by avoiding acronyms, jargon, and inside jokes. Reporting that "I called SEAC about CWA, and they sent me the CRS report" will confuse and intimidate people. It's easy for those who know a topic to speak in shorthand, and in that context it can be useful, but remember that not everyone has your in-depth knowledge.

Reaching Agreement

A large part of sharing ownership and responsibility for an idea involves making compromises: on goals, on methods, and on the language you use when discussing the issue in public. This may mean a broadening of your idea, like expanding a city cleanup effort to include people from another school or neighborhood. It may also mean narrowing the focus to address only those parts of your original idea that the group can agree on.

The decision-making process that you use will depend on the size of the group. Voting on project ideas is always a good idea for large groups but is very formal and sometimes can lead people who are in the minority to feel as if their voices aren't being heard. When you're in a smaller group where members are familiar with one another, try consensus. Consensus—coming to a general agreement through discussion rather than cutting off formal debate and taking a vote—conveys a very empowering sense of ownership and unity on the group. The danger of consensus is that the most vocal members push their ideas through by dominating debate, but this should be rare in a small and familiar group. Find the best balance for your organization: One successful group I know uses voting to decide on big, semester- and year-long projects and consensus for weekend and small-group projects.

Reassure members who might feel that their voices aren't being heard—those in the minority on a major vote or those who feel they "gave in" for the sake of consensus—that their ideas are important, too. Offer them the chance to look into their idea in more detail and bring it up again at a future meeting. Talk about the aspects of the chosen project that address their specific concerns, and give them the chance to focus their work there. Show them the ways in which their contributions are vital to the group's work.

In bringing your project idea into focus and defining the group's priorities, you may be pleased to discover new approaches and ways of strengthening your efforts. But even if you feel that the group's goals are a step back from what you were hoping for, accept these ideas for the time being. This will enable your group to get started on something, at least, and you may find that ideas discarded early in the process will return later as you reevaluate and plan further projects. At the same time, don't concede so much that you are no longer comfortable or enthusiastic about what is going on. Don't ask more of yourself, as far as compromise goes, than you would ask of others at the meeting. Don't ask less, either.

Narrowing Your Focus and Setting Priorities

The workshop programs presented by Earth Train in 1992 gave some great ideas on how to use group memory in the decision-making process. Working with materials from Interaction Associates, Inc., facilitators in Earth Train's workshops used a two-step process to bring a long list of project ideas down to manageable size. First, with group approval, they combined similar ideas in order to eliminate duplication. Then they used what was called the *N/3* method to prioritize.

To use *N/3*, divide the total number of ideas on the list by three and give each group member that number of votes; for example, twelve ideas on a list give each person four votes. Each member can then cast votes for his or her four favorite ideas. The top vote-getters are discussed further by the group, and some are developed into project ideas.

Write down your goals in "action statements," saying what you want to change and how; and "reason statements," explaining why each action should be a priority for your school or community. Think of these as the terms in which you will describe your effort to the rest of the community. Use short, snappy sentences preceded by bullet points and be as specific as you can about how you want these changes to be made. Like group memory, do this on the blackboard or on a piece of paper that everyone can see, and solicit suggestions on wording from everyone. This is a step beyond group memory, putting things in more formal language and narrowing your priorities to those you plan to address in the short term.

From this list of goals you're going to draw two things: a mission statement and an action plan. Your mission statement should be at most a few sentences long and should explain your group's identity, goals, and methods in simple sentences. Think of your mission statement as the definition that would follow your group's name in the dictionary. A good example is: "The Springfield Community Cleanup Team, a group of middle school and high school students, works to improve the quality of the city's streets and parks through weekend cleanup efforts and by encouraging community members to keep the city clean by properly disposing of or recycling their garbage."

Keep Your Focus

Even if there are several things your group can agree on, you may wish to pursue only one at the outset—particularly if these goals are not closely related or if you don't have a large group to work with. Beware of your group's mission statement starting to look like an octopus. Of course people in your group are going to have strong opinions on a variety of issues, but unless you maintain your focus on a single issue or family of issues (for example, the local environment, bias crime in school), your group will appear vague and be difficult for the public to understand. It could also succumb to one of the biggest pitfalls for new groups: trying to do too much at once and overstretching personnel and material resources.

Unless you're an overarching student organization such as a stu-

SUCCESS STORY

Fighting Homelessness—Strings Attached

Penn Musicians Against Homelessness was founded in 1988 under the direction of University of Pennsylvania student Brian Fan. Based on the belief that a commitment to the community near campus should be part of students' urban education, PMAH brings together student classical musicians for the benefit of West Philadelphia's less fortunate. At the outset, the twenty-five-member group focused solely on performing—holding classical concerts on and near campus, and donating the proceeds to local charities benefitting poor communities.

PMAH continues to hold such concerts, but it now boasts 150 members and a variety of other projects. The group has taken its performances "on the road," giving concerts in homes for the elderly, the Children's Hospital of Philadelphia, and at the openings of homeless shelters and community centers in the area. It has participated in benefit concerts for AIDS research and recently initiated an ongoing music education program that links members with underprivileged elementary school students in West Philadelphia. Members have also participated in renovating a house and initiated a joint music education project for children with the West Philadelphia Improvement Corps.

The move beyond performing has been an important one for the group, says outgoing PMAH director Jennifer Lynch. "We have built closer ties with members of the community, beyond just writing a check each semester," she says. "We've also brought members' commitment to the issue of poverty into the realm of direct action offstage."

Lynch urges others who organize performance-oriented benefit groups like PMAH to be sure members have the opportunity to participate in the community directly—to know where their money is going and to make connections and build mutual respect with the people there. PMAH has learned, she says, that the best way to appeal to a certain community—children or the homeless, for example—is to create a show specifically for that audience and to involve them in the production.

"By bringing in homeless people to speak at our shows, we educate our audience and build connections with the people we work with," says Lynch. "It's as important to teach your audience about the problems as it is to pass their money along to those who need it."

---

dent council that can assign task forces to a variety of issues, maintain your focus. It's perfectly acceptable for the "Green Club" to have a position on the differential treatment of female students in science class; it may be going too far to expect the club to organize an event on this issue. Endorse other groups' efforts if your organization's consensus supports them. Collaborate with them if it's appropriate, but maintain your own focus.

Goals in hand, make a plan. Remember that meeting and talking aren't activism: You've come together for a reason, and your purpose in discussing the issue is preparing to get active on the issue. The next step in the process, then, is deciding what kind of action(s) your group wants to undertake. The next chapter, along with the material in Part Two, will give you guidelines for organizing. One thing must be emphasized here: *Make your actions appropriate to your goals.*

This decision will often be obvious. If you're trying to get legislation passed, grassroots lobbying is your tool of choice. If it's an environmental cleanliness issue you're dealing with, direct action and community education will probably be most appropriate. Sometimes you'll have to think a little harder about what strategies you want to adopt. Be creative. Read the "Success Stories" throughout this book and the chapters in Part Two for more good ideas.

Too often new groups jump at the chance to have a rally or a protest, even when that is not the most appropriate way to reach their goals. Rallies are overdone, and other, more appropriate actions are underutilized, which often hurts the legitimacy and effectiveness of many environmental and social justice movements. If it's attention you want, go join the theater.

There is definitely a place for this kind of publicity-generating action in the process of working toward most goals, but it should almost never be the first thing you do. A rally or protest is a confrontational act and will probably put you on adversarial terms with the very individuals—legislators, school administrators, or private firms—whose cooperation you need most. Think hard about your goals and about whose help you'll need to make them happen.

Dividing Responsibility: Committees

The next chapter will talk in more detail about delegating responsibility for specific aspects of your project—such as publicity, procuring materials, and cooperation with other groups—to individuals and groups within your organization. The basic unit of subdivision is the committee. A committee should function in the same way as the group, meeting to coordinate activities and keeping its members abreast of their responsibilities and the needs of the project. Subcommittees are sometimes useful in enabling committee members to further focus their efforts, such as when your fund-raising committee is working on two difficult grant applications. Committee chairpeople should report to the group leader or the person overseeing the project on a regular basis to discuss what has been accomplished, what must still be done, and where potential trouble spots lie. Be ready to divert extra time and resources to crucial committees when unforeseen needs arise.

Don't overdo committees. Committees should be organized in response to need; for example, if your funding comes solely through the student union, you won't need a fund-raising committee. Extraneous committees are a drag on your group's resources and can cause people to lose enthusiasm because they don't feel they're contributing anything. Committee meetings can also become a major drain on time, wasting hours that could better be used working on direct action, lobbying, or even your schoolwork.

Two things should be kept in mind when forming committees: interest and resources. Each person will have something he particularly wants to do or a knack for a certain aspect of the work. As decisions are made and the time comes to delegate tasks, let people volunteer to do what interests them. If you can, try to familiarize yourself with people's particular interests, background, and resources before making committee assignments. This will help you decide who is most appropriate to lead or serve on certain committees, and enable you to avoid assigning an award-winning writer to the food committee. Many larger groups ask new members to fill out information sheets detailing their talents, interests, and resources; these are kept on file for future reference.

Keeping in Touch

Before you adjourn your first meeting, decide and announce when your group or certain committees will meet next. Recap what was discussed during the meeting, what actions were decided on, and who volunteered to do what.

Without a contact list, you don't have an organization. Make sure you've passed around a sheet of paper to get each person's phone number and campus address; this is information you can use to contact them and to establish a "phone tree" when needed. Be sure people have your name and phone number, and those of other group leaders, in case they want to get in touch. Thank everyone for coming, and end with a positive remark about what you're all trying to do.

Your Next Meeting and Beyond

The frequency and structure of future meetings will largely be determined by what kind of action you're trying to take. It may not be necessary for the whole group to meet if committees can work independently on different parts of the project and if they keep each other updated. During the time just prior to your event or project, you'll need to meet more frequently as a group and make sure the lines of communication are open.

Regular meetings are probably a good idea because they allow a group to stay current with what its members are doing, maintain open lines of communication at a social level, and make members feel that the group is a constant part of their lives. Keep in mind, however, that if you have regular meetings where there's often nothing new to discuss or no project in the works, you will risk losing people's interest. The ideal frequency of meetings probably falls somewhere between weekly and monthly; it will depend on what you're trying to do, how many people are in the group, and whether or not you see each other in other settings such as classes or on sports teams.

Try to get yourself a regular place to post information. This could be the corner of a classroom, a designated bulletin board in the student center, or anyplace you can post meeting information, brochures, a sign-up sheet, and newspaper clippings. A consistent meeting place will also help avoid confusion. The more people who know where to find you and find information about you, the more easily potential members can learn about your group and maybe decide to join.

Evaluating

As the last people file out of the room, sit back and take a deep breath. Congratulations. You've just successfully led your first meeting. Even if things didn't go exactly as you'd planned, don't sweat it. The people with a genuine commitment to what you're trying to do will come back.

Evaluating your first meeting involves thinking not only about what you should do differently in the future but also praising yourself for the things you did well. Developing a personal style of leadership comes as much from realizing and reinforcing your strengths as from working to change the things that you aren't so good at yet.

Give yourself time to relax after the meeting by getting a cup of coffee, going to the gym to work out, or whatever works for you. Sit down later in the day—possibly with a friend who was also at the meeting, or with your other organizers—and ask yourself questions like: Did the meeting start on time? If not, how can we encourage promptness in the future? (The best way is often simply to start on time even if not everyone has arrived; there are few things more embarrassing than walking into a meeting late, and most people will do it only once.) What helped make discussion flow? How can we make that happen again? If the discussion was full of

Meeting Evaluation

Meeting Date ____________ Topic ________________________

Things that worked well	Things to improve for next time

The best thing that happened in today's meeting was...

Concerns

Recommendations

lulls or discontinuities, what are some ways to avoid them in the future? What are some ways to "kick-start" conversation in such a situation? (Shorter time limits on agenda items, jumping into a stalled conversation with an innovative idea of your own, or asking people who haven't spoken for their input are good ways.) Think about what would be the best way to run meetings in the future: Is your group able to work effectively in an informal setting? Should you try to organize your debate with Robert's Rules of Order? Or is there some happy medium that will work most effectively?

What was said during the meeting that really made the group feel good? What negative things were said, and how can these be turned into positive statements? How can interpersonal conflicts—whether preexisting or sparked by the day's debate—be prevented so they do not affect your ability to work together? Part of the answer to these questions is to emphasize the "professional" over the personal when meetings are convened and encouraging calm dialogue—possibly mediated—between those in conflict outside the meeting. The details will depend on the exact nature of the conflict.

Coming out of the meeting, did you feel as though the group was headed in the direction you envisioned? If not, should you try to steer things to your way of thinking or see where the group's consensus leads?

Try to do some form of evaluation after every meeting. It keeps you on your toes and can help you recognize and head off conflicts before they undermine your efforts. The meeting evaluation worksheet (see the example on the previous page) is another good way to organize your thoughts.

Whether you're feeling euphoria, despair, or ambivalence after your first gathering, remember the immortal words of Abraham Lincoln: "And this too shall pass." You're going to have good and bad meetings in the future. I won't lie to you and say that it gets easier, but rest assured that your techniques for facilitating meetings and leading actions will become more practiced. You'll develop your own style, appropriate to the group of people you're leading and what you're trying to do, and things will run more or less smoothly—not because they're easier but because you manage them better and roll with the punches. Even when things get rougher, they'll always be interesting.

4

Taking Action

Now we get down to the nitty-gritty—the process of actually planning, organizing, and executing your project or event. I'll start by speaking generally about planning—the important stuff that everyone needs to think about—and then talk in the next four chapters about the specific actions you may want to incorporate into your strategy. Finally, I'll address the needs and considerations that come with some of the most common types of action. As with all the ideas in this book, adapt the useful ones to your specific project and community in the ways you think will work best. For more detailed thoughts on a broad range of issues and actions, be sure to read the excellent chapters in Part Two.

Asking the Right Questions

It's easy to rush off in search of action, to hold a poorly planned rally, to attend a meeting or two, then to stop and go back to your "life before activism" as if nothing had happened. But if you want to be an effective activist whose work actually makes positive changes in your school and community, you need to plan your actions in terms of your goals, not the other way around. These are the questions you should ask yourself and the order in which you should ask them when you plan every action.

1. **What is your goal? What do you want to change?** Define your goals in specific, measurable, and achievable terms.

Read those three words again. Your goal(s) should be *specific,* describing exactly what you want to change. "Cleaning up the environment" doesn't count, but "getting local businesses to recycle and to cut down on their use of hazardous cleaning materials" does. So do "replacing Styrofoam and plastic with paper products in the school cafeteria," "getting Congressman Smith to support renewal of the Clean Water Act," "having an elected student representative with full voting rights on the school board," and "decreasing the number of racial bias incidents among the youth in the community."

Your goals should be *measurable.* This gives you something specific to point to as the outcome of your work. People love numbers; show them some. Think about the above examples in this light: Decreasing businesses' use of hazardous materials *by how much* and *by when?* Increasing household recycling in your community *by what percent* or *of what specific products?* (And saving those households *how much money* in the process?) Your congressman's vote will be measurable: a yes or a no. Student representation on the school board: At the end of the year, the seat is either there or it's not. And recognizing a change in the number of bias incidents is obvious.

I'm not saying that less tangible things—heightening community members' awareness of the connection between personal actions and environmental outcomes, defusing underlying racial tensions at your school through dialogue—are any less valuable. They may in fact be more important in your situation; they are an important part of the changing of people's minds that must precede the changing of their actions. Remember, however, that it is both rewarding and easier to prove success when you can point at something and say, "We did that."

Finally, your goals should be *achievable.* Too many student activists end up convincing themselves that they can't do anything because they set their goals too high at the outset. You are not going to save the planet; don't expect to. But you will have a visible positive effect on your community with each success, and along with other student activists around the world, you will exert an overall positive influence on the planet and on the people you come in contact with. It is often good to start your group off with a small project—something very achievable, that gives you a victory—and then build on that shared success by going for the gusto your second time around. Remember that results are not always obvious. Changes in environmental policy, for example, won't show up "on the ground" for a number of years. Ecological revival, like its destruction, will be a slow and incremental process.

2. How do you get there? What must happen to effect this change in your school or community? The answers to these questions will seem painfully obvious: They involve getting people to change their actions, getting your school to change its policy, or getting your representative to change his vote. But think in more specific terms: Your chances of success will be much greater when you approach the powers that be with a detailed proposal that outlines the benefits for them. Do a little legwork. Point out to your high school that if they buy recycled paper products from company X, they will save Y amount of money because of the difference in price between Styrofoam and recycled paper, and an additional Z dollars because paper will create a lower volume of trash and decrease what they pay for waste removal. You get the idea.

Imagine a best-case scenario: You go to the local dry cleaners and ask them to cut down on hazardous materials usage. The proprietor says, "Okay, I will. But how?" If you've done your homework, you'll be able to hand him a sheet of paper explaining less hazardous alternatives, their relative cost, and where he can get them. Otherwise, you may lose your chance.

Don't waste your time aiming your efforts at individuals or organizations that can't help you or that aren't in a position to make the changes you're looking for. Find the source of the problem or the potential solution and direct your actions toward it. There's nothing more embarrassing than walking in to talk to your municipal parks director, getting halfway through your pitch, and hearing, "Um, this is the parking office. Parks and recreation is upstairs."

Another important question to ask while in the planning stages: Has your idea—or something like it—been tried before? With what result? If possible, talk to the people who orchestrated that earlier attempt. Find out what they went up against and get their advice on how (or whether) to deal with those opposition forces. Evaluate their effort and think about how you can improve upon it in order to achieve success. Ask for their research and sources; if there is legislation drafted, ask for a copy. This may save you a great deal of time.

3. What actions can you take to make these changes happen? I've said it before and I'll say it again: Tailor your actions to your goals. If you want to change people's behavior, community education and dialogue are the ways to go. If you want to change a legislator's vote, it's grassroots lobbying. Try cooperation-building measures first and save rallies, civil disobedience, and other confrontational tactics for the time when diplomacy fails.

So we have our three basic questions: What's your *goal?* What has to happen to get there? What *actions* by you will make it happen? You probably dealt with the first two questions during the early part of your meeting. The rest of this chapter will talk about identifying and accessing the resources available to you and using them to best advantage toward various efforts.

Identifying Resources

Goals and resources are the two major factors to consider when it comes to planning your action. We've already talked about goals: Make your action appropriate to what you're trying to achieve. The resources you have at your disposal and the resources you think you can reasonably obtain will play a big part in deciding what actions you can and should take.

As clichéd as it may sound, your most important resource is knowledge. Knowing what you're talking about and knowing where the problems are and what the best solutions are is the foundation on which your effort must be built. Without it, it's hard to make a cogent argument for your viewpoint, and you may not do right by those you are trying to help. That's why we read, research, and keep up to date on what the issues are and how people are trying to affect them. Inform yourself from accurate, respected sources; then use your knowledge to inform others and guide your actions.

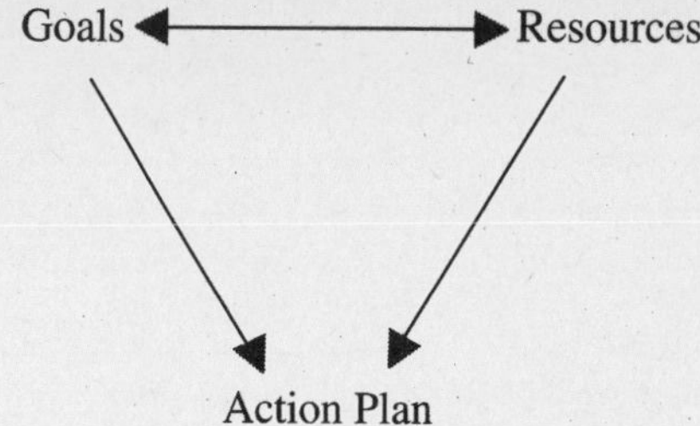

Your goals will determine the kind and amount of resources you need. Your resources, especially when they're limited, will have an effect on how you realistically define your goals. The interplay of these two elements shapes your action plan.

Tangible resources will fall into two categories: personnel and materials. Both are necessary, and the ratio in which you have access to each of them will be a big part of determining what kind of action you should take. For example, in high school I worked alone on a project to bring a Russian high school student to my hometown for a month. Although I had no personnel resources, some things were available to me—a photocopier to mass-produce fund-raising letters, school permission to send them home with every student, and my father's letterhead to make our correspondence with the Soviet embassy look very official. That enabled me to make my project happen almost single-handedly. A large group of people without those resources probably would have had a more difficult time than I did alone. On the other hand, a human rights effort coordinated by a group of students at my college had very little in the way of material resources, but they were able to use a phone tree and an information table in the post office to motivate more than one thousand calls to Congress in support of a cut in aid to Indonesia. That's something I couldn't have done alone despite all the resources I had at my disposal.

So start off by determining the resources you have access to. Poll members as to what they think they can contribute in the way of contacts, such as a writer for the local newspaper who could help you get publicity, the owner of a nightclub who might host a charity event, someone with a pickup truck who could help with weekend cleanup and recycling drives. These factors should also be considered when you are assigning members to committees.

You don't have much money, so you need to use your imagination. Fund-raising, which I address more thoroughly in Chapter 8, is difficult and time-consuming. Seize every opportunity to get "in-kind" donations—contributions of goods or services rather than money. Take advantage of any opportunities you have for free stuff: Find out, for example, if anyone in the group has a parent who would let you use an office photocopier if you supplied the paper (or if you didn't). Ask to use the school's computer lab after hours to lay out all your publicity materials. (And maybe even get a little extra credit!) See how environmental testing on the local river can be worked into your biology class, and then use school equipment for that, too. How about that small, funny-shaped room in the corner of your school building—can it be used as a student counseling center or as a meeting place for your steering committee?

From Strategy to Structure

Once you have your basic plan of action, you need to fill in the details, to write out the plan in a step-by-step format. Next to each step note the date by which you want to have achieved it. For basic projects your action timetable will have just a few items on it and probably a single date of completion, with maybe one or two intermediate steps. More involved projects will require more steps and possibly more "fudge time" in case you face delays—for example, in getting bureaucratic permission for your project. Put the timetable up for the whole group to see.

Let's say you're planning a letter-writing campaign to convince your senators to support a piece of environmental legislation. What organizational structures will you need to make this plan happen? In other words, what does your group need to do in order to get people in the community to write letters? Break your action plan down into some basic categories: logistics (reserving space to set up a table in the school cafeteria, at the mall, et cetera; clearing your plan with the principal, mall manager, and so forth), basic materials (paper, pens, envelopes, stamps, a table and two chairs, a coffee can for donations toward postage costs), informational materials (a one-page handout explaining what people should write about and/or multiple copies of a form letter for them to sign, a poster to put above the table), publicity (press release, public service announcement, a letter to the editor about your effort), and staffing (getting members of your group signed up to man the table during certain hours of every day). The specific categories you come up with will depend on your project.

Committees

Assign each of these categories to a committee (the less glorious name for "task force") or individual in your group and let them hammer out the details. Use the survey I mentioned in the last chapter—or a more informal discussion of what various members are interested in or have a knack for—to put the knowledge and skills of your group to best use. This information becomes important as you plan your action and divide up your limited resources, personnel, and other items. Knowing what people are best at and what they want to be doing is the way to keep them pointed in the right direction and to use their talents most effectively.

This is particularly important when selecting committee chairpeople. Encourage members with more experience or who have done something related to the task at hand to lead committees. Remember also that the chairperson is in a leadership position; consider the ability of these individuals to interact with members of their committees—to lead by delegating tasks and to maintain enthusiasm. Most important, choose committee leaders you know you can trust, people who can accept responsibility and be counted on to carry out tasks assigned to them. At the outset, have a system of regular "check-ins" so that an important task isn't left undone due to forgetfulness or poor coordination.

Committee membership will be more self-selecting. People will naturally gravitate toward the committees that interest them or where they think their talents will be best used. Each committee should be of a size appropriate to its tasks. For example, one person with a car and some cash can handle your stationery needs; ditto (minus the car and cash) for writing press releases. Logistical arrangements will involve more legwork and can be divided up among a larger group of people. The committee list shown here, from the 1995 Youth Environmental Summit in Loveland, Colorado, is a good example of an effective, well-defined organization for a major project.

YOUTH ENVIRONMENTAL SUMMIT

Committee Organization and Responsibility

Sponsorship: The Sponsorship Committee's responsibility is to raise the necessary funds to host the Summit. Members set up and deliver presentations to foundations, businesses, and service organizations, solicit donations of both cash and in-kind, research and follow through on grant proposals, and host fundraising events within our communities. The Sponsorship Committee works diligently to make sure the Summit has the necessary funding to see our dream become a reality.

Selection: The Selection Committee's function is to set the criteria for attendance at the Summit, research and locate interested students both nationally and internationally, and select participants based on their completed application. Our goal for this Summit is to have two students from every state in the United States and two students from every country in the world. To date we have received qualified applicants from thirty states and fifty countries.

Speakers: This committee is responsible for locating and confirming all keynote speakers and workshop presenters. Since "committed to action" is our theme this year, we want speakers to be individuals who have been proactive and can inspire others to step up and lead. Our workshop presenters will be professionals and youth with skills and expertise in different environmental issues. They will work with and teach smaller, more interactive groups of fifteen to thirty students.

Media: This committee coordinates all aspects of media communications, from sending out press releases to working with reporters. It is essential that our country and world be aware of what is going on with the Youth Environmental Summit and how today's youth are making a positive impact on our world.

Housing and Transportation: This committee is responsible for coordinating housing and ground transportation for the Summit. While in Loveland, participants will stay with local families. We are continually interviewing qualified and interested families within our community. The Housing Committee will coordinate transportation, facilities, and food for the time spent in the mountains.

Food: The Food Committee is responsible for locating local and national companies to donate food for Summit participants. Host families provide both breakfast and a sack lunch for the days we are in Loveland. This is a tremendous help, but we must still provide two breakfasts, two lunches, eight dinners, and snacks for over five hundred.

Y.E.S. Kit: This committee compiles the Y.E.S. kit, a resource book, calendar of events, and action planner given to all participants to help them achieve their goals and to get as much out of the Summit as possible. The Y.E.S. kit will include "how-to" computer disks, world flag, itinerary, articles concerning the environment, detailed descriptions of workshops and keynote speakers, a planning and action guide, environmental facts, resource lists, suggested reading list, collected poetry, list of sponsors, an address book, and note pages for each day. Also included will be the Cultural Handbook, written by elementary school students, in an effort to better understand and promote cultural respect throughout the world.

Expo: This committee plans and coordinates Eco-Expo, a mini World's Fair showcasing environmentally sound organizations, their products and programs. Various university and professional representatives will have booths to show participants the career options available to them in the environmental field.

Events: This committee is responsible for planning events for the Summit participants. Our goal is to make these events action oriented, educational, and fun! This committee has already scheduled tree plantings and *Buckminster Fuller's World Game.*

Organization was a major strength of the Youth Environmental Summit. This is a good example of dividing and defining responsibilities effectively.

Encourage close friends to work together if they want to, but be sure that sharing a committee assignment doesn't mean just another chance to hang out with one another. When it looks as if people are gravitating toward "popular" or high-profile committees, stress that every aspect of the project is important and that writing the press releases is meaningless if there's no activity to advertise. Specifically encourage certain people to be involved in the tasks that you think will suit them best or where there is a particular need for more attention. Encourage committee chairs to keep everyone involved in the process and to draw out reclusive individuals, just as you try to do in your meetings.

Of course, the biggest determinant of how many people work on something will be the size of your group. If there's just a handful of you, each person may find himself designated a committee. (Don't worry; it's not as huge as it sounds.) If the size of your group permits it, however, try to encourage formation of committees that contain a wide range of experience levels; this is a good way to get newer members involved in the process and prepare them to cycle into leadership positions later.

When you plan actions, be sure to take into account the limitations of people in your group—especially time. As students you have to divide your time among some combination of academics, sports, work, and social life—as well as activism. Time is one resource that's really at a premium, and there are going to be periods when other things in your life have to take precedence. This means you should seek projects that maximize your effectiveness in a minimum amount of time. Taking a longer view, it also means you should try to structure a group where members can pick up one another's slack when necessary and a communication network sufficient for this to happen easily.

The Buck Stops Here

Every project should have one person—or at most two people—who serves as coordinator and makes sure everything comes off as planned. This individual's job is to make sure that the project is running smoothly, that all the little easy-to-forget details are being taken care of, and that action is taken to shore up any part of the effort that is lagging behind—whether by her own actions or by seeing to it that someone else fills the breach. Each committee chairperson should report to the coordinator on a regular basis, especially between meetings, and should ask this person for help when it's needed. Remember, though you may have organized the group, you will not always be the project coordinator.

The project coordinator should also be the single person with complete authority as a negotiator with outside organizations and individuals. A big part of your group's credibility will be its ability to live up to its promises. If someone in your group makes commitments on behalf of the group that the group isn't prepared to keep, you're going to look bad when you have to back out. The key words for the project coordinator are *responsibility* for commitments made to those beyond the group and *monitoring* of the group's progress toward its goals.

Some progressive organizations reject this hierarchical structure, advocating a more easygoing system of collaboration among "equals." They seem to associate hierarchy with the "dominant paradigm" of Western, male-oriented society that has resulted in much injustice through misuse of power. But at the level we're talking about—an organization of well-meaning individuals, often friends outside of their activist cause—you will almost certainly find a cooperative atmosphere without thoughts of rank or superiority. And if your group leader is a megalomaniac, that's probably not something that "horizontal organization" will do much to solve anyway.

Put simply, it's better to have a single person—or two people who communicate very frequently—with the final responsibility for the group's actions. This will avoid the misunderstandings that occur when members make promises, and most important, it will ensure that everything gets done because there's a single mind that knows what's going on in all parts of the project organization.

Always maintain open lines of communication. Go out of your way to seek updates from other members of your group. Make evaluation an ongoing process. And keep an eye out for anything that might get lost in the division of labor. It is best to have a base of operations that's accessible to everyone—even if it's a bulletin board. Keep a checklist on the wall of what needs to be done to make your event happen and have each person initial items they've taken care of. (Initialing—and not just a check mark—should be done *after* the task is completed, to avoid confusion.)

If your group is engaged in activities where public knowledge would be a problem, such as a surprise rally in the dean's office, a public checklist is, of course, a bad idea. A good rule of thumb about secrecy: The fewer people you want to know about something, the fewer copies of the document (that is, checklist, press release) should exist and the more control you should exert over how and to whom it is transferred. (Electronic mail, especially, provides a dangerous chance for your secret to be "blown wide open" by someone forwarding a confidential message to a large group of people. Be careful.)

Making the News

Chapter 7 will deal much more completely with how to take best advantage of the opportunities the media present for your group. We'll spend just a few minutes here on how press relations play into your organizational structure.

To deal effectively with the media—getting them to take you seriously and to keep coming back for more—you must present a professional and organized image. Have a single spokesperson who is both articulate and knowledgeable about the subject. Keep in mind that reporters are not only looking for good quotes, they're also going to need background information and data on your issue. Your spokesperson should have that or at least know where to find it so he can get back to the reporter with the information as soon as possible. He should also be someone who can think on his feet (able to answer "curve ball" questions on camera) and can keep a cool head and not get flustered when being cross-examined by an unfriendly reporter.

Refer all press inquiries to the spokesperson and name him as your contact in all press releases. If you want to divide this responsibility between two people, make the second individual a "media coordinator," responsible for receiving press inquiries, directing interviewers to the spokesperson, and laying his hands quickly on any background information requested. This could also be the person in charge of writing and faxing press releases.

Self-generated Publicity

Depending on what you're trying to do, the best press may be what you make yourself: leaflets, posters, and other informational materials. They are the best way to represent yourself to the community directly, in the "first person," without the selective or biased approach you may find in media coverage. They are also visible reminders of your group's existence—meaning they can help attract new members and others interested in the issues you're working on.

Leaflets are small sheets of paper, usually one-quarter to one-half the size of a standard page, that explain your effort and the reasons behind it in short, dramatic prose. These are most useful for encouraging individual or community action, especially when they include a "here's what you can do" section. They can be handed out on street corners, in the lunchroom, at the mall, to members of the crowd at your rally, or almost anywhere else. (Depending on what your leaflet says, you may be prevented from passing them out in places posted "no soliciting"; and, of course, you should get permission first if you intend to hand out leaflets in school or in a place of commerce.) The Springfield Environmental Club's "SAVE IT!" leaflet is eye-catching and informative, as is "A Place to Talk."

Posters can advertise meetings, events, or a current letter-writing drive, or just be designed to get attention for your issue. They should be brightly colored, simple in design and content, and easy to read from far away. Don't try to go into a lot of detail in posters; save that for leaflets, press coverage, or the speakers or activities at your event. See the clean, to-the-point job the National Child Rights Alliance did with their Youth Summit poster. The "Day of Action" poster uses startling facts to get attention.

Information sheets usually include more information and go into more detail than leaflets. They are particularly useful during let-

"[WE] CANNOT TREAT THE EARTH AS SOMETHING SEPARATE FROM HUMAN CIVILIZATION; WE ARE PART OF THE WHOLE TOO, AND LOOKING AT IT ULTIMATELY MEANS LOOKING AT OURSELVES."
— VICE PRESIDENT AL GORE, EARTH IN THE BALANCE

OUR MESSAGE: The earth is ours, and we deserve it to be left in good condition.

OUR PLEA: "Environmentalism" is not a huge concept, it is a series of small changes that each of us — me and you — can make. Please give some of your time this week to...

- **PARTICIPATE** in Springfield Environmental Club's recycling program. Bring glass, plastic (numbers 1 and 2), aluminum cans, and newspaper to the loading dock behind the school every Saturday between 9 a.m. and 2 p.m. We sort your recyclables and take them to the recycling center for you; the proceeds benefit our projects.
- **USE LESS WATER.** One fifth of American water use is non-sustainable — that means we're drawing on water reserves that aren't being replaced. But by installing inexpensive water-saving showerheads and sink faucets available at most hardware stores, you can cut your water use by half... and save money. Take an hour this weekend and make the switch.
- **SUPPORT** the student campaign to retrofit lighting in our school system to compact fluorescents. Contact your school board representatives and PTA leaders and let them know that the expenditure this year is worth the $150,000 more the school will be able to spend on students every year.

For more information contact: **S.E.C.** • c/o Student Activities • Springfield School District • Springfield, SD
MEETINGS EVERY THURSDAY AT 3PM IN ROOM 111

Flyers can advertise services, solicit attendance at an event, urge personal action, or provide background on a problem—such as a flyer of "fallout facts" to distribute at a rally against a toxics incinerator. Sized about one-quarter page, they are

Talk It Out!

We all have times when we just need to talk about something, but it's not always easy. Friends are busy, or don't understand.

A PLACE TO TALK is just that —a comfortable, non-judgmental space where you can air your concerns to patient, understanding individuals. Not adults, not psychiatrists, just people like you who want to listen.

Whether there's something on your mind or you just feel like chatting, stop by Room 211 any day during third or fourth period or lunch. We're here for you.

Parents

Relationships

Grades

Sex

Teachers

Friends

The Future

Confidential...Understanding

A Place To Talk

a good way to disseminate information if you have the person power to distribute them broadly.

ter-writing drives and other lobbying efforts. They provide everyone you're bringing into the project with the same information, including "talking points" for them to bring up when contacting their legislators. Such information sheets can also be provided directly to, say, congressional staffers as a quick and easy way to brief them on the issue you're bringing to them. Use simple sentences with bullet points, and include charts or graphs if appropriate. Stick to the facts, or if your material is campaign-related, present your issue in a "pro/con" format. The East Timor sheet is a good example.

In election years, groups all over the political spectrum print non-partisan voter guides. These can be a powerful educational tool when you're working on lobbying during election season or when you want a handy way to convey your representative's record on certain issues. (This information is also available from organizations like Project Vote Smart, listed in the Resource Directory.) Most groups are more than happy to provide voter guides to anyone who asks. Be sure to go to an organization that's near you on the political spectrum: Even "non-partisan" ones are geared in their language and structure to help one candidate or another.

As you design your materials, take a look at information you've received from national organizations. These groups have experience at presenting issues cogently and simply, and will provide a good example for what you're trying to do with your own issue.

All the materials you produce should include the name of your organization, a brief summary of your mission, and a contact name, phone number, and address. Try to make everything look like it goes together. Like the parts of your mission statement, there should be a visible, logical link among the materials you distribute. Think about creating a logo for your group and putting it on all your materials as well. This will be helpful in creating that link and can give your group more credibility by making you appear more established and professional. Keep your logo fairly simple but avoid what I call "the clip art look," a cutesy or very standard logo that looks like you took it from a book. If there's an artist or graphic designer in your group, have her create the logo.

YOUTH SUMMIT

"By Youth - For Youth"

April 8, 1995

NORTH CAROLINA CENTRAL UNIVERSITY HAYTI CULTURAL CTR.

Youth from around the nation will be coming together on **April 8, 1995**, for an all-day summit **BY AND FOR YOUTH**. On this date in Durham, North Carolina, Youth leaders will present a Youth Bill of Rights for the consideration of summit participants. Some of the issues to be addressed include: ⇨

- AIDS • Racism • Child Abuse
- Student Movement • Environmental Issues
- Free Speech for youth • Psychiatric Abuse of Youth
- Homeless and Runaway Youth, AIDS Orphans • Child Labor and Poverty
- Militarism in Schools • Queer Youth

Youth from India will also participate in the event to raise the issue of child labor exploitation worldwide. Summit youth also hope to involve youth from the Brazilian street children's movement as well.

Contact: Jim Senter
NCRA
PO Box 61125
Durham, NC 27705
919-682-5509
or
Kate Barnhart
JimSenter@delphi.com

Initial Participating Organizations (partial list) include: • Students and Teens Opposed to Psychiatric Abuse • Kids Helping Kids • The Sanctuary • Youth for Philippine Action • Progressive Student Network • Third Wave • People's Association for Rural Development (India) • Children Opposed to Rape and Molestation • Florida Coalition for Peace & Justice • Youth Peace / War Register's League • Coalition of Peer Educators (COPE) • Youth Education Life-line (YELL) • Children's Rights of Pennsylvania • Human Coalition • American Association of Young People • American Association of Former Foster Children • Human Coalition • The Quaker House

Get this ⇨ *Also: Featuring - The only student EVER to be arrested for publishing an underground H.S. Student Paper. And Rutgers University Association of Black Law Students Representative on racism in education and more!*

Look for versatility in posters: NCRA also printed this double-sided, adding an application form on the back and using it as a mailer to interested students.

Concerned About Rape and Domestic Violence? *Newt Gingrich Isn't.*

In fact, his "Contract with America" aims to repeal the 1994 Violence Against Women Act.

The Act provides $1.6 billion over 5 years for police training, battered women's shelters, domestic abuse hotlines, and aid to sexual assault victims. The Act also expands victims' forms of legal protection and recourse.

*While cutting the Act, Newt's budget includes **$72 billion** for 442 fancy fighter planes built in his district. Major General Jay Garner says the F-22 is "the wrong airplane" and its advanced capabilities "while impressive, [are] unnecessary."*

Newt thinks 10 F-22's are more important than fighting violence against women. Do you?

Sources: Robert Shepard, "Female Agenda Takes Long Way To Become Law," *Chicago Tribune*, Sunday, September 25, 1994, Womanews, 1; Robert Scheer, "Hey, Sucker, Wanna Balance the Budget?" *Los Angeles Times*, Sunday January 29, 1995, Opinion, p.5.

Join in a National Day of Action

Wed., March 29 ◆ Noon

Cornell ◆ Willard Straight

What made this poster so effective was its combination with other posters on campus, each focusing on the effects of a particular part of the contract with America (e.g. environmental issues, student aid, civil rights). By doing this, the group was able to bring in a broad range of individuals with varying interests in the cause.

East Timor

Tell Congress to Take a Stand Against Indonesian Genocide

The Facts:

BY DAVE COOK—THE WASHINGTON POST

• In 1975, with the blessing of then-President Ford, Indonesia invaded East Timor on the eve of its independence. Thousands of Timorese and five foreign journalists were killed.

• Since then, Indonesia has carried out a brutal military occupation of the half-island nation. Many Timorese have been herded into camps where, despite widespread malnutrition, they are forced to grow coffee for export.

• **At least 200,000 Timorese — almost one in four — has been *killed* during the Indonesian occupation.**

• The U.S. continues to provide Indonesia with more than 100 million taxpayer dollars each year, plus nearly half a billion dollars in commercial arms sales. These sales are in fact illegal under a 1958 law that says the U.S. may not sell arms to countries engaged in external aggression.

The Opportunity:

• There are currently several bills in Congress to oppose the Indonesian occupation of East Timor. Rep. Ron Machtley (R-RI) is drafting a bill that would cut off all aid to Indonesia, and has co-sponsored a bill that would cut more than $3 million in IMET military training. Another congressional office (Tony Hall, D-OH) is working on a separate bill to curtail U.S. contributions to Indonesia.

Call your Congressional representatives and ask them to support the IMET cut and the Machtley bill when they come to the floor.

Things to emphasize when talking to Congress:

• Austria, Canada, and Holland have all suspended aid as a result of the November massacre. The U.S., under the Foreign Assistance Act, links aid to human rights as a matter of policy. The U.S. must take action consistent with this policy.

• When speaking to Republican congresspeople, remind them that U.S.-backed genocide is a non-partisan issue and that suspension of aid has bi-partisan support.

• If questions of IMET are brought up, remember that the U.S. has been providing military aid to Indonesia since 1955, and in that time millions of civilians have been killed by the Indonesian army, not just the 200,000 people who have died in East Timor.

• The U.S. has been quick to support UN sanctions against Libya and Iraq. Why has the U.S. worked *against* moves to sanction Indonesia? (A UN resolution was defeated in early March by pressure from the U.S., Japan, Australia and Canada -- Indonesia's largest trading partners.)

• Remind them that UN actions are being taken in Cambodia. Why not in East Timor? In per capita terms, the genocide in East Timor has been worse than that in Pol Pot's Cambodia.

Contact: EAST TIMOR ACTION NETWORK/RI • Box 1930 • Providence, RI 02912-1930

This information sheet makes a good handout for letter-writers and a handy "cheat sheet" for organizers manning the campaign table.

Budgeting

This is usually the easy part. Your treasurer says, "We have no money." You nod and say, "That's too bad," and move on to the next agenda item.

The process of allocating resources is important because yours are so limited. You'll often see "creativity" referred to in this book. In the context of budgeting, this means doing more with less, cutting corners, and adjusting priorities to do the best you can with what you have. Budget considerations will be part of any project-planning process, but they should never be the only way that you define your limits. It's as if you're looking at the project in both directions—the "ideal case" of what you want to do and the "reality" of what you can do with the resources you currently have on hand—and finding a realistic middle ground that takes into consideration where corners can be cut and what kind of support you think you'll be able to generate. Look for places where creativity or a little extra time can make up the difference between what you can afford and what you want to do.

Start by drafting your ideal-case budget, one that looks at your project idea and says, "Here is how we can do this, with only top-quality materials, speakers, and transportation." This will take a little research. Call around to find out what things cost. Ask your parents or teachers what kind of expenses might be involved in what you're trying to do, including "little" things like parking fees when you drive someplace and easy-to-forget things such as telephone bills. If you don't anticipate these costs, they'll come out of your own pocket; after a while you won't be able to afford doing that.

Now go back through your dream budget and see what you can do without and what you can replace—for instance, using photocopied posters instead of professionally printed ones, picking speakers up at the airport instead of paying their cab fare, and providing a full hour break instead of serving lunch at your day-long teach-in (as long as there are places for people to go for lunch). It's like that old adage about packing for a vacation: "Pack everything you want to take, then put half of it back." After a project or two, this will become second nature.

This kind of accounting will also be an ongoing process as you evaluate the progress of your fund-raising. Sometimes you have to make tough decisions, like doing without a speaker who can't come because you can't afford to fly her in or planting fewer trees because of the cost of saplings.

Part of budgeting is making smart choices. If you're having materials printed up—T-shirts, banners, and the like—shop around for the best prices and make a good pitch to printers to give you a break because of the worthiness of your cause or because you'll let them put their logo in the corner of the materials. Getting donations, particularly in-kind donations, will be an important part of much of your work.

Negotiating

Getting from here to there will almost always mean interacting with people whose permission, support, or influence you need. Sometimes the relationship will seem adversarial, as when you're trying to change the position of an unfriendly legislator. Just as often they will be amicable—talking about goals with a possible coalition partner, for example—or neutral, what salesmen call a "cold call" where you need both to inform someone about your work and to ask them for help.

Yours is the high road. In planning the personality of your approach, prepare to strike a balance between confrontation and conciliation. The exact ratio of the mix will depend on how much initial agreement there is between you and the powers that be. Sometimes you will need to present forceful, emotive arguments in order to overcome deep disagreement between you and the person across the desk. Sometimes all it will take is a combination of praise and an appeal to common sense—for, say, a congressman to take his "caring for kids" sentiment one logical step further, to protecting the environment. The more you and the other party seem to agree at the outset—in other words, the less you have to nudge the other party to achieve what you want—the less confrontational you should be.

Remember that you carry moral strength in your movement and

in what you are trying to do. Your youth and your commitment to these goals is a big part of your appeal to those beyond your group. As you begin to work with those people, try to expand your community to include them. Let the persons in power buy into your dream because they want to identify with your group and your strength. Your visceral appeal, even more than your brilliant tactics, will draw in those who want to share your vision. But this is not everybody.

The first rule of negotiating is to know what you want and to maintain your focus on goals throughout the process. Decide what you want to get out of the negotiation: a changed vote, permission to hold a demonstration in the town square or to cross someone's property en route to an ecological site, or the use of an empty classroom for group activities. Think in terms of the "best-case scenario." Now figure out where you can give a little: avoiding harsh rhetoric in the future if your politician votes your way, being off the property by sundown, taking responsibility for cleaning up your space. Think of these as "drop-back" positions to be offered in order to get what you're looking for.

For example, if you're trying to put together a one-day environmental justice colloquium on your campus, you'll probably go to someone in the dean's office as well as faculty in the environmental studies and political science department. You may decide to go into these meetings asking for full funding of your project and some of the secretary's time in making the logistical arrangements. Maybe you'll get only half of the funding; that's an acceptable "step back," and it's a heck of a lot better than nothing. The successes of your first meeting will determine your goals going into the second meeting.

Negotiation is your tool to get as close as you can to your best-case scenario by offering small concessions on your side. At the risk of presenting an incredibly trite analogy, think about negotiation being like trading baseball cards in elementary school: your Babe Ruth (say, a public campaign of embarrassment or boycott against a polluting company) is worth ten of their Mario Mendozas (say, limited or cosmetic changes in company policy). Negotiation is a game of bargaining, of give-and-take, until terms are reached that are amenable to both sides.

Remember that you can't take back an offer once you've made

it. Stand firm and give only a little at a time, unless it becomes clear that the other side will not budge. When negotiating, "no" means no only when they've said it three times.

Begin by establishing what the discussion is and is not about; this will keep negotiations on track and prevent surprises that might put one party on the defensive. As an example: "Thank you for taking the time to meet with us, Superintendent. We're here to talk about the school district's recycling program. We would like to present our case for expanding the program and want to hear your perspective on how that might be possible." This statement establishes both the topic and the tone of the meeting: You're demonstrating your interest in what the superintendent has to say, but you are also making it clear that you know your stuff and have done your research.

Here are some ideas on more "hard-nosed" negotiating:

Make sure that meetings with the powers that be are "open-door" meetings—that what is said is official and on the record (meaning you can go to the press with it), that more than one representative of each side is present, and that both sides acknowledge the right of others (such as the student body) to know about what went on. This will avoid a war of believability if one side does not follow through on agreements made. (Otherwise, it's your word against theirs, and they're bigger than you are.) Go in with notes to be sure you don't forget anything that needs to be discussed, and take notes during the meeting. Write down questions as they occur to you; be sure to ask all of them by the end of the meeting.

Ask to negotiate as a small group—say, three students. The ability to back up one another will make it harder for the people you're talking with to be overbearing or intimidating, or to try to fool you with their savvy or word games. When you negotiate as a group, be sure you have discussed your plans and positions in advance and designate one person as primary negotiator. The others can present portions of the case for your position and of course can offer input throughout the process. When in the negotiating situation, avoid moves that your compatriots don't expect. Always present a united front. If you have a disagreement with someone in your party, present it to those present as "another alternative" rather than starting a dispute within your group in front of "the other side." If necessary, ask for a few moments to confer privately during the meeting.

Sometimes you'll find yourself facing a very politically charged situation. Perhaps what you're doing appears to challenge the authority of the powers that be, or maybe they are just reluctant to put responsibility in the hands of students whose only goal should be (in their minds) to learn what you're taught. Anything that has the potential to make someone—perhaps a principal or dean—look bad or even that could reflect badly on "their turf," like wanting to do an anti-bias program in a school where the principal doesn't want to believe there's racial tension, will put officials on their guard and make it more difficult to get what you're looking for.

Begin by demonstrating genuine interest in working with these individuals. Join their little committees or start off by proposing a joint project that could not meet with rejection. This is why a friend of mine says that tree-plantings are the best first event for a student organization: Who could object to a tree planting? And once the trees are planted and the amicable relationship has been formed with officials, they've shed their wariness of your group and may even be feeling genuine moral support for you and your efforts. That can only make it easier to take further steps toward the kind of meaningful change you're looking for.

As has already been said, you should know what you want before going into negotiations. Now for the important corollary: Know what you're getting when you leave, and be sure the person on the other side of the table knows as well. Get a concrete commitment, with a timetable, for whatever each side is promising to do or not do. Once you've reached consensus on the issues at hand, draw the discussion to a close with a statement such as, "So, Dean Tanner, we've agreed to work together on this environmental justice colloquium, with funding coming half from your office and half from our student activities budget. We will do all the legwork and publicity for the event, and you will make arrangements for the room and deliver the opening remarks. Does that reflect your understanding of our agreement?" Before you leave the room, be sure that everyone knows what has been decided and, if appropriate, that you've scheduled a specific time when the additional details will be coordinated.

Follow up the next day with a brief note thanking the person for meeting with you and reiterating the agreement reached.

Get It in Writing

If your agreement involves receiving funding or sharing expenses for a project, ask for a signed letter confirming the arrangements made or even a "memorandum of agreement" that outlines the terms of your agreement and is signed by representatives of both parties. Be careful, though: If you sign for a student group that does not formally exist, you may be the one held liable for the terms of the agreement if your group can't come through. Discuss such measures with your advisor or a knowledgeable adult before signing anything. There's nothing wrong with asking to take a copy of the memorandum and bringing it back the next day; don't be pressured otherwise.

Rolling with the Punches

Okay, so you can negotiate and make your pitch to the community and even keep your own stuff together in the process. But what happens if all that doesn't do you any good? We've all come face to face with brick walls in our time as activists. What those of us who stick with it have learned is that there's usually a door somewhere, and even when there's not, we'll probably be able to come up with some grappling equipment.

If you find no success even when offering concessions or compliments to the powers that be, seeking media support, or whatever, first take a step back before frustration gets the better of your diplomacy. Talk over what happened with other leaders and the people that are closest to you. Ask for input at the next meeting. Regroup and find another way to approach the problem. Look again for faculty support or go to your parents and try to rally parental support within your school or community. Look outside your school to local firms and service clubs that might be able to provide everything you hoped to get from your first source. In short, always have alternatives.

This points to another important item for student organizers: Always have some kind of contingency plan. Be prepared to drop back to a less ambitious project or even a very different issue if you reach the end of your rope on plan A. Have an idea of what direction you might go so you can redirect your volunteers' efforts quickly and avoid losing momentum. Your group will need strong, well-considered leadership at this time. Stick to your democratic principles: Bring plan B into focus through discussion and move forward on it with the support of members.

The old adage, "If at first you don't succeed, try, try again," goes double for student organizing: It's not always easy, and sometimes it's remarkably difficult. Keep your eyes on the prize, maintain a positive attitude, and convey that attitude to the people you're working with. Be flexible: Roll with the punches and always have ideas about other directions you can take your group if things aren't working out.

5

Changing Policy: Helping Government Do the Right Thing

Many activists focus their efforts on the "policy arena"—legislative and governmental processes where rules and regulations are made. While the drafting and passage of legislation can be a painfully slow and often frustrating process, there is an undeniable excitement to having one's words and goals end up on the books as law. Likewise, preventing a harmful or unjust law from being passed—especially over the wishes and efforts of environmentally malicious corporations—is a heartening example of democracy at work.

The legislative strategies in this chapter are applicable to almost any level of government, but you will probably find the greatest effect at the local (municipal) or state level. National campaigns are out of reach of individual youth activists, although you definitely should not hesitate to use these strategies to encourage your congressional representatives to support national legislation that is important to you. In particular, you can serve as a vital link in national grassroots efforts like those organized by the Sierra Student Coalition and 20/20 Vision. Contact these and similar groups, which are listed in the Resource Directory, to join their networks and stay up-to-date on their national campaigns.

Also keep in mind that references here to "legislation" and "legislators" may not mesh with the rules and protocols of the body you're trying to affect, particularly if it's a smaller government such as a town council. Early in the process, make a point of asking legislators or their staffs some very basic questions: "What's the step-by-step process for getting a resolution/bill/motion through the body? What deadlines will we have to meet, and how quickly will things have to move once our motion reaches the floor?" And, of course, "How can you help us?"

Ask and Ye Shall Receive

Always be specific about what you want your legislators to do. In the words of a friend of mine who has worked on Capitol Hill for a number of years, "Any elected official will nod, tell you you're interesting, and make you feel important. You have to tell them exactly what you want them to do—to 'close the sale' with a call for action—if you want to make anything happen."

Also remember that there's more to ask for than just a vote for or against a bill or amendment. Ask your legislator to sponsor, cosponsor, or introduce legislation on your issue, or to send a "Dear Colleague" letter to other legislators urging them to do the same. If you can't get the legislator to agree with you, ask him to abstain from voting ("take a walk"), refrain from working against your position, meet with experts or affected individuals, or work for a change in wording that allows you to meet halfway.

If you find yourself having a great deal of trouble getting binding legislation passed, try for a resolution. A resolution is a nonbinding statement of the interest or desire of the legislature (for example, "The legislature urges citizens to participate in community recycling efforts") and can be a good first step toward subsequent legislation of a more substantial nature.

Another interesting strategy is to introduce legislation that you know won't get passed but do so in a way that makes legislators look bad for not passing it or that exposes the "underside" of what they're trying to do. A good example of this tactic was the "Boxer amendment" introduced by Senate Democrats—including California's Senator Barbara Boxer—during debate on one of the 104th Congress's crown jewels, the GOP's legislation prohibiting "unfunded mandates." The Republicans wanted to prohibit the U.S. government from enacting regulations regarding health, safety, the environment, and so on, without reimbursing states for the cost of enforcement—a move that would gut most regulations that protect the basic security we all enjoy. In response, Boxer and company introduced an amendment prohibiting the "unfunded mandate" legislation from affecting regulations that protect the health and safety of children. The defeat of this amendment forced the Republicans on record as endangering our nation's most innocent citizens. Ouch!

Take Aim

The first thing to find out when you want to change policy is: Where is this type of policy made, and where can you have an effect on it? Much environmental regulation occurs at the national level—the Clean Air Act and the Clean Water Act being two good examples—but some legislation allows states and localities to pass different rules as long as they aren't weaker and don't contradict federal statutes. Talk to legislative staff members in your congressman's district office or in your state capital, or to other knowledgeable individuals, to figure out where to target your efforts.

You may also find that there is more than one way to do what you want. For example, if you're trying to prevent a polluting industry from building a plant in your community, it may not be reasonable to change environmental regulations in time to stop them. But go to your municipal supervisors and see if it's possible to change zoning laws (rezone the site as residential property, for example) so that the potential factory site is no longer legal for that use. Such action doesn't address environmental issues *per se,* but the effect is the same if you are successful.

Seek Allies

Affecting the legislative process effectively is not something you'll be able to do alone, particularly if you're new at this. Seek help in developing the legislation from a conceptual standpoint (for example, figuring out exactly what actions or groups you do and don't want to target, and making sure your legislation doesn't contradict something already on the books unless that's its intent) and in drafting the final version. The language and format you use will be important: Have someone who knows help you out. This help could come from your legislators and their staffs, from knowledgeable individuals at a local university, or from resources accessible through another group acting in the public interest.

If a law like the one you want to pass already exists, then the problem is in enforcement. Find out what agency is responsible for seeing that the law is obeyed, and find out why that agency is not doing its job. Pressure it to do so—either through a grassroots effort, by mounting a media campaign to expose the wrongdoing, or by asking your representative to "lean on it."

Do a little research—check voting records available at the state capitol or city hall or inquire of legislators and legislative monitoring groups like the League of Conservation Voters—to find out which legislators have supported similar legislation in the past. If no one has actually sponsored legislation in the right vein, see who has been an outspoken advocate of your issues or of related issues. They may be interested in helping you; often they have staff members who worked on earlier legislation and so can be valuable resources. Make an effort to meet and talk with these staffers, and try to make them feel included in your efforts; such people are very strong allies to have.

The surest way to get a legislator's attention is to contact your own. He is the one you and your parents elected (even if you didn't vote for him), and he knows he'll have to answer to you again in a year or two. While he may not be the environmental or social justice champion you're looking for, he will be eager to please his constituents and can either point you in the right direction or agree to sponsor or support something you have put the time and effort into drafting.

Seek out nongovernmental organizations (NGOs) in your community that might have an interest in what you're doing or could lend you their expertise. These will often include local chapters of state and national organizations, such as Public Interest Research Groups (PIRGs) and the National Conference, or service clubs that have a political action wing. Explain to them what you are trying to do and ask for their help in terms as specific as possible. Ask if they have lobbyists in the state capital (or wherever you're hoping to effect change) that you could contact for help in reaching

SUCCESS STORY

A Youth Voice in the Legislature

Seeing a need for greater representation of youth concerns in the Colorado Legislature, Eileen Burke and Monica Loseman, then seventeen, joined forces in 1993 to seek passage of a resolution on the topic. Loseman, who was copresident of the State Student Council, and Burke, a longtime advocate of youth representation in Congress, formed a committee of Student Council members in the Denver-Boulder area.

The group drafted a resolution calling for annual youth forums in each legislator's district; it was then put into formal language by the Legal Services Department of the state legislature. Drawing on the combined networks of the committee's members and with the help of a professional lobbyist from the Colorado Student Association, the group found a number of cosponsors from both political parties. Students around the state were given information about the resolution, as well as instructions advising them on how to contact legislators.

The resolution—which was passed on the last day that the Colorado Legislature met in March 1994—contains a variety of "whereas clauses" expressing the need for and interest in greater youth representation in the state, and a "be it resolved" clause encouraging legislators to give greater attention to youth issues and, with the help of student leaders, to organize and hold meetings with the youth of their districts to discuss issues of concern.

Burke, who graduated from high school in the spring of 1994, calls the resolution "a starting point." She has passed her resources and contact lists on to younger students now entering leadership positions in the committee, who she says are mapping plans for stronger legislation *requiring* legislators to hold youth meetings.

---

legislators. Always make it clear that you are not trying to "muscle in" on the organization's territory, that you will not take advantage of their access to legislators, and that you will not use that access in a way that might jeopardize it (like acting offensively toward the legislator during a meeting). This is one place where your affiliation with another large organization would be advantageous, since it will see in you the same legitimacy that the chapter receives from *its* national affiliation.

If you think it would be useful, seek a more formal "working relationship" with the other organization. This may enable you to work with them on multiple projects, particularly in the context of trading support—that is, they'll help you out if you'll assist their grassroots campaigns. Working with a grassroots campaign to support legislation that's already in the pipeline is also good practice when you want to orchestrate your own campaign. If your issue and theirs have a lot of common ground, perhaps you'll even be able to convince them to include some of your language in their bill in exchange for a coordinated effort.

Show the Advantages of Your Proposition

The key to getting support for what you're trying to do is to show why it's a good idea from as many angles (e.g., environmental, economic, impact on local residents) as possible. Make sure to back up your arguments with facts, and be able to cite their sources whenever possible. Remember the difference between fact and interpretation; in addition to your facts, find some background resources that include interpretations and analysis of the issues involved—by local experts or in published works by national figures such as Ralph Nader and Noam Chomsky. (Be aware of how the reputations of public figures can affect your argument when you draw on their work: If your opposition is likely to attack such individuals' characters or positions on other issues, be prepared to respond.)

One of the most useful arguments to have on your side is an economic one. Often, you may not seem to have it. When you're arguing against a public works project that will bring jobs into the community, you're setting yourself up to be on the losing side of the environment-versus-development battle. (For one thing, this is a false dichotomy set up by proponents of "development"—the people who used the spotted owl "issue" to make it look like environmentalism is allegedly destroying the logging industry.) Respond, depending on the specifics of your case, by addressing quality-of-life issues like pollution-related health risks; possible damage to the existing, traditional economy; moral issues surrounding environmental destruction (for example, "It's just not right"); and local aesthetics. In making your case, provide alternatives to the legislation or project at hand and express willingness to work toward those alternatives alongside your opponents.

Of course, if you can find a way to have economic issues on your side—supporting something that involves bringing government money into the community or expanding on the above "traditional economy" argument to bolster your arguments in favor of a certain measure—run with it.

Think also about arguments that you yourself might not make. If you're opposing a dam project on the local river, you may be concerned about biodiversity—the beavers and egrets that will lose their homes—but another likely by-product of the dam might be the destruction of local fishing or rafting grounds. If this argument will get local sport enthusiasts on your side, it's worth making and repeating.

While you're at it, appeal to notable individuals in the community (business leaders, educators, and so forth) to lobby your legislator or "go public" in support of your effort. The support of such individuals will have a strong influence on your legislator. If you're going to be setting up a table outside a house of worship, ask the clergy to announce your effort from the pulpit.

Letters to the editor can also have a particularly strong impact as lobbying tools. Legislators or their staffs read the newspapers every day; the district offices of most U.S. legislators clip anything that mentions their name and fax it to them each morning. Because it is a public appeal for specific action by the legislator—meaning that the community will be watching her action on the issue and that someone (you) is willing to discuss it in a very public way—a letter to the editor carries a great deal of weight.

"The Best Defense"

Anticipate what your opponents are going to say about the issue and prepare a complete response to every argument they have. People are always looking for ways to catch environmentalists off guard or make them trip over their own arguments. This doubles your responsibility to know your subject from "all sides" as best you can.

Research the opposing position and take a look at the issue based on their priorities. To prepare your responses, hold a debate within your group and have several members act as opponents to your position. This will also give you a chance to explore areas of mutual agreement: However small these may seem, they can become the seeds of a win-win agreement if you ever find yourself able to interact directly with those opposing you. Writing up a pro/con fact sheet will also be helpful; such a sheet can then become part of the publicity material (like leaflets and posters) used to encourage people in your community to take part in lobbying on the issue.

Use the System to Your Advantage

Often, particularly in the case of environmental legislation or new building projects, regulations require a public hearing on the issue, allowing local residents to voice their concerns. These hearings usually end up as a formality because no one attends, and sometimes they are simply not held despite regulations. If you are opposing such a project, find out when the hearing is and attend it; use the grassroots strategies below to bring people out in force. Ask to testify, particularly if you know the issue well or if you represent a part of the community that will be affected by the decision. If a hearing is mandated but doesn't seem to be forthcoming, demand it; threaten to report the developers and your legislator or local supervisor to whatever entity is charged with making sure hearings take place if it isn't held in a satisfactory time and location. If the law provides only for a "period of public debate" during which it is the responsibility of citizens to convey their concerns to the agency, use the same grassroots lobbying strategies you would with pending legislation.

Like hearings and periods of public debate, environmental impact studies are usually mandated as part of the permission granted to developers. Ask for copies of study results and other statements; look closely at them—or ask an expert to help you do so—for inaccurate information or misinterpretation of data. If it's appropriate, publicly challenge the statement (before the relevant governing body). This will usually force the developers to conduct another study, resulting in greater expense to them and more delays to the project. Tactics like this that delay projects and increase expense and inconvenience to developers can be among the most useful you'll find for postponing or preventing environmentally harmful development in your area. Don't be afraid to "throw the book at them."

Political Support

Okay, let's get back to the lobbying side of things. The first question that will come to your legislator's mind when you approach him is, "Why should I support this?" The political translation of this question is, "What is it about this bill that will make my constituents remember my action when election time rolls around?" Think about possible answers to that question. Is your effort feel-good legislation, like declaring a local Youth and the Environment Day? This is something that will help your legislator's image as a nice guy who cares about his constituents. (The political analogy is "kissing babies.") Are you seeking support for a youth center in your community? This could bring outside money into the community—read "jobs."

Unfortunately, not all political efforts are so facile. Are you trying to prevent the construction of an incinerator near your town? Back to the old environment-versus-development conundrum: The issue presents your legislator with a tug of war between economic interests (the project will bring jobs and money into the community and probably promises to be clean and safe; the firm may also be one of the legislator's campaign backers) and environmental and moral ones. These are battles which business—with its money and access that the nonprofit sector can never match—has an annoying tendency to win. Time to bring your legislator back to his guiding principle: getting reelected.

Demonstrate Community Interest: Grassroots Lobbying and More

To motivate your legislator, you have to motivate members of your community to contact him and express their support for what you're trying to do. The way to a legislator's heart is through the ballot box. Show him that his voting constituency is interested in the issue, sufficiently interested that the issue could be a "defining" one for his public image, and even the wealthiest political contributors will have trouble buying his agreement.

The first step toward community action is awareness. You have to inform people about the issue, about why it matters to them and about what they can do about it. Don't forget that last part. It's easy to get people to listen to you for a few seconds and even to get them worrying about an issue, but you must provide them with a way to express that concern right then and there.

The easiest community to motivate will be that group of people most affected by the legislation or project at hand. This may mean people who live near a proposed waste site or the parents of children who go to school near one. If it's social or economic policy you're addressing, the most affected may be working parents, the unemployed, or young people. The nature of the affected community will determine your strategy: If your community is politically underrepresented—for example, the young, recent immigrants, and many poorer communities—a voter registration drive may be the first step to empowerment. (In registration drives, it's best to avoid advocating a particular policy of ideology; save that for the next step.) If the community is already organized around some other entity—the PTA, a church or community organization, the student union—access these groups as a venue for your efforts.

Use a combination of educational and attention-getting tactics as appropriate to your issue and community. These may include rallies or other demonstrations, a media campaign, or a community education effort that ties in with grassroots lobbying. Gauge which will be the most effective in your community and which your group is equipped to do within the necessary time constraints. Be creative.

If you think your community will be receptive to the idea—in other words, if you think it will be worth the time and effort—organize an event that includes individuals knowledgeable on the issue. Invite your legislator(s) and ask them to speak as well. This will force them to articulate their position and defend it, and to respond directly to constituents' concerns. Try to keep the event focused on the issue at hand; some people, given the opportunity to address their legislator directly, will go far off topic. As with meeting strategies outlined in the previous chapter, make an effort to keep the discussion on course.

"By the People"

If you've attained the legal age limit (eighteen in most states for most positions), consider running for office yourself. It's a great way to get press for the issues that are important to you. Getting directly involved in the campaign process will be an exciting move for your organization. But beware: If you are representing a nonprofit organization (even just as a local chapter), partisanship may be illegal. You may have to break away and create a separate "committee to elect John Doe" if you want to run. (And if your name is John Doe.)

Running for office is also a good chance to make contacts in one of the political parties. This will be useful, in the short run, because you'll have familiar ears to bend with your lobbying efforts and, in the long run, if you want to stay involved in politics. Remember that if you run for office, you might just win. Be prepared to shoulder those responsibilities or don't waste your time on the effort.

WORDS OF WISDOM

A Revolution of Values

I am convinced that . . . we as a nation must undergo a radical revolution of values. When machines and computers, profit and property rights are considered more important than people, the giant triplets of racism, materialism, and militarism are incapable of being conquered.

A true revolution of values will soon cause us to question the fairness and justice of many of our past and present policies. True compassion is more than flinging a coin to a beggar: It is not haphazard and superficial. It comes to see that an edifice which produces beggars needs restructuring. A true revolution of values will soon look uneasily on the glaring contrast of poverty and wealth. With righteous indignation, it will look across the seas and see individual capitalists of the West investing huge sums of money in Asia, Africa, and South America, only to take the profits out with no concern for the social betterment of the countries, and say: "This is not just." It will look at our alliance with the landed gentry of Latin America and say: "This is not just." The Western arrogance of feeling that it has everything to teach others and nothing to learn from them is not just. A true revolution of values will lay hands on the world order and say of war: "This way of settling differences is not just." This business of burning human beings with napalm, of filling our nation's homes with orphans and widows, or injecting poisonous drugs of hate into the veins of people normally humane, of sending men home from dark and bloody battlefields physically handicapped and psychologically deranged, cannot be reconciled with wisdom, justice, and love. A nation that continues year after year to spend more money on military defense than on programs of social uplift is approaching spiritual death.

. . . There is nothing, except a tragic death wish, to prevent us from reordering our priorities, so that the pursuit of peace will take precedence over the pursuit of war. There is nothing to keep us from molding a recalcitrant status quo until we have fashioned it into a brotherhood.

—Rev. Dr. Martin Luther King, Jr.,
"Declaration of Independence from
the War in Vietnam"

A Letter-writing Drive

The classic tool of grassroots lobbying is the letter-writing drive. This involves setting up a table somewhere in your community—at the mall or the grocery store, in the lobby of a church or temple after services, or outside a local factory at shift-changing time—where you and your group can explain what you're trying to do and provide passersby with an instant way to make their voices heard. This is a particularly good outlet for high school activists: Make up a handout or a transparency for the overhead projector and ask each teacher to give ten minutes of class one day for students to write letters. When instructing people on how to write letters, keep in mind the following guidelines.

Handwritten letters carry far more weight with legislators than do preprinted form letters. Provide visitors to your table with a fact sheet that includes recommendations on what to write, including a specific mention of the resolution they are asking the legislator to support. Have plenty of copies of this fact sheet so that interested people can take a copy away with them. (Be sure your group's name and contact information also appear on the fact sheet.) Tape a few copies of the fact sheet to the table, some of them facing out to the writers and some facing you so that they can act as a "crib sheet" when you give your pitch. Also have a poster that states in simple terms what you're doing there—e.g., URGE SENATOR SPECTER TO SUPPORT MILITARY CONVERSION ACT. WRITE LETTERS HERE. SPONSORED BY HARRISBURG INTERFAITH PEACE COMMITTEE—and try to place it someplace where it will be visible (perhaps on the wall behind you) rather than on the front of your table where it will be blocked by people's legs.

Provide table visitors a sheet of paper and a pen, and ask them to write a brief letter based on the information you provide. Make sure they put their return address on the letter; envelopes are thrown away by the legislative staff. If possible, have writing paper and envelopes of varying sizes and styles; this will make your effort look even less contrived. When the person has finished writing, have him or her address an envelope to the legislator. Thank the person and take the envelope and letter back to mail later. Don't let visitors walk away with their letters because many will forget to mail them. (Of course, do this very politely!) Ask for a contribution toward postage. Don't forget to make a pitch for your group as well. Tell visitors the time and location of your next meeting, and have plenty of flyers for the taking.

Most grassroots lobbying guides offer the following suggestions for letter writers, and you may want to share them with table visitors:

- Begin by thanking the legislator for favorable action, if appropriate, or mention an area of agreement. (This is establishing common ground or "buttering them up.")
- Limit topics to one or two crucial things. (This will be the function of your fact sheet.)
- State your reason for writing based on personal experience and/or give the reasons why *you* support given legislation.
- Use your own words: Encourage letter writers not to copy word-for-word from your fact sheet.
- Ask legislators how they plan to vote. Ask a question that requires an original answer since this may encourage the legislative staff to do more research on the issue.

You may find it easier to type a form letter or postcard to your legislator and simply ask passersby to sign a copy. While this is less effective than handwritten letters, it's much better than nothing. As before, make sure that the signers write their address on the letters, address an envelope, and give a contribution toward postage.

Once your letter-writing drive is done, mail the letters a few at a time over the course of about a week. This will also make letters seem more spontaneous and less like part of a campaign.

You may be thinking, "What about petitions?" I've found that petitions are almost useless. The action involved in signing a petition—simply writing one's name—is not a demonstration of commitment or concern about an issue, and legislators know that. There may be situations at the local level where the population of the community is small enough or familiar enough to local policymakers that they will take a petition seriously. Otherwise, petitions are just for show.

Three other strategies for motivating grassroots lobbying—phonebanking, canvassing, and letters to the editor—will be discussed in Chapter 6.

Ultimately, your lobbying strategy will depend on whether or not your legislator and members of your community support what you're trying to do. When you're working with a legislator who is already on your side, public praise and thank-you's are the way to go. If your legislator is undecided—a "swing" vote—that's the time to focus your efforts on a grassroots lobbying campaign, write letters to the editor, and encourage your contacts in the media to write articles about the issue that present your arguments to the community. Even legislators who oppose you can be convinced to abstain or fight within their own party for more moderate language if you can show the political support in the community. The toughest part comes when your community is undecided or opposes your efforts; in both cases, public education and vocal support for your initiative is the way to go. If you're up against your community, you have the additional task of making sure that it's *your* voice that's loudest in legislators' ears. Don't see obstacles—see challenges!

Timing

They say timing is everything. Think about what else is happening in your community and in the legislature while you're conducting your lobbying effort. The best time to introduce new legislation is early in the spring, at the start of the legislative session. Election years are an especially good time. Your measure will pass just in time for the legislator to be fondly remembered on election day.

Also keep in mind the opportunity that legislators have to kill a bill (without losing face) just by tabling it or failing to act before the legislative session ends. Keep leaning on your legislator and redouble your lobbying efforts if closing day is approaching and it looks like your bill may be overlooked.

If appropriate, try to coordinate your effort with other things happening in the community: local festivals, the visit of a big-name speaker, or other popular events. Also remember that there's an element of luck involved. If it weren't for a long, hot summer—spurring public discussion about the greenhouse effect—the Clean Air Act might have had a tougher time getting renewed in 1990.

6

Community Education: Teaching to Take Action

Community education—distributing information (and interpretations thereof) designed to change people's actions or attitudes—is an excellent opportunity for youth activism because the tools you need are simple: facts and background on an issue, the strength of your convictions, and a little creativity in conveying your message. It's an opportunity to change people's minds about an issue, to introduce them to new ways of thinking about the world around them, and to influence them to act on behalf of themselves and their surroundings.

As with the legislative efforts addressed in the previous chapter, you should always know what actions you're asking for and be explicit in explaining them to people with whom you interact. Remember that awareness does not necessarily lead to action; you have to ask for what you want.

In defining issues for your audience, always think of yourself as answering their question, "Why does this matter to me?" The answers for this question will be different depending on the segment of the audience you're attempting to reach. My earlier example of sport enthusiasts opposing a dam project shows one way to visualize an issue from another's viewpoint. What would be some ways to portray the same issue to your town's elderly community? Maybe something about "destroying the traditional, historic character of the region." (How about appealing to your local newspaper for an article about their childhood memories of the river and how those memories would "drown" in the dam project?) Would the same argument wash in your town's upper-class neighborhoods? What kind of appeal might work there?

Follow these same guidelines when you're trying to appeal to members of your community to change their own actions—say, urging them to recycle plastics, to "shop green," or to participate in a town-wide racial unity event. Use "if . . . then" statements to explain the benefits of their action and the problems that come with inaction. Whenever possible, explain the direct impact *on them* in graphic (but true) terms. Besides presenting facts, use dramatic examples of the real impact of the problem on real people. (A good example is how, during the health care policy debates of 1993, President Bill Clinton always told horror stories of misfortunes that have befallen uninsured individuals.) Because people often make judgments in terms of "better or worse" rather than "good or bad," use comparisons when making your point. This is an extension of what was said earlier about knowing your opponent's arguments and crafting rebuttals that use their own language and logic against them.

Keep your arguments simple and make positive appeals, particularly when dealing with issues that people may find depressing or unsettling. If you're talking about military conversion, for example, turn the focus away from potential job loss in your community and instead encourage dialogue on ideas for retraining and retooling local defense-related industries and attracting new economic opportunities to the area.

Venue Menu

You'll need to focus your limited resources and efforts on whatever outlets will give you the greatest access to your most appropriate audiences. So the first question to ask is, "Whom are we trying to reach, and where are they?"

When your audience is your fellow students or younger students in your community, the obvious answer is school. Think about the best ways to reach your peers within the school environment. If your high school is anything like mine was, the answer is not "in class." Doing a class presentation was like looking out into a sea of glazed-over eyes—at least those that were open. What are some nonacademic, yet still organized and manageable outlets at your school? Maybe the answer is a special assembly conducted with the permission of your principal. Maybe it's a presentation during halftime at basketball games or posters on the cafeteria walls. The geography and social atmosphere of your school are unique, and no one knows them better than you. Use them to your best advantage.

If you're trying to reach your parents—or, more broadly, the middle-aged consumers and property owners of your community—the answers will be very different. Try asking your parents for ideas if they're willing to lend their counsel. If not, just watch them, and you'll get many of the answers you need: Where do they go? What do they do? What kinds of ideas and styles appeal to them? Canvassing and phonebanking that focus on "family neighborhoods" would be a good start. Going to community organizations such as churches and temples, the Rotary Club, or the PTA with an educational presentation would be another. How about the offices of pediatricians, dentists, and orthodontists? Put together an informative booklet on your issue and ask permission to put it in every waiting room in town. You'll reach many parents and probably a handful of interested teens as well.

In summary, look at the community you're trying to reach and see where they go. Think about what kind of materials and information would be most accessible to them (and what language it should be in). That's how to tailor your appeal for maximum effectiveness.

Strategies

Most of the materials you will use for your community education project—leaflets, posters, and information sheets being the most common—have already been discussed. When you're using them to encourage some kind of concrete action, remember to be specific about what you want consumers to do. If you're trying to generate action that represents a lifestyle change—for instance, getting people to use less water—try designing a "permanent" giveaway item like a graphically appealing sticker that reads TURN

IT OFF WHILE YOU BRUSH AND SHAVE which can be put on the bathroom mirror. This is also another place for your group's name and logo to appear.

Media Appeals

The media are, for obvious reasons, a particularly powerful tool for efforts like these. Chapter 11 talks about media strategies in much more detail, but here are some specific things to think about vis-à-vis community education projects:

- Generate awareness of the power of small lifestyle changes by setting an example. Strive for media coverage like, "Student drivers at Middletown High are saving hundreds of gallons of oil each year by keeping their tires fully inflated, and they're urging adults to do the same."
- When interviewed, give quotes in "if . . . then" and other formats intended to persuade readers to act as well. Encourage the reporter to end the article with an appeal for reader action or to accompany it with a sidebar along the lines of "here's what you can do."
- Aside from getting attention for yourself, try to get local papers and television stations to cover the issue in a news article or editorial opinion. Call up editors and producers and offer them whatever background information you have; if you're comfortable doing so, offer to write the newspaper article yourself.
- Write a letter to local newspapers encouraging action and inviting responses from citizens on both sides of the issue.
- If your local media is half the problem—perpetuating wrongheaded ideas or acting only as a soapbox for local government or industry—try publishing a media-busting periodical of your own, your own private *Adbusters*.

If you have the facilities and know-how to produce a video about your issue, explore the options available to you through public access television. Find out what format the station needs before you

SUCCESS STORY

Passing on the Wisdom

In 1993 four high school students in Buenos Aires, Argentina, set out to educate children about environmental issues, which don't get much attention in Argentinean schools. The group called themselves CONECO, an abbreviation for Concientización Ecológica (Ecological Awareness); *con eco* also means "with an echo," reflecting the group's hope that their ideas would be passed on. They began by researching environmental issues with the help of local experts. Based on their research, they developed an elementary curriculum in seven parts: waste, energy, deforestation, animal extinction, and air, water and noise pollution.

After writing summaries of each segment, CONECO devised lesson plans that got young students involved in the process through participatory activities. Their materials, which ranged from posters and puzzles to video presentations, engaged students' senses, and the group built and decorated a "mailbox" where the children could register their written responses and ideas at the end of each lesson. They also created a small three-dimensional model of an ecosystem that included a forest with animals, a river, and a small city. This model was a graphic part of each lesson. During the segment on water pollution, for example, participants would pour paint into the "river." On deforestation day, students would rip out the trees from the model. By the end of the seventh lesson, the model was completely trashed—a striking demonstration of the combined effect of environmental destruction.

Despite the fact that they were offering a free service, at first CONECO had difficulty convincing any local elementary schools to allow them to teach their one-day-per-week, seven-week course. Once they had their first school, however, the rave reviews they received from teachers, students, and administrators spread through the community. The principal also wrote a very complimentary letter that they were able to show to other schools. By the end of their first seven-week presentation, the group had requests for their program from nearly twenty more schools.

CONECO continues to teach its program in local schools. In addition, the four young women who founded the group, all now seventeen, are trying to bring in a second generation of young teachers. They are also working on a newsletter and a children's book about ecology.

---

begin. If possible, ask to be featured one day on community-focused programming that already exists. Decide if reaching the very limited audience that watches public access television is worth the effort you would have to put into it.

Phonebanking

Phonebanking—an event where your group makes calls to support your legislative or community action goal—is an efficient way to reach a large number of individuals with a minimum of effort and expense. Phonebanks are useful not only for advocating community action and legislative advocacy but also as a way to explore public opinion and even recruit volunteers. Use them to encourage attendance at an upcoming event, request a specific action like calling one's legislator, or to "get out the vote" on election day. If you're calling outside your local area, remember that long-distance charges add up. Find out the rates, figure out how many calls you can afford to make, and be sure you've raised the necessary funds.

The group atmosphere of a phonebank is one of the things that make it a lot of fun. Find a place with at least as many phone lines as you have people, plus at least one line to receive incoming calls; good places include law and real estate offices, churches and temples, and other well-staffed organizational centers (like your university's administration building). If such a workplace is not available, have volunteers make the calls from their homes. Even then, try to have a central location where volunteers can "check in" (get their phone lists and scripts) and "check out" (report back on the evening's calls).

Who is called depends on the issue at hand. Try to get membership rosters from pertinent groups you work with, or ask national organizations for a list of members in your area. If you're targeting students, begin by using lists from other campus organizations; if you have the time and resources, try to reach every student in the campus directory.

The best time to make calls is in the evening, between about six and nine o'clock. Never call adults after ten; college students can usually be reached later at night, but never after midnight unless it's a number where you've gotten no answer earlier in the evening. If you're calling people in other states, don't forget the possible difference in time zones.

Draft a phone script for volunteers to use. Make it brief, and if you're encouraging a particular action, be specific. Begin the script by identifying the caller as a student volunteer representing your organization. Concisely describe why you're calling—a few "bullet-point" facts should do it—and move quickly to tell the listener what he can do to help. Emphasize that you're not trying to sell anything. Include a few strategic pauses or questions with easy answers, to give your audience a break. Encourage callers to ad-lib in addition to using the phone script, but remind them to stick to the issue and be brief. No call should take more than five minutes.

Have everyone practice the script using role plays within the group. This will be important to develop callers' ability to think on their feet and respond to unexpected remarks.

If someone says you're interrupting their dinner, apologize and offer to call back later. Devise a set of symbols for callers to use on their phone lists; symbols should designate things like wrong number, message left, negative response, positive response, send information, call back later/tomorrow. Encourage listeners who respond positively to join your efforts.

At the end of the evening, tally up the results of that day's calls. Depending on the issue and the script, each volunteer should be able to reach between twelve and twenty people per hour. Write down the names and addresses of people who asked for more information; if possible, address the envelopes immediately and drop them in the mail the next morning.

Phonebanking can be discouraging. Expect to be hung up on or brushed off rudely; this will happen and is not a reflection on you or your pitch. If someone in your group has done phonebanking before, ask that person to be available to volunteers who have questions or experience strange calls. Give volunteers the chance to take short breaks for relaxation or to vent about a particularly unpleasant call. A centrally located spot with food and drink is a nice idea. Remember: Happy volunteers are productive volunteers.

Canvassing

"Pounding the pavement, pressing the flesh" was the traditional cornerstone of political campaigning before the media age. Canvassing—going door-to-door with information on your issue, perhaps seeking funds or signatures—can still be a very effective way to reach private citizens. It gives you a chance to be at your most convincing, going face-to-face with someone to share information and your sense of commitment to change.

Guidelines for canvassing are much like those for phonebanking. Prepare a script ahead of time and practice it with members of your group; this will help you develop the ability to speak naturally and fluidly about your topic. Try to avoid carrying the script with you—it looks unnatural. Instead, give yourself adequate practice and try to memorize a few catchy phrases to use every time. Begin by introducing yourself and deliver your argument simply, convincingly, and as briefly as possible. Include a few "strategic pauses" to catch your breath, and use a crib sheet (notes, not full sentences) if you need to. Speak clearly and distinctly, and try to "speak their language," what is appropriate to your audience. Avoid slang and profanity.

Maintain a positive attitude no matter what the person you're speaking to says. If the person strongly disagrees with you, don't get into an argument or allow yourself to be verbally battered. Calmly thank the individual for his time and move on. Trying to convince such a person of your views is a waste of your time and energy.

Be prepared with enough material for the canvass. Obviously, this means having enough flyers and other informational materi-

GREENING YOUR GREENBACKS

As a generation we are fulfilling the wildest dreams of vendors and advertisers to the tune of $2 billion a year. As activists we might as well use the power that we wield to meet our own ends as well. On the day-to-day level, that means buying the products of environmentally and socially responsible companies and avoiding the products of those who are not. A good guide for the basic consumer is *Students Shopping for a Better World.*

As organizers we have the chance to do even more. We can convince local businesses to lessen their negative impact on the environmental and improve their standards on questions like workers' rights and equal opportunity. These appeals can be made in a positive way and, if not adequately addressed, can be backed with the threat of a boycott—getting people to take their business elsewhere until changes are made.

When organizing a boycott (or girlcott, the feminist alternative), the key is participation. A boycott is fundamentally a public-education effort: "Don't shop at ——— because . . ." Provide alternatives. People are not willing to "go without" in the interest of the greater good, particularly abstract ideas like the environment. Getting people to make the intellectual and emotional connection between how they live and what's happening to the planet is one of the foremost responsibilities of our generation, but that's a matter of incremental change and not of short-term, intense changes of habit like those a boycott demands.

Focus, don't try to keep half a dozen boycotts going at once, because people will lose track of where they're "allowed" to shop or what products they shouldn't be buying. Also be aware of how boycotts can spread. Participating in the boycott of a large conglomerate like Gillette or Pepsico means avoiding half of what's in the supermarket. Keep it simple and focus on smaller, local firms to maximize your effectiveness.

When you get the chance to state your case directly to business, focus on how your proposal will benefit the company. In the words of Peter Allison of Eco-Logical Solutions, Inc., "emphasize that *the bottom line of green is black.* In other words, most environmentally sound business practices save money. The logic is simple: If you reduce waste by recycling or source-reduction (using less material in the first place), you pay less to have it hauled away. If you install lights that use 75 percent less energy, you save 75 percent of your lighting bill. If you eliminate a material used to make or package a product, you don't have to pay for it." Show how your proposal will not hurt the performance of their product or service but may help it. Tell them that improving their environmental practices will be good for their image in the community and among their own workers, then work with them to improve this image when they do what you ask.

Changing business practices requires patience. First, you are a non-employee going up against that monolithic idea called "that's just how we do it here." Second, businesses often plan in the long term; if you're looking for a change that involves the firm's budgeting practices, you may not see the results of your change for a quarter (three months) or even a year. Be prepared to work with businesses on their turf; in our commerce-driven society, it's something that must be done sooner or later.

---

als to leave one at each stop. If you have something that identifies you with a national organization or one that's known in your community, carry that with you as well, and be prepared to show it to skeptics. Don't forget the less obvious things: maps and pencils (to mark "not home," "send info," and so forth) if you're canvassing outside your own neighborhood, a flashlight for after dark in rural areas, and so on.

Agree on a starting and ending point for all canvassers and a time by which everyone will return. Apportion the streets and neighborhoods as equally as possible, and be realistic about how many houses you can reach in your allotted time. Twelve to fifteen per hour is reasonable.

Travel in pairs. There's no reason not to be safe. Also, avoid canvassing too long after dark; the later it gets, the less likely people are to open their doors for you and the less visibility you have to watch for potential dangers. In all cases, stop by 9:00 P.M. unless you're canvassing inside college dormitories. Carry a whistle or some other noise-making device that could be used to draw attention to you in case of an emergency.

If possible, wear something—a button, T-shirt, or name tag—that identifies your group. Dress nicely and appropriately for the community in which you're canvassing. Try to look like you "fit in," and people will be more likely to take you seriously; also try to look "safe" so people will be comfortable opening their doors to you. Usually this means a more conservative look than you would exhibit among friends; men with long hair should tie it back, for example.

The *caveats* for canvassing are also much the same as for phonebanking: Be prepared to deal with rude individuals, to have the door slammed in your face, and to have disheartening conversations with people who genuinely believe that change is impossible or undesirable. This has always been, for me, the "psychological" danger of canvassing, because the power of a face-to-face interaction goes both ways. A few encounters with people who are convinced that what we're doing is futile will shake anyone's resolve. Always stay as positive as you can, give yourself little pep talks between houses, and take a break when you need to. Remember: They're wrong.

Events

A well-attended, informative event is a powerful tool for getting community members to feel they have a personal stake in what's going on with your issue. Events involve more advance planning—making arrangements for your venue, seeing to the logistical needs of invited speakers, dealing with security if necessary—but are worth the effort if you can reach a sizable audience. A successful event is proof of your group's talents and ability to work together.

Consider whether the response you'll get is worth the time invested. Informational events are not necessary for all types of community education drives. Getting people to recycle, for example, does not require the sage advice of David Brower live and in person. Events are especially useful when you're introducing a new concept for which people need more background. Economic conversion—retooling the military-industrial complex to meet consumer needs and encourage global peacemaking—is a good example of something that can't be explained in a leaflet. Bringing together a panel of knowledgeable individuals to discuss the issue, however, can help your whole community understand where you're coming from. Events are also a chance for more vivid presentations on what would otherwise be "dry" issues. Wilderness advocate Lenny Kohm, for example, has done more for public awareness of the plight of Artic National Wildlife Refuge with his multimedia slide presentation than a thousand flat black-and-white newspaper articles.

Organizing an event is similar to organizing a demonstration from certain logistical standpoints. Check out the guidelines in Chapter 8 for more details.

Presenters

The steps needed to arrange for speakers will vary depending on where you plan to get them. Often, the best speakers are young people like you. When it comes time to express your concerns, no one can do it better, and you'll surprise yourself with your ability to reach your audience.

When you want to look for speakers beyond your own group of friends and adult supporters, ask the same people who helped do your research whom they recommend. Ask your faculty advisor. Also try local universities and service organizations, or local branches of appropriate government agencies.

If you're not sure where to find individuals qualified to speak on your topic, contact national organizations that work on the same issue. They may have contacts in your area to whom they can refer you, and many have a speakers bureau that you can contact. Be aware that many speakers—particularly those on the level of a national organization's bureau—expect payment (called an "honorarium") for their service; if you're not able to pay them, be up front about it and ask them to waive the fee for your group. If you want to bring in a big-name speaker, try getting funding by working with another local service organization or through your school. (Most schools have a speakers fund that often goes unused because no one plans any events.)

Communicate with your speakers well ahead of time. Ask what materials they need: a slide projector or blackboard, for example. If you can't provide it, let them know that early on and help them make alternative arrangements. Let the speakers know what to expect: how large the audience will be and what kind of people will be present, whether they will have a podium, how long they will be answering questions, and whether or not authors will be asked to sign their books after the event. Basically, do all you can to prevent surprises on the night of the event.

Speaking events can range from a presentation by a single speaker to a political debate or workshop-style panel discussion. Be as creative as you can within the confines of your budget and facilities. Sometimes a single lively speaker is all you need. Consider combining a speaking engagement with a workshop program that gets participants more personally invested in the discussion.

Find a presentation that will appeal to your audience. There is a growing number of individuals and groups out there—like the YES! tour—that combine music, pictures, and audience participation to educate and empower viewers on environmental and social justice issues. See what's out there or bring together local talent to produce something of your own. If you're working on diversity issues, pool the resources of local ethnic organizations, performing groups, and restaurants to create a weekend-long cultural fair that pulls in all corners of your community.

Sticking to the issues, political-style debates can be fun as long as they don't become a circus for political performers. They'll also have a large appeal just before elections, which is also when you are most likely to get candidates' enthusiasm as well. Use questions from a moderator or the audience to keep debaters "on-issue." Be sure your moderator is neutral and has the authority to quiet both the audience and the speakers if they get out of hand. Try to bring debaters together ahead of time so they can meet and socialize before they take on the role of adversaries.

Panel discussions can be an interesting forum because they

get several knowledgeable individuals together to discuss the issue. Participants in a good panel will include representatives of varied interests—politicians, environmentalists, businesspeople, and private citizens, for example. This will encourage a lively debate of issues, making the event more interesting and compelling speakers to clarify their positions and respond to those who disagree. Have a moderator—a respected faculty member, local television personality, or even a qualified member of your group. The job of the moderator is to keep debate focused, ask questions that lead into various points of discussion, and recognize plenty of audience members during the question-and-answer period.

Filling the Seats

Getting people to attend is another challenge. Hold the event in a central location that is familiar to most members of the community: your school auditorium, the recreation room of a local church or temple, the gazebo in your town park. Take into account questions of acoustics (avoid high ceilings) and comfort. Also, if you're planning to include small-group workshops in your event, be sure there is space for groups to spread out; ideally, try to have available for their use several nearby rooms or, if you're outdoors, a large grassy area.

People are likely to attend an event when someone they know has been part of putting it together. Involve as many people as you can in the planning and organizing of the project. If appropriate, ask another group to cosponsor the event.

Try attaching your event to something else that people are likely to attend—church services, a concert or school play, sporting events—unless that means being overshadowed in such a way that your message will fail to come through. Consider who your audience will be: If your event involves a video, speaker, and letter-writing action about the human rights situation in Haiti, seek a time and location that's accessible to the local Haitian-American community.

Finally, advertise your event widely with posters, a calendar listing in area newspapers, and public service announcements on local radio stations. If you're in a position to do a mass mailing—for example, "box slips" in a college or boarding school mail room—this is another effective way to increase awareness of your upcoming event. "Box slips" should be more like posters than leaflets. Give just enough information to get recipients interested.

We Learn by Doing

People will feel more involved in the event and retain more of the information that they're given if they take some active part in the program. Look for ways to make your event interactive. Encourage audience members to think critically and participate in the discussion. This will give them a greater stake in the outcome, and they are less likely to feel like they're being lectured or manipulated. Role-playing exercises and other "issue games" are one way to do this; having the audience break up into discussion circles is another. As you research the issues and look at what has been done before, you should come across materials that include workshop ideas, discussion topics, and the like. High school and college curricula are often good sources for debate and activity ideas.

Try to look beyond "buzzwords" and discourage the casual use of jargon or invective when it hinders real dialogue on the issue. (In short, try to go beyond the television-talking-head level of analysis.) Focus on the issue and avoid going off on tangents or associating certain policy ideas with political personalities or parties. Focus on the topic, not the political gaming that surrounds it in Washington or your state capital.

It is particularly important in a public forum to approach your topic from an objective viewpoint. Programs that begin with certain presumptions about any politically contentious issue—that welfare reform is a bad idea, for example, or that environment should always come before economic issues—lose half of their audience before they've even begun. Showing a willingness to hold your own beliefs up to honest scrutiny will increase your clout with people who wouldn't give you a second glance if they felt you were beginning with a set of presumptions that they did not share. As mentioned earlier, keep discussions on course, try to draw out silent participants and tone down extremely vocal ones, and make every effort to defuse conflict constructively. Use "group memory" to make sure everything that's brought up is recognized and has a chance to be considered.

Watch the Clock

Think realistically about how much time people are willing to give to your event. Start on time—never more than ten minutes late unless you're expecting many more people to arrive—and don't let the event drag on. Shoot for under ninety minutes in length, less if it's a young audience (high school age or below). Two hours is an absolute maximum unless you intend to plan a half- or full-day program of workshops and other activities. In this case, keep each workshop or speaker under two hours and be aware that "fifteen-minute breaks" can take up to half an hour. Try to vary your program. If you have two speakers and a dramatic workshop, for example, put the workshop in the middle.

Before the event, ask speakers if they are willing to stay around even later to continue the discussion with interested audience members. If possible and appropriate, hold a reception after the event—"wine and cheese" or "cola and cookies"—to encourage a more personal level of interchange. This should occur in a different location or at least a different room so that there is a clear division between event and reception, and so you can clear out of the auditorium and let the technical crew close up.

If a mess is left from papers or other materials used as part of the event, assign several members of your group to clean up; this will help you stay on good terms with the people who own and operate your venue. Remember, diplomacy is just as important with the janitorial staff and technicians as with your keynote speaker.

Change Will Come

Expressing your concerns to the community in a way that allows them to share in your emotion and participate in your fight is one of the most important things you can do as a student activist. We, the readers and writers of this book and the people we work with, are vital to creating a sustainable planet. But it is not enough for us alone to change and act. Changing the minds and actions of those around us, in our own communities, is a necessary step.

Seek innovative combinations of these community education strategies. Think also about how they could work alongside a legislative or direct action effort. Creativity, along with a strong sense of what's most appropriate for your school or community, will be your strongest ally.

7

Direct Action: The Hands-On Approach

"Direct action" has an exciting ring to it (like "task force") and on the surface is self-explanatory. Rather than trying to change people's minds or legislators' votes, though these can be important adjuncts to direct action efforts, you are doing things that have a direct positive effect on the place or group you are trying to help. The field of direct action is probably the broadest available to you. If it's something you can *do*—be it building nesting stations for endangered birds, turning vacant lots into vegetable gardens, starting a peer counseling or mediation project at your school, or collecting and distributing food for the homeless in your city—it's direct action.

It is not possible to anticipate and describe all the projects you could undertake. Some of the best are contained in this book as "Success Stories." There are thousands of others: school cleanup projects that bring together people of diverse age and racial backgrounds; aid projects that provide needed supplies and moral support for refugees abroad; and community development weekends that inspire such enthusiasm that they outlast the group that created them. The more you learn about what else is going on out there, the more ideas and adaptations you'll discover to apply to your own community.

What's more, these projects can be educational, both for participants and for those who see what you are doing. Something as simple as a weekend graffiti-removal project may inspire others to develop similar efforts in other parts of your city or beyond. Beach cleanups *do* make some people think twice about what they leave behind in the sand. Try making this educational aspect a part of your action. Bring leaflets or coordinate a cleanup with a rally, both to draw more people to your cleanup and to draw more attention to the trash issue.

You know what you want to fix, and maybe you even have some ideas about how to fix it. If you don't, someone does—a teacher, religious leader, or local official who's just yearning for a vivacious, directed group like yours to come along.

Defining Your Constituency

Begin by identifying who or what it is you're trying to help and what kind of help is needed. If you're working on a local cleanup effort, familiarizing yourself with your "constituency" may be as simple as looking out your window. If you're engaging in a more intricate environmental effort, this may mean talking to local conservationists and experts in the field to find out how to reduce the population decline of a local species or resuscitate a wetlands ecosystem faltering under the strain of local industry, or something simpler like where's the nearest place to recycle polystyrene. It may also mean doing some research and observation of your own. If you decide to base your action on your own examination of the problem, try to follow scientific methods so your study is something you can show to others as a valid examination of the problem. (Also, your biology teacher will love you.)

If your constituency is an identifiable population group (such as the homeless) of which you are not a part, go talk to them about what their real needs are. All too often organizations that set out to help "the poor" or "people with disabilities" fail to really listen to the needs of their constituency, and to have members of that constituency genuinely involved in the planning and decision-making process. A woman I met some time ago—a mother of three who has been on welfare for a number of years—told a story about a nearby middle-class church group that wanted to help out people in her community: "I was glad to be part of their steering committee because I thought it would give me a chance to really articulate our needs. I told them the public housing program moved us around a lot and that we needed more stable housing in order to have the stability to get on our feet. So they decided to hold a book drive for our kids. I went to the next meeting and said again, 'We need mortgage assistance so we can get a place to call our own from which to better our situation.' They arranged for our children to have free piano lessons. This went on and on."

While this story is so extreme as to be absurd, it illustrates my point very well: Your resources are limited. They—the individuals or group you are trying to help—know what they need most. Begin with a dialogue that educates your group on the issues and the needs facing that community. If it's a community of which you're a part—like students at your high school or college—many of these questions will shake out early on as you recruit and organize your peers. Nevertheless, make a conscious effort to talk your ideas through with people representing all facets of your school community.

Bringing people from outside your school or peer community into the process will mean being flexible with meeting times and locations. Do so to the extent that this is possible. It will be worth the effort from the standpoint of your knowledge and, perhaps even more important, your legitimacy within that group.

Mitigate possible opposition by talking to others who will be affected. Think about others who will feel the impact of your planned action. If they consider your actions as causing harm or as a potential for harm to them or their lifestyles, they may form a formidable opposition to your efforts. If you're setting up nesting platforms or building an environmental education "walking tour" of a local wilderness area, think about the individuals living near the wilderness whose scenic views will be marred by the appearance of human-made structures. If you're a group from the suburbs working with inner-city youth, take into account the feelings of the people who live around you, particularly if you're going to be bringing unfamiliar people into your community.

Bring these people into the process in whatever way you can. By conveying some ownership to them and making them feel part of decision-making, you will likely be able to bring possible adversaries around to your point of view. Let them feel that they've had a hand in making the effort happen. If we're using the wilderness example, this means going to nearby homes to explain your proposal, to explain why it's important to the health of the area as they know it, and to ask them to be part of your effort. Their direct, personal interest in the area makes them important to what you're doing. Let them know that in positive terms. Especially when what you're doing involves a lifestyle change for some peripheral group, make an effort to speak of positive alternatives and outcomes, and to think in their language when conveying your arguments.

To return to the suburban–inner city example, it's vital to remember that perception is even more important than fact when it comes to how people approach an issue. Violent media images have trained many in our parents' generation to be fearful of inner-city residents, particularly people of color. It's wrong, but it has happened and one of your first challenges in dealing with this would be to overcome the myths that have created the inaccurate image of "troubled kids" from the city or "spoiled kids" from the suburbs. The very simple process of introducing your urban compatriots to members of your community will do much to dispel such stereotypes. Remember as well that this dichotomy works in reverse, and such inaccurate perceptions and tendencies to mistrust exist along many divisions in our society—race, class, and geography being the deepest and widest.

This brings us to another term you're likely to hear in this context: NIMBY. It stands for "not in my backyard." NIMBY—the idea that if something bad has to happen, it should happen to someone else, somewhere else—is something you'll often be able to use to your advantage. Protesting the arrival of a polluting industry project in your area is a good example of such a scenario. When your project involves bringing unfamiliar groups into your community, NIMBY will be your adversary. The inclusive tactics outlined above are the most effective way to face and surmount that challenge.

SUCCESS STORY

Bringing Prairie Back to the Prairie State

The environmental club at Wheaton-Warrenville South High School in Wheaton, Illinois, recently brought sixty acres of prairie back to the Prairie State. Created in 1989 and now consisting of about twenty regular members, VERTERRA—Latin for "green earth"—has spearheaded an effort to return their school's expansive grounds, except for its athletic fields, to their natural condition.

The prairie project began in 1994 when the school's biology classes studied a small area of preserved prairie near the school and learned that human expansion had shrunk the prairie of Illinois to only 0.1 percent of the state's territory. VERTERRA, which has benefitted from strong support from faculty sponsors and school administrators, felt that the school should make a commitment to preserving the state's original wildlife. Under the guidance of a local conservation design firm that they approached side-by-side with school officials, the group figured out what flora and fauna should be incorporated into the prairie and created a three-step plan to bring back the prairie by the spring of 1996—beginning with the planting of prairie grasses and flowers in early 1995. The deal was that the school would provide the funding and VERTERRA members would do all the physical labor. The plants are expected to draw native wildlife back to the area, reestablishing a complete ecosystem. Teachers—of not just biology, but also of English and art—are already planning exciting curricula that involve hands-on activities for students of all grade levels.

While planning the prairie project, VERTERRA faced some opposition from fellow students concerned about the cost of the project and looking for other ways to spend those monies, and from nearby residents concerned about dangers posed by native animals returning to the area. The group responded with an educational campaign carried out by erecting tables at local ecological fairs and coverage in sympathetic local newspapers, the school paper, and the school's newsletter for parents, and by stressing the importance of the prairie and the nonexistent threat from predatory or disease-carrying animals. VERTERRA has won state and national recognition for this and other projects. They've inspired others, too: One year later a nearby school engaged the same conservation design firm to reestablish prairie on its land.

Facilities

Just a quick mention of something that harks back to the beginning of this chapter: Plan ahead when it comes to facilities—the location and equipment you'll need to carry out your effort. Have contingency plans, especially if you're counting on something like an in-kind donation that you're not sure will come through.

Always find out whose permission you need to be somewhere—on state park lands, in a capitol meeting room, and so forth—and get that permission early on in the process. Telephone a few days before your event to confirm that those arrangements are set and to restate to whoever is in charge your time of arrival and planned activities. The exception to this rule is when you're doing something that involves defying the powers that be. In such a case, secrecy rather than permission may be your primary goal in the planning stages.

Successful direct action conveys on your group an immediate sense of accomplishment. These are activist tactics that really mean making a difference to the people and the ecosystem around you. They are also the strongest ways to make a point about your issue. Actions do indeed speak louder than words. Use direct action strategies in tandem with an educational campaign or a legislative effort to maximize your impact in the long term.

8

Demonstrations: Taking It to the Street

Demonstrations can be an effective way to exert significant public pressure on an individual or institution that has failed to meet your requests or expectations on a certain issue. They can also be useful as part of a community education effort when they are designed to express advocacy for certain actions, legislative or otherwise.

Several strong caveats must be added to those remarks, however. A demonstration is, in almost all cases, a confrontational act. As a public embarrassment of the individual or group whose actions you're disagreeing with—your school's trustees, your congressional representative, or a local business—it will probably make them angry at you. If you're not able to generate enough public pressure to make them change their actions, you may lose your chance because of that emotional response. There are exceptions, of course. You may be able to go to them after a protest and say, in effect, "Now work with us, or we'll hold bigger and bigger protests until you do."

There's also a certain public distaste for demonstrations. Although the 1960s were before our time, there remains in the United States a cultural memory of that era that often includes a tendency to blame "radical" antiwar and civil rights demonstrators for the painful divisions that rent American society then. Expect to be told to "work within the system" and not to "make waves." If this reaction is extreme, your action could generate public sympathy for your opponent, particularly if that opponent is popular within the community or region. It's strange to think that even though you are in the right, you could be viewed as the aggressor, but it's possible.

Finally, demonstrating alone is not activism, although everyone seems to think it is. Collegiate activists today, cursed with the same theatrical bug that infected our parents, are quick to protest and slow to work through the system. In a way this is understandable: Rallies and protests give an immediate sense of accomplishment, and they avoid the frustration of working slowly through the bureaucratic morass that may stand between you and what you're after. But often what's accomplished is the demonstration rather than the goal of real change that it was supposed to represent.

In my mind, one of the best examples of incorporating a rally into an effective policy change effort took place at Brown University in 1968 and 1969. (May this be the only time I cite an example from the 60s!) A group of students, including undergraduate government president Ira Magaziner, wanted to change Brown's curriculum: eliminating core requirements, instituting a pass-fail option to encourage students to explore unfamiliar disciplines, and establishing other specialty courses. Magaziner and his fellow organizers spent almost three years pounding the pavement, visiting every undergraduate and every faculty member to explain their proposal and get each person's input. With the legitimacy that those actions conveyed upon Magaziner's group, they were able to organize a rally that brought almost all four thousand Brown students to the main green on two consecutive days while the faculty was voting on the curriculum changes. Their success was primarily a result of the years spent pushing the proposal and reworking it based on faculty and student input; their ability to generate a rally of such proportions during the faculty decision-making process was the "topper" that convinced the faculty of student enthusiasm for the program.

Kinds of Demonstrations

What are you trying to say? What's the difference between a rally and a protest? We sometimes use these words interchangeably, but it's very important to know what you're doing when you take to

SUCCESS STORY

Keeping the Costs Down

In January 1995, the Southeast Pennsylvania Transport Authority (SEPTA), which serves the greater Philadelphia area, announced a plan to raise mass transit rates, including those for students. The increase of $2 per week for a roll of tokens didn't sound like much, but it was a big deal to poor students who had no choice but to ride SEPTA to school each day.

Asian Americans United, an advocacy organization working on issues of concern to the Asian-American community in Philadelphia, rallied students around opposition to the fare increase and started an aggressive campaign against it. Just two weeks before the final vote, AAU sent out flyers and made posters to educate the public on what the fare increase would mean to poor students. Allying themselves with other organizations representing mass transit riders, group members also spoke eloquently about the problem at a series of SEPTA hearings. "We might not be able to go to school [after the fare hikes]," one student said, "but we will learn a lesson—who this society thinks is important and who it thinks should be thrown away. Is this really the lesson you want us to learn?"

The group also held a speak-out at one of the magnet schools that draws students from all across the city. At the rally, the divide between students was obvious. Those to whom the issue mattered were enthusiastic, and those who weren't walked right by. Although disappointed by the lack of solidarity from their counterparts—some wealthier, some not—the group continued its efforts.

When the SEPTA board met to vote on the proposed rate hike, students packed the room. The students faced haranguing from board members, who "acted like they were giving us lessons about the 'real world' . . . that we should go home and learn about budgets," according to organizer Lai Har Cheung. "We were making a concerted effort to work with the board, who were trying to make young people pay for their budget problems, but their remarks told us they had a lot of growing up to do."

Although they didn't reach the board members' hearts, the organizers must have reached something. Bowing to intense student pressure, the board engineered a fare increase that spared the students. Since the vote, students active on the rate hike issue have stayed together and begun organizing to advocate welfare reform legislation.

---

the streets. My simple guideline is that you rally *for* something and you protest *against* it. For example, a group of students who marched in front of a Denver hotel during the Western Hemisphere economic summit held there in 1995 were very careful to say that they were not protesting the free-trade agreements but rallying *for* strict environmental protocols. This was wise. One of their chants was "Free trade, but how? The right way, right now. Save the earth."

There are all kinds of demonstrations, and each one sends a different message. A *vigil* implies that you're waiting for something—the expelling of a student guilty of hate crimes, for example. It is usually quiet and often held at night with candles. Chants are not appropriate. Vigils can also represent mourning—for people suffering human rights violations or a natural disaster abroad, for victims of domestic violence, or something similar. Choose a location appropriate to your issue; when it's a conflict between students and a school, the president's or principal's house is a popular destination.

A *sit-in*, or occupying an office or building, represents a more forceful demand and implies that you will not leave until the demand is met. It can be more vocal. You can be asking for action—like the 1995 sit-in at a Rutgers basketball game that demanded the ousting of the university president—or demanding some kind of statement, like an apology or the release of information to which you feel you have a right.

If you're going to have a *march*, make the very motion of the march represent part of your message. March from school to the proposed incinerator site to show how close it is and to show that *students* are against the plan. March from a housing project to the state capital, representing the arrival of constituents to demand their rights as well as a vivid reminder of the "quality" difference between rundown public housing and the opulence of the capital complex.

Planning

The key to being taken seriously is to demonstrate organization and continuity in your rally program. Plan extensively and in great detail. Have a single person whose job is rally coordinator and who is responsible for delegating tasks and overseeing their completion. This probably should also be the person who deals with authorities before and during the rally.

If you intend to have a series of speakers, go to them beforehand and discuss what they're going to talk about. Based on this information, arrange your list of speakers so that there is some sort of topical continuity—good segues, if you will—from one speaker to the next. An example would be to have the first speaker talk about the importance of a certain wilderness area to the community and the bioregion, the second speaker discuss how local industry and non-point-source pollution affects the wilderness, the third speaker talk about how local businesses and families can change their consumption habits to decrease the community's negative impact on the area, and the fourth speaker talk about ways to become actively involved in protecting and revitalizing the area. This kind of logical flow of speakers will strengthen each one's argument because of its place in the matrix.

Talking to speakers ahead of time will also give you a chance to weed out those who are likely to take an inappropriately harsh stance and thus risk alienating listeners and even members of your own group.

Try to have a diverse group of speakers in as many respects as possible—race, gender, age, social group, faculty/student, and so on. This will increase your ability to reach various segments of the community. If possible and appropriate, seek the participation of notable individuals in your community (politicians, popular business people, club leaders). Even if they speak only long enough to give an endorsement or just send a letter of endorsement for you to read, if their participation is appropriate their names will bolster your legitimacy in the eyes of your audience.

Make a schedule and stick to it. Type up a timetable of the event that includes speakers, chants, and any other actions (such as a march) that are going to take place. Indicate how much time each speaker gets, then distribute a copy of the timetable to individuals who are speaking, leading chants, or otherwise involved in the rally. Have someone stationed in the front row of the audience to cue speakers when their time is running out. (This is an effective way to get rid of belligerent or otherwise inappropriate speakers once they've begun their tirade.)

Know when to end your event. Don't let things drag on. The assembled crowd will just get tired of standing there or decide they're too hot or too cold, and drift away. If you have a sense that this is happening, try to shorten the rest of your speakers' time and bring the event to a close. In my opinion—and there are those who differ—the strongest time to end a rally is when most of your crowd is still there and interested. Let them go away talking about the issue, and it will stay in their minds longer than if they walk away feeling overloaded.

In all cases, do not confront counter-protesters or authorities. Shouting matches can easily escalate and get out of control, and violence is always a harmful outcome. Make your point without being offensive. Criticize the action and not the actor, to paraphrase the Reverend Martin Luther King, Jr., and you will ultimately earn respect for standing firmly and peacefully in your convictions.

Notify Officials

Let relevant individuals know what you're planning. This will include the police (speak to the chief or sergeant of your local precinct), your school principal or college administration officials, the owner of any property that will be affected by your event, and others who would have the power to break up your event or attempt to arrest you or have you arrested. Contact your local branch of the American Civil Liberties Union (ACLU) or the national ACLU office in Washington, D.C., and clarify what your legal rights and responsibilities are when it comes to demonstrating. If you anticipate any trouble, try to have a lawyer or law students on hand as observers and advisors.

Staffing

There are several ways in which group members who are not speaking should be involved in the process. In addition to the "cue person" mentioned above, station group members at the periphery of the crowd to talk up the issue and explain the purpose of the rally to members of the audience, particularly late arrivals. These volunteers could also be charged with distributing leaflets or buttons, collecting signatures on letters or a petition, and letting people know about your next group meeting.

Designate one individual to be your representative for the media. For more details, see the discussion about spokespersons and press packets in Chapter 11.

Anticipate that police will respond to any large gathering of people. Assign a single person—possibly your rally coordinator, although that individual may be dealing with keeping speakers and chants moving along—to speak for the group to police and other officials. This person should be a calm individual who can explain the purpose and program of the rally and assure police that there will be no trouble. Try to have this person be the same individual who contacted officials in the first place, so he or she can remind them of this and provide the names of the officials notified. Make sure your entire group knows who that individual is and can immediately refer officials to him or her.

If there are places where the crowd should not spread to—off the curb and onto the street or onto someone else's private property, for example—station group members there. There's no need to anger neighbors, risk charges of trespassing or destruction of property, or put crowd members in physical danger. If you think they'll be useful, put up ropes or other barriers in addition to stationing people there.

Setting the Stage

There are a number of things to consider when choosing a site for your demonstration. Most often you'll want it to take place right in front of whatever firm or institution you're protesting—the university administration building, the district office of your congressional representative, or a local business. Rallies are best held outside. You'll be seen by more people (many of whom are likely to join the crowd, at least for a few moments), you'll be less confined if the group grows too large, and it won't get stuffy from all the people. There may be situations where this will not be the case—a sit-in at the principal's or dean's office, for example. If you have an indoor event, be sure the media knows exactly where to find you; post people at the front door of the building and at all strategic turns to point them in the right direction.

Here are some other things to consider when selecting your exact site:

- *Size.* You want your crowd to look big. A smaller area filled with people is much more impressive-looking than a larger area that's only sparsely populated. Estimate how many people will attend your rally, taking into account whether you'll have a central location that will draw many extra people between classes, and plan accordingly.
- *Timing.* Try to target your rally for a time when the individuals whose policies you're trying to affect will be around. This could mean during a congressional recess for your U.S. senators, midmorning for university officials, during an evening city council meeting, and so forth.
- *Visibility.* Can you be seen from major thoroughfares or from the windows of the building you're in front of? Have someone stand on the spot where you plan to put the speakers' podium and walk around the area, checking their visibility. Also think about the "photo op" you're giving the media. Try to have your backs to the building where you're protesting so they can photograph both you and it effectively. Use stairs to your advantage to make the group appear larger or to place yourselves above an assembled throng. Try to avoid having the sun behind you, in the crowd's eyes.
- *Sound.* If you are using a megaphone or other amplification system, test it out before the event. Be sure you get a clear sound, with plenty of bass so it carries better. Avoid narrow spaces between buildings that may cause a bad echo. As when checking vis-

ibility, walk around and see how the sound will carry; keep in mind that a large crowd of bodies will deaden the sound a bit.

- *Accessibility.* Choose a location that will be accessible to people with physical disabilities, if at all possible.
- *Weather.* What will you do in case of rain? Consider having either an alternative site or a rain date for your event. If you don't, think about how you will protect your sound system and make sure you have access to a tarp (or, in the worst case, a big umbrella) to shelter your speakers, including when they're waiting to go on. Inclement weather will seriously cut down on your attendance, but the dedication it takes to demonstrate in very bad weather will also impress some people.
- *Legalities.* We talked a little about this earlier, but you should look into what you'll need in the way of permits for your public gathering. It would be a waste of time and energy (yours and the police's) if you overlooked this and the police had to disperse or arrest you. Obviously, if surprise is crucial, you'll have to dispense with this step, but you should also be prepared to face the consequences.

Civil Disobedience

Civil disobedience—intentionally breaking the law in order to make a point about its morality or the morality of the system it upholds—is a serious step for any activist. Particularly for a young person, a criminal record could have detrimental effects months and years down the road. There are too many issues involved in civil disobedience, from legal counsel and "passive resistance" to moral choices, to effectively address it here. If you are interested in learning more about these issues, I strongly recommend the *Handbook for Nonviolent Action* published by the War Resisters League.

Done well, demonstrations can be an important way to express how committed you are to your goals and to display unity on a certain issue. Approach demonstrations with a sense of humor as well as a sense of theatrics, and remember that they should almost never stand alone in your activist repertoire.

WORDS OF WISDOM

Cast Your Whole Vote

Under a government which imprisons any unjustly, the true place for a just man is also a prison. The proper place today, the only place which Massachusetts has provided for her freer and less desponding spirits, is in her prisons, to be put out and locked out of the State by her own act, as they have already put themselves out by their principles. . . . That separate, but more free and honorable ground, where the State places those who are not *with* her, but *against* her [is] the only house in a slave State in which a free man can abide with honor. If any think that their influence would be lost there, and their voices no longer afflict the ear of the State . . . they do not know by how much truth is stronger than error, nor how much more eloquently and effectively he can combat injustice who has experienced a little in his own person. Cast your whole vote, not just a strip of paper merely, but your whole influence. A minority is powerless while it conforms to the majority; it is not even a minority then; but it is irresistible when it clogs by its whole weight. If the alternative is to keep all just men in prison, or give up war and slavery, the State will not hesitate which to choose. If a thousand men were not to pay their tax-bills this year, that would not be a violent and bloody measure, as it would be to pay them, and enable the State to commit violence and shed innocent blood. This is, in fact, the definition of a peaceable revolution, if any such is possible. If the tax-gatherer, or any other public officer, asks me, as one has done, "But what shall I do?" my answer is, "If you really wish to do anything, resign your office." When the subject has refused allegiance, and the officer has resigned his office, then the revolution is accomplished. But even suppose blood should flow. Is there not a sort of blood shed when the conscience is wounded? Through this wound a man's real manhood and immortality flow out, and he bleeds to an ever-lasting death. I see this blood flowing now.

—Henry David Thoreau,
Civil Disobedience

9

Keeping the Ball Rolling: More Thoughts on Meetings and Diplomacy

Sharing Responsibility Effectively

It is clear when you look at the amount of work that goes into planning and executing a major project that you can't try to do everything yourself. Dividing responsibilities, however, raises some worrisome questions: Whom should you trust with various tasks? How much can any single person be asked to do? Will the others come through, or will they drop the ball?

The ability to gauge the enthusiasm of group members and other fellow activists is important because it will allow you to work with many different types of people while always attaining a quality outcome to your efforts. The intuition involved is one of the hardest things to explain because it combines knowing the concrete parts of members' lives—commitments to other projects, family issues, what they've done (and failed to do) in similar efforts in the past—with a more esoteric ability to read people's commitment in their body language and vocal inflection. This latter part is hard to describe, and it's something you will learn only through experience.

As your group discusses the division of tasks, make it very clear what each job involves in terms of responsibilities and time commitment. It's easy to divide up a list of one-line items like "arranging for speakers," "transportation," and "media relations" by writing one person's name next to each, but this often results in an unbalanced division of labor. Some things may not get done because those responsible didn't realize it was part of their job. To avoid such complications, write down the components of each of the major task areas and allow for the division of larger tasks among several people.

For example, when someone volunteers to do "media relations," nod acceptingly but say, "Okay, so you'll take care of calling newspapers and radio and television stations, type up a press release and fax it to them, and also assemble a press packet on the issue to be handed out at the event. Will you have time to do all that?" Give the volunteer an option, like: "Do you want someone else to assemble the press packet?" And ask if the volunteer also plans to be the group's official spokesperson at the event. This all needs to be done with some tact. Avoid a tone of condescension or disbelief, and keep in mind how easy it is to volunteer to do more than you're capable of doing.

New Members: Starting Small and Developing Commitment

If a member of your group is new to projects like the one you're doing, let him start small by doing just one or two things or by working with a more experienced member. This policy will give the new member a chance to demonstrate his level of ability and commitment; it will also be self-affirming for him as he proves himself able to be part of your group. Make a particular effort not to diminish the task or accomplishment with words like "only," "just," or "small." Don't say, "Mark, since you're new, why don't you just greet people as they arrive and hand out information on the project?" Instead, be positive: "Mark, we need someone to greet people when they arrive and to hand out information on the project. This would be a good chance for you to get to know people and practice talking up our work. How about it?" This attitude will make Mark feel that he is an important part of what you are doing and will make him more likely to stay with the group and perhaps take on a larger task next time.

Allow new members to expand their responsibilities incrementally, easing into their commitments to the group. Allow them to move at their own pace. This doesn't mean waiting for them to volunteer; it means knowing the difference between encouraging

WORDS OF WISDOM

Feeling Involved, Playing a Part

I've never been the kind of harried, mercurial individual that comes to mind when you hear the words "campus activist." The most important steps I've taken involve providing the supporting impetus for a project and relying on others for help. "Catalyst" might be a good word to describe my role—making arrangements and coordinating others' roles in bringing a project to fruition. Working with a group called Student Action for the Earth (SAFE) at my college, I didn't even feel I deserved to be viewed as a committed member. I just sat at our booth at the arts festival, wearing the recycling hat I made in high school, but I enjoyed the feeling of doing something simple and of value to the group.

From this and my other experiences organizing similar projects, I learned that you don't need to be Mr. Capability or know everything to start becoming involved meaningfully. It can mean something to you just to latch on and learn to depend on the others in the group for what you may lack in clarity and skill. It teaches you to see others as your help, as you struggle to be a help to others.

—John Lauffer,
Middletown, Pennsylvania

people to do more and pressuring them. Part of your job as a leader is to make people *want* to take on more commitments. Positive language, praise for accomplishments, and constructive criticism are the best way to do this. Cajolery and "guilt tripping," while sometimes effective in the short run, will create a negative atmosphere and decrease people's enjoyment of the project. In the long run, the group and its efforts will suffer.

If you are organizing a project based on the ideas in this book, you are already demonstrating a great deal of commitment to something that you care about deeply. Remember as you organize a group around your effort that not everyone will feel as strongly as you do and that many will have other priorities. Also remember that people like my friend and fellow activist John Lauffer, whose words appear on the previous page, will be as important to your success as your most dynamic leaders. Be sure to make it "okay" to demonstrate varying levels of commitment. Don't demean those who can give only a few hours a week, a little bit of phone time, or even just their attendance at your events. When you make the work into a competition of members to demonstrate the greatest commitment to the project, you will drive away people whose time—even when limited—is very valuable. These are people who, once gone, will never have the chance to develop a greater commitment through continuing involvement in the group.

What if you start someone off with a small task and he fails at it? Examine first the reasons for his failure: Was he sufficiently instructed on how to do the job? Did something else come up in his life? (And if so, why didn't he contact you and bow out?) Or was it a question of his lack of interest or commitment to the cause? This is an easy assumption to make, but think hard before you do. If someone doesn't do well in his first effort but still seems committed, try him out in another capacity. It may simply be a matter of finding his niche in the group.

Striking a Balance: Specialization versus Dependency

Generally, as you will discover, activists must be jacks- and jills-of-all-trades—able to handle fund-raising, planning, organizing, and publicity while still doing homework and avoiding the wrath of family and friends who are frustrated by the time spent on the project. With this in mind—and perhaps already in the realm of your own experience—seize the opportunity to work with a group of people and allow each to develop her own role in the group "machine."

It is important to remember the difference between working consistently with people in a certain role (which gives you very competent people doing jobs at which they have a great deal of experience) and fully depending on them, which leads to collapse when these people leave. Specialization and consistent division of tasks is usually something to encourage, but not to the point that your group becomes dependent on key people to get the job done. Eventually, in some situations, these people won't be there, so make sure there is always someone who can fill the gap.

Always be sure that the people who are consistently involved in a particular part of a project's development don't lose sight of the group aspect or the larger importance of your effort. In other words, avoid making your press liaison feel stuck next to the fax machine (where he hasn't seen a tree in weeks) or making the person who does all the driving feel she exists only behind the wheel of her car. Group meetings are a good way to maintain the social aspect of what you're doing and keep everyone in touch with the dialogue on group priorities and community issues.

As a last word on the idea of specialization: You'll discover there's a certain comfort in the predictability of group members' fulfilling those tasks at which they are most practiced. Don't assume, however, that people will always want to do the same tasks or that what someone does in your first project is necessarily what he'll be best at in the long run.

Let people try their hand at several things as you get started. Give them a chance to develop new skills. Find out what they're best at and try to increase their understanding and respect for what is involved in various aspects of the group effort. In all this joy of self-discovery, be sure that the web of responsibility doesn't get broken. Maintain communication and give people a chance to share tips on things they've done before.

Dealing with Difficult People

Everyone brings some combination of personal interests and needs to an effort like yours. Usually this is positive; diverse concerns and viewpoints will help your group clearly define its priorities and will give members the chance to think about issues and reconsider their own views in the process. You may, however, encounter people whose personal agendas can get in the way of what you and your group are trying to do. Sometimes these will be group members, and sometimes you'll come across them when working with other organizations. Descriptions of several "types" are given below, along with suggestions on how to deal with them.

As you read these descriptions, realize that these are *facile* labels applied to traits that almost everyone—you and me included—has exhibited at one time or another. These attributes are not necessarily negative; indeed, they can sometimes be harnessed to the benefit of the cause. As you consider this list and deal with people who fit these descriptions, remember the intrinsic value of each individual and of his contribution to the effort. Always seek conciliation first, exercise diplomacy, and don't allow interpersonal friction to hinder your efforts.

Zealots and experts: Some people need a great deal of acknowledgment for their knowledge and commitment, and they may go out of their way to get it—or at least to get some attention.

The zealot is very vocal about her commitment to the cause and will often hold very extreme views. She may go beyond the kind of strong view that can be refreshing and useful in a discussion to the point of making other members uncomfortable. Allowing the zealot to direct the formation of your group's opinion and political affiliation could push you to the fringe, alienating others within and beyond the group. A public opportunity for her to express these views as a member of your group could discredit you in the public eye; counting on her personal diplomacy in a confrontation with the powers that be is downright foolish.

Sometimes the zealot's tendency to pull discussions off course can be mitigated by effective monitoring on your part: limiting each speaker's time and reminding the entire group of the need to come to a consensus. If this doesn't work and if you feel the need to confront the zealot about the disruptive nature of her opinions, do so in private, one-on-one, so she doesn't feel ganged up on. Attempting to embarrass her in front of a group will put her on the defensive, resulting in a counterproductive and possibly volatile exchange. Acknowledge her commitment to the cause, praise her opinions, and remind her that the entire group must be comfortable with decisions and actions taken. Some action is better than none, even if it doesn't fit her opinion of how much should be done. Also reiterate that not everyone can do as much as she does but everyone can do something as long as they feel it is valuable. If the opportunity exists, you might want to suggest that she join another group as well—giving her the chance to "double" her own commitments—and act as liaison between the two. Be wary, however, of the opportunity this will present her (and the other group) to pull members away from your organization. If this begins to happen, it will become more important than ever to demonstrate to all members that your group is very active and that making a commitment to its work *is* the right thing to do.

The expert wants recognition of his knowledge on the subject at hand; as a result, he will often go on and on about the issue. (In class we'd call this person a teacher's pet or "brown-noser.") This behavior will drag discussions out and could intimidate or simply bore less knowledgeable members.

The expert's fault is not in knowing the facts—we should all know as much as we can about the issues we're working on—it's the way he chooses to demonstrate his knowledge. Suggest that he direct this energy into assembling a fact sheet on the issue to distribute to the group and at events, or ask him to prepare a summary of relevant legislation for the next meeting. Maybe he can be the one to draw up your group's bylaws and constitution. In the context of the meeting, encourage brevity by maintaining time limits on agenda items and even on individual speakers. Be sure to acknowledge others first so they get their chance, but try not to make the expert feel ignored. If you find yourself in a situation where the expert is rambling on, look for any opportunity to jump in and reclaim the floor. Even an expert has to breathe once in a while!

Analyzers and nitpickers: Similar in behavior to the expert, the analyzer will talk an issue to death, always attempting to find more angles of attack. Sometimes this is the product of a reluctance to act; sometimes it's just because the analyzer loves a good debate more than the action that your group is trying to focus on. As with the expert, the best way to keep an analyzer from dominating group discussions is to stick to your agenda and recognize other speakers. On a more concrete level, you could ask the analyzer to draw up a fact sheet interpreting the pros and cons on relevant issues for your group (say, environmentalists) and the other side of the issue (polluters) and see where common ground lies.

A nitpicker is an analyzer who takes a very critical view of others' ideas. He can find a problem with any argument and seems to be in search of a perfect solution where none exists. Remind this person and the group that no solution will be perfect. Taking action means accepting compromise within the group and with those on the outside. Try to avoid having the analyzer and the nitpicker take part in public debates on the issue because the annoying nature of their approach will often do more to damage your group's argument than the potential accuracy of their remarks. This can be difficult in a small group, but it should be possible to encourage these individuals into less visible roles while urging others to be the public voice of the group.

Sometimes you'll come across someone who seems to begin every statement with the words "I think I speak for everyone when I say . . ." Such people attempt to make their own opinions preeminent in the discussion by giving the impression that they speak for others; when a group is full of quiet people unwilling to challenge such self-confident assertions, they can often succeed.

Begin discussions—particularly those involving a large diversity of opinion, like a public debate on the issue—by outlining some basic rules of play: respect for others' right to their opinions, allowing others to finish their statements, attacking ideas and not individuals, and (if appropriate) confidentiality. This will usually help head off Mr. "I think I speak for everyone." If not, quietly remind him that each participant should speak for himself only and not make assumptions about the feelings of those around him.

Spotlight seekers: Some people may get involved in your group for reasons of personal gain. Don't deceive yourself that activism is full of altruists devoid of their own motives. It isn't the cutthroat world of big business, but you're quite likely to come across people looking for their fifteen minutes of fame or the next rung on the ladder. Three types of these people are publicity hounds, political gamers, and résumé padders.

Publicity hounds want to see their name everywhere, even to the exclusion of the group. Put this individual in front of a camera, and he'll say, "Look what *I* did. *My* project is saving the earth!" This devalues the time put into your efforts by other group members and paints an inaccurate picture of your project

SUCCESS STORY

Encouraging Personal Action at School

The students of SCOPE—Students Concerned about Our Precious Environment—have slowly but successfully built up a culture of environmentally responsible action at their high school in Middlebury, Indiana. Their effort is a good example of how small efforts can garner support for further projects, and how once you get the ball moving someone may pick it up for you.

The group began recycling paper and aluminum cans in 1992, setting up a community-wide collection center at school and hauling the recyclable materials to nearby Elkhart. After raising money selling environmental theme T-shirts, SCOPE was able to replace its weekly trip to Elkhart with a dumpster for recyclable materials and began paying a local waste-management firm to take care of the hauling. Group members hope the school will soon take responsibility for the firm's small monthly fee. In just three years, the SCOPE project has sent more than twelve tons of paper to the recycling plant instead of the landfill.

Since that success, SCOPE members have used a poster campaign to encourage their classmates to conserve energy by riding bicycles or carpooling to school, and added short "eco-facts"—most drawn from the *50 Simple Things* series and similar books—to the school's afternoon announcements. During Earth Week each year, a reward system is also part of the scheme: Each time students carpooled to school, they received one entry in a drawing for tickets to a local amusement park. Riding a bike to school netted five entries each day.

SCOPE's Earth Week projects also include lunchtime games—pitting students against one another in one-minute can-crushing or six-pack ring-cutting races—that offer a chance at the free tickets as well as a subtle education in environmental issues. The group has also coordinated with fellow students who refill school soda machines each week to take and cut up the dozens of six-pack rings—potentially lethal to animals and fish—generated each time a machine is refilled.

in the eyes of the press, and thus of the community. Think twice before letting this individual be your spokesperson. His enthusiasm for attention may make him tenacious in seeking attention from the media; this may be helpful to your cause. On the other hand, what good is a little more press if it doesn't accurately reflect an appropriate distribution of credit for your successes? This is a decision you'll have to make. As an alternative, try making the publicity hound the group member quoted in your press release (see Chapter 11); this will get his name in front of the press, where he wants it, while still serving exactly the purpose you want it to.

Political gamers get high on the idea of power and the control it gives them. They will try to turn the process of organizing into a political struggle within the group, and perhaps beyond. This could set up some volatile conflicts among group members if the gamer tries to play them off against each other, and between your group and another group or the powers that be if the gamer becomes your negotiator. Ultimately, this could result in a challenge to your leadership. Confront the political gamer carefully. Give her some acknowledgment for her talents, perhaps even a chance to lead part of the group. Do your best to avoid a direct confrontation of an adversarial nature; this would be unpleasant and could have a ripple effect in your group.

The résumé padder is harmless but annoying. He's the kid who is a member of every organization in school so he can list them on his college application or résumé. Beware of a lack of commitment and recognize that others watching him "role-play" may suffer a decline in genuine commitment. Mitigate that development by not showing your own resentment of the résumé padder's presence. The best way for you to do this is to laugh it off: If the padder claims to be doing more than he is, so what? Anyone who matters will know who is really doing the work in your group. No one can be forced to take part in a volunteer activity.

A last word on "types": The priority in what you are trying to do is *action* and effecting real change. Don't get bogged down in the personal and political because it will only get in the way of bringing your group together to make a difference. Expect the occasional difficult interpersonal situation but recall that people also represent the value of what you're doing. Focus on those that inspire you. Remind yourself to relax a little. Maintain your self-respect but remember that ego will only get in the way of working with the kind of diverse, focused people you're likely to encounter on this journey.

Keep It Fun!

You're dealing with weighty topics, with things about which you are genuinely concerned and in which you have some emotional involvement. It's sometimes hard to avoid being grim and serious as you focus on your activist efforts, but you have to—for your own sanity and for the enjoyment of the rest of the group. The satisfaction of a job well done, which comes only after the hard work and not always then, may not be enough to keep a large pool of people involved on a regular basis.

It's challenging to maintain a very sociable atmosphere in meetings while also making effective use of your time. Do your best. Also, see if you can reserve your meeting space for a few minutes before and after the scheduled meeting, to give people a chance to hang out and chat. (This is something you should take part in as well. Don't be a distant leader!) Afterward is usually a better bet, since it prevents conversations from delaying the beginning of your meeting. Knowing they'll be able to have some fun hanging-out time after the meeting will also encourage people to focus on getting things done efficiently.

Less formal meeting situations—like a breakfast meeting or a "working lunch" on the weekend can be pleasant diversions for smaller groups or subcommittees. Be sure, however, to avoid excluding members who can't afford to go out to lunch or whose dietary needs would prohibit it. Don't make food a constant theme, either, because not everyone is comfortable with it.

If it's appropriate for your group, plan social events that are completely independent of your work. See a movie, go dancing, celebrate someone's birthday. Encouraging friendship and camaraderie in your organization will help people enjoy being part of your efforts, so they'll stay with it. Celebrations after group successes are especially rewarding and can tap group enthusiasm if they become an informal brainstorming session on your next project.

The Power of Words

The labels used to denote "types" above are as useful in this context as they are potentially hurtful when used against people in name calling. Think about all the situations you may find yourself in as an activist: leading a group discussion, attending a school board meeting, negotiating with local businessmen or political figures, speaking to the press, and more. Think about how you would speak and act differently in these scenarios. What words might you use in your group meeting that you wouldn't let slip when speaking with your principal or legislator? What would you say instead?

Activism gives us the opportunity to speak in evocative, emotionally-charged language: to seek *liberation,* to embrace *truth,* to build a *better future,* to foster *harmony* and *understanding,* and to combat *injustice* and *prejudice.* If you're doing right by your lofty goals, using these words is appropriate. Always think about the emotional punch these words will have on your audience, however. If you go to your principal with a proposal to do a project to combat *racism* in school, that's a word you'll have to use. But realize that your principal will probably take it personally. People don't want to associate such words with "their space." Soften the blow with conciliatory language, acknowledging that the principal himself is not seen as a racist and demonstrating your willingness to focus on the issue and not impugn the school. Talk in detail about what words you should and should not use when promoting and carrying out the project; unless softer language underplays the seriousness of the problem, *racism* can become *prejudice, bias,* or even *misunderstanding.* Be prepared to compromise on words as a first step to moving forward in any cooperative effort.

There is no magical formula for appropriateness. It's mostly a question of good judgment on your part, based on knowing your audience and tempering your language and actions to suit it. Also try to avoid "misappropriating" language—angering a group by using phrases they see as uniquely theirs. For example, there are very few cases of human rights abuses or mistreatment of individuals that can stand up to a comparison with the Holocaust; attempting to draw this connection is likely to anger the local Jewish community.

Be aware of how the language you're using crosses over into other issues. I was thinking recently about what a school community might do in reaction to a student suicide to bring people together in a supportive atmosphere to heal emotional wounds and discourage others who might be considering suicide. I thought about a "rally for life"—then realized that a rally for "life" could bring out people carrying pictures of aborted fetuses and chanting "Don't kill me, Mommy." This would hardly be what school officials were looking for when planning an event based on what the word "life" meant to them. What other words could they use instead?

The debate over abortion rights gives the most salient and ongoing example of the use and misuse of language. Think about these words: "Pro-life," "anti-choice," "pro-choice," "abortionist," "fetus," "unborn child." Your opinions on reproductive choice will determine which of those words you use, and it's as easy to tell someone's opinion about the issue by their language as by their professed beliefs. When you find yourself confused about what language to use in a debate, remember the intransigence found on both sides of the abortion debate and how it's reflected in language. Seek a common vocabulary based on mutual compromise with your opponents before attempting to move forward with discussion.

R-E-S-P-E-C-T

If anyone knows about the negative power of labels and the assumptions that go along with them, it is we—"Generation X." At every step of your efforts you can expect to collide with people who will look at you and see only the media image of young people in the 1990s: confused, dysfunctional, self-centered, and resentful. To these will often be added whatever assumptions can be made about your race, your gender, or your (presumed) religious convictions. (This goes for "majority" as well as "minority" groups.)

These are prejudices like any other, and the best way to combat them is through action rather than words. Don't just say, "We're not like that," because that is just what adults will expect you to do. Prove yourselves. There is nothing more effective than taking action contrary to what is expected of our "sedentary" generation—by being effective activists and achieving real change. This is another reason I counsel against simply going out and rallying over an issue. Crying and stamping our feet is exactly what is expected of us as "children" in this "adult" world.

Try to avoid having such generational, ethnic- and gender-based assumptions made about your group by seeking diversity in those areas. In a political organizing guide published in 1992, a friend of mine counseled that "any organization that doesn't include women, minorities, and a full mix of people with different economic backgrounds is setting itself up for problems." While I think that's an overstatement, his point is valid. You should seek the participation of a diverse group of your peers because it will mitigate some assumptions that might otherwise be made about you and because it will often lead to a more balanced and fully representational consideration of issues within your group. Just make sure the people who are a minority in your group don't feel that they are being used as tokens; they won't stay around if that's the case. Diversity is the right thing to do. It is being mentioned in this context because it is also a large part of how you will be perceived by adults, by various minority groups, and by the media.

As for a more direct strategy, sometimes anticipating people's assumptions and turning those assumptions back at them can be effective if done in a good-natured way. I've occasionally begun presentations by saying with a smile, "I am not disenchanted, I'm not carrying a handgun, and I do not watch 'Beavis and Butthead.' " Although the last part is a lie, my little joke is a quick and direct way of reminding my audience that I am an individual as well as a young person; by listing some of their own biases about me before I begin, I may prevent those biases from getting in the way of their hearing what I have to say.

Ultimately, the best way to avoid generational and other prejudice is by earning respect. Know your subject, speak eloquently, and be willing to listen and consider the perspectives presented by older people—as long as they are more productive than "when you're older, you'll understand." Explain yourself fully, be open to compromise, and progress will be possible.

10

What Next? Keys to Effective Follow-up

This chapter talks about follow-up: what to do when you reach the end of your planned project in order to provide closure, monitor the maintenance of what you've already accomplished, and prepare for future efforts. In the heady celebration of victory—or even the agony of defeat—these are the easiest things to forget, yet no action is complete without them. They constitute some of the most important steps you can take to maximize the effectiveness of what you've done and set the stage for future efforts. Follow-up falls into three categories: Diplomatic and publicity follow-up, logistical follow-up, and evaluation and redirection.

Apply these guidelines to situations where you've completed the goals you set out for yourself or where you've achieved some abridged or modified set of goals. Apply them also to situations where you did not manage to do what you wanted to do. You may be tempted to use the word "failure" to describe such a turn of events—because failure is often how it feels. Instead of "failure," try "setback"; you've encountered a temporarily insurmountable obstacle between you and your goal. This may mean you have to find a new way around the obstacle, to work harder to convince the obstacle to get out of your way, or to find a new goal and work toward it. Remember that you learn more from "failure" than from success. Now it's time to go back and apply your newfound wisdom to a campaign that will be successful.

Public Images: Packaging Your Success

Declaring success brings you a well-deserved good feeling and can be an important source of increased legitimacy for your group. You're proud of what you've done. Show that pride in a way that doesn't make you appear arrogant or self-aggrandizing. Bring others into your victory. Arrogant pride says, "Look what we did," as you point at yourselves. Universally uplifting pride says, "Look what *we* did," as you spread your arms wide and indicate the whole community that is your audience. When congratulated, smile modestly and say, "Well, we couldn't have done it without everyone's help." It's true.

If the culmination of your work is the creation of some new service like a peer counseling or mediation program, publicizing its availability will be your primary means of "declaring success." Use posters or an announcement in the community service column of local newspapers, and encourage local press to report on your success. It's almost like marketing yourself as a business would, except you usually don't have to pay for your "ads." Remember that creating the service is a pale victory if no one shows up!

If, on the other hand, your effort is something that will occur incrementally—like increasing recycling and decreasing trash volume in your school or community—think of some publicity methods that could simultaneously indicate your success to date and encourage others to participate in the future. How about a "thermometer" indicating the percentage of local households recycling, with future goals and dates marked on it? The thermometer, drawn on poster board with levels indicated (and amended weekly) in bright red marker, could also include facts about recycling and contact information for your group. How about "gold stars" or "eco-hero" bumper stickers for those individuals and families who participate? What are some other examples of this kind of inclusive publicity?

Once you've had the chance to evaluate your successes and setbacks and can look toward planning a new project (see below), state these new goals as a "view of the future" or "upcoming goals" when interacting with the media or publicizing yourself. Realize the need that people have to rest and process the

WORDS OF WISDOM

The Real Gifts

Somebody asked Pete Seeger a question about how he felt about all these years of being involved in things like this, and he sort of answered me because he knew my commitment to things. He said, "You know, Harry, my involvement in a cause, benefit, march, or demonstration, I'm not sure it's made a difference . . . but," he said, "I can tell you one thing: Involvement with these issues means you're involved with the good people. The people with the live hearts, the live eyes, the live heads." Just think about it in terms of your lives. . . . Who are the people who are your best friends? Who are the people you keep coming back to? Who are the people who make your life worthwhile? Usually they're people who are committed to something. So in the final analysis, commitment in and of itself—irrespective of whether you win or not—is something that truly makes your life more worthwhile.

—Harry Chapin,
in an interview with Bill Ayers, WPLJ Radio
(New York's Power-95 FM)

changes that have occurred—this goes for members of your group, too—but use the afterglow of your success to maintain momentum.

If it's a setback that you've experienced, try to find a positive spin on it in order to maintain and redirect momentum within your group and beyond. Describe your effort as postponed or declare partial success. You might say, for example, "We're pleased that our lobbying effort brought this important environmental issue to public awareness. Although Congressman Jones didn't support our position with his vote, we look forward to continuing to keep the public abreast of the movement for higher emission standards and will urge the congressman to support future legislation." If you can name this future legislation—that is, find something else that's in the pipeline and do a little background

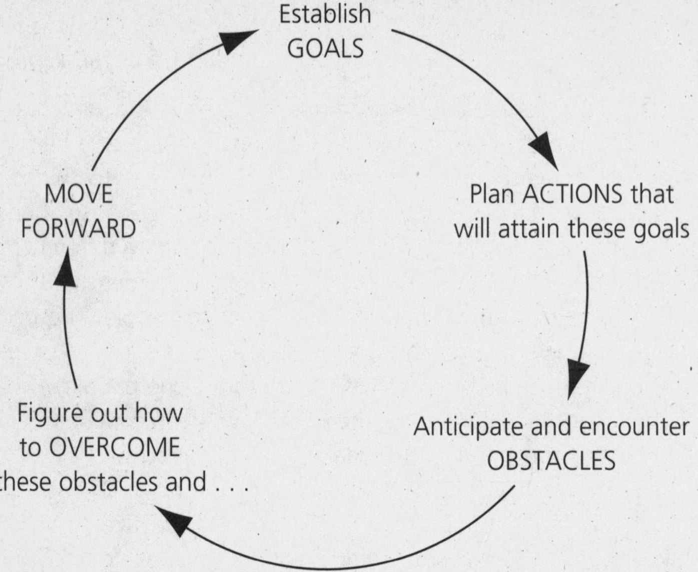

research—you can redirect the public focus immediately and possibly even use their sympathy to your advantage.

How about declaring partial success as a complete success? If you were trying to get a student onto the school board as a voting member and got the seat but not the vote, you could declare this a success: "There will now be a student voice on the board." Remember that declaring complete success as opposed to qualified success in a situation like that may mean cutting off your ability to work toward further progress on the same issue. Revising your goals after the fact may also seem dishonest. It's up to you.

Back into the Fray

The most important question when you face a setback is how you and your group will represent this development to yourselves. You're upset and disappointed, and that's normal. Deal with that in whatever way works best for you. When you're ready—and again, don't wait too long or you'll lose your momentum—go through the evaluation process above. Decide what changes you should make in tactics, goal, or "angle" (this may include pulling back to a more intermediate goal for the time being) and begin again.

Think of this setback stage as the middle of your effort—a sort of reevaluation "on the fly"—while also recognizing the ways in which it is an ending and a new beginning. If the changes you're making are large, return to step one and draft a new set of goals and plan of action. If it's more a question of strategy, bring your current efforts to a close and redirect your energies to something you think will work better.

. . . Where Thanks Are Due

Thank everyone. Period. Every person or entity involved in the success of your project should receive a note, a phone call, or a personal message of thanks from you and/or the members of your group with whom they interacted. This increases their sense of having been part of the project; it helps you stay on good terms with them, and it makes it clear you appreciated their help and aren't taking advantage of them. In the same way, it helps you cultivate allies for future efforts.

Thank-yous are in order even if you were not successful. These thanks will be more of the shrugged shoulders, "better luck next time" variety, of course, but they may also be worth sympathy points if you can maintain momentum with your benefactors.

It's always tempting to use a thank-you note to pitch your next project—trying to get helpful individuals to jump right in again. I recommend resisting this temptation because it can often make recipients feel as if they're being railroaded into more involvement than they had originally agreed to. If you wish, end your note or phone call by saying, "I look forward to working with you again sometime" or "I'll keep you posted on our future projects." Then wait a few weeks before going back with a new request. This will give your patron a chance to "rest" but not to lose enthusiasm, and will give you an opportunity to pull together an impressive new proposal. If you have funds left over and your project was quite large, a certificate or small gift—something appropriate to your specific project—may be in order for those individuals who were most involved and who did not enter the project because of a preexisting friendship with you: in other words, those individuals who "went above and beyond" in their work with you. Your ability to provide gifts like this will depend on your resource base; these individuals will understand that as well.

Celebrate a Little!

A simple event—a potluck evening or pizza party—is all that's needed. But this is a way of conveying your mutual appreciation for one another and for your supporters, and a chance to set aside the stresses of your effort and just be sociable.

Finally, take a few moments to acknowledge those individuals at the periphery of your efforts—your parents, friends not involved in the project, or others who might have felt slighted for time because of your other focus.

Logistical Follow-up

Remember that even victories require continued monitoring and advocacy. If your group is moving on to another project, establish a monitoring committee for past projects to take care of this kind of follow-up. This may involve those who were most involved in the completed effort, particularly if they feel a personal commitment to seeing it through and other talented individuals are prepared to lead the charge on your next effort.

The most important step in the legislative process is the drafting of regulations and the implementation of programs that occurs *after* the vote is taken. Monitor these rule-making and enforcement processes, and let the bureaucrats know that you're watching. Their power over the process—to help or to hinder the intentions of the legislation—comes from their relative invisibility. Knowing they're being observed and evaluated by a citizens' group may be a new experience. Keep your legislators and sponsors apprised of the program's progress, especially when you need them to "lean on" bureaucrats to keep them honest. If possible,

SUCCESS STORY

Making a Difference in Mexico

At the ripe old age of nine, Carolina Garcia Travesi Gonzalez of Tamaulipas, Mexico, took a course on consumers and ecology at her school. Her interest sparked, Carolina founded the Ecological Children's Club at school the following year. With the help of publicity posters in schools and local stores, the group grew from seven members to eighty in its first few months, bringing together students from across Ciudad Victoria, halfway between the Texas border and the Gulf of Mexico.

The group began by giving presentations in schools, libraries, and summer camps. Their message to peers was to take personal responsibility for the environment: They talked about how students could conserve water, protect trees, and convince their parents to cut down on the use of toxic cleaners in the home. They taught a simple method of recycling paper that allows children themselves to create new paper from old. They also worked with state and local officials to plant hundreds of trees in poor neighborhoods; this was coordinated with environmental education projects in the neighborhood, where children were encouraged to "adopt" a tree and care for it. Individual students negotiated the projects with school and government officials and the media, and the group came together to carry out each planting or educational project.

Bringing everyone they worked with into the project and making them feel part of the club's work was central to the group's success. "We never asked for money. We only asked the state government office for trees, or the radio stations and newspapers for free advertising. We had full collaboration from everybody, and we believe it was that way because we didn't ask for money, just for their time and action," says Carolina.

Unfortunately, Club Ecologista was eventually hijacked by a local politician, who came in with promises of assistance and ended up organizing events through his office and bringing in young people who were not part of the club for his "photo op"—then had municipal workers do the tree planting! The club dissolved, but many of its members continue their work in a less formal setting.

Carolina, now twelve, sits on Ciudad Victoria's municipal ecological committee and is seeking a place at the table of a federal committee on environmental education. She continues her own educational campaigns and is working with activists in India to have two children's environmental books published in Mexico.

---

ask for a seat or two on the oversight committee in charge of the process. (This is the step where special interests, particularly business, wield a great deal of power and can often defeat the very legislation that you just saw passed.)

Likewise, community education projects—particularly when they involve effecting "lifestyle changes" like recycling and decreasing water use, but also including attitude-changing educational efforts—require maintenance to make sure people don't go back to their old ways. Conduct an occasional telephone "survey" of people who were involved to see if they are still involved, do a new postering campaign one to three months after your original effort to remind individuals of the commitment they made, or write a letter to the editor for the same purpose. If you are in a position to know who is not keeping up with the effort—for example, if you're the recycling collectors—send a note to remind them or just ring the doorbell to ask where their recyclables are. If you see a participation problem developing, prepare another low-intensity grassroots campaign to get things back up where they belong.

If it's a direct action effort you're engaged in, the challenge of maintaining commitment falls on your group. If a need still exists for the service you're providing, don't stop just because you feel you've made your point to the public or the powers that be. Keep up with your responsibilities; that's what it takes to hold on to the gains you've made and demonstrate that you are truly serious about your own effort.

Commitments made to other organizations or to those opponents with whom you reached some compromise must also be maintained. Don't renege on your end of a bargain—whether it be to support another organization's next fund-raising drive, to tone down your rhetoric against school personnel in exchange for concessions, or to participate actively in the solution you and your adversaries agreed upon. This is a crucial part of confirming your credibility, keeping hold of the gains you've achieved, and building toward future efforts. If it turns out that your opponents are the ones backing out on the deal, this is a moral victory for you and will provide more ammunition if you decide to go public about it. (Keep in mind that the *threat* of going public will often have more influence on getting your adversary to keep up his end of the bargain than the actual *act* of doing so, particularly if it's a public effort that put him in the hot seat in the first place.)

Evaluation

It is important for movements like ours to be able to adapt their strategies and goals in order to maximize their overall effectiveness. This can be an uncomfortable process, but if undertaken with the idea that questions of strategy should be divorced from judgments of participants' personal characteristics, it can be inoffensive and extremely helpful to the overall success of your effort. Focus on questions of utility, with the idea that you are not only looking back but also looking forward at ways you can apply your conclusions to future efforts.

Although it is being addressed here in the "follow-up" section of the book, evaluation is a useful tool at all stages of a campaign. Don't be afraid to ask for members' input throughout the process, while being aware that "switching gears" too many times will leave both your group and the public somewhat confused as to your goals and methods. Also, keep a brief ongoing journal of your actions and how you felt about them at the time. Looking back at this can be a useful way to evaluate the structure of your campaign time line.

Shortly after completion of your project, devote a meeting specifically to evaluate what was done and talk about possible strategies for the future. Be sure to solicit everyone's input; this is

Project Evaluation Worksheet

Project Title __________ Dates Carried Out __________

Group Name __________ Your Name __________

Strategy/Activity	Effective-ness (0-5)	Things to keep for next time	Things to improve for next time

People/Groups Worked With	How were they helpful/harmful?	Recommendations

Other Comments __________

By filling out this form, then discussing what you wrote, your group can bring together everyone's ideas on how future projects should be different, and how they should be the same.

part of "conveying ownership," as mentioned in Chapter 3. First ask what happened: What went right and what went wrong? What strategies were the most effective, and which ones could you have done without? Then ask why this was the case. Why was one strategy more effective than another? What does that say about the characteristics of the community you were trying to reach? Finally, reflect on how these revelations should affect your future efforts. What types of action might have worked better? How could you improve on even those efforts that were successful? Should you try the same strategy again—that is, will it be effective in the same place a second time? A third?

Consider some of these same questions in relation to people you encountered. Why did you have trouble reaching person X but not person Y? What did you say to person Y that made him an ally? How can you adapt that approach to other individuals in the future? What could you have said to person X that might have positively affected someone of her personality type or in her position? Remember that the answers to these questions will often hinge on less tangible elements of individual personalities. Still, this information may be useful if you can discern the sources of these traits and thus be able to anticipate them in future diplomatic efforts. Finally, keep in mind who was helpful and who wasn't. The helpful ones are people you should approach again, while the unhelpful ones—unless you come up with what you think will be a more effective approach—probably aren't worth your time.

If you hold an event such as a teach-in or a local youth conference, prepare a questionnaire beforehand that asks participants to evaluate each part of the program and offer ideas for future programs (a sample appears on the next page). Distribute this questionnaire near the end of the event, asking the participants to take a few minutes to fill it out before they leave. Tally up the results and see what was well received and what was not; use this information as a starting point for the discussion questions above. Written evaluations can also be useful within your group as a catalyst for discussion.

"Close Encounters" Workshop Day Evaluation

Name (optional) ________________________________ Grade level 8 9 10 11 12
School ____

Please rate each activity:	Best........Fair........Poor				
Morning session (Introductions)	1	2	3	4	5
First workshop facilitator's name___________________________	1	2	3	4	5
Keynote speaker James Todd	1	2	3	4	5
Second workshop facilitator's name___________________________	1	2	3	4	5
"Art for Unity's Sake" Creative Project	1	2	3	4	5
Final plenary session	1	2	3	4	5

What event or workshop did you find most interesting and informative, and why?

What event or workshop did you find least interesting and informative, and why?

What event or activity that we *didn't* have would you like to have seen at this event?

What suggestions would you make for future workshop programs? What should we keep and what should we "throw away"?

Overall, what was your impression of "Close Encounters"?

Other comments:

Thank you very much! We're glad you attended.

Please give this form to a facilitator on your way out.

Always give event participants a chance to evaluate their experience. A combination of "ratings" and open-ended questions gives everyone a chance to give some input. Consider their suggestions when planning your next event.

Looking Ahead

If you've reached an ending point, think about ways of expanding your efforts. This may mean seeking new members by recruiting volunteers or expanding your group's membership constituency to include students at other schools, community members, or others outside your current sphere. Set some concrete goals for yourself: networking with students at ten other schools in the area, getting twenty more people to participate in planning and carrying out your next event, bringing in five adults from the community that represent different churches where you could base future events. Approach these goals in the same way you approached your project: Figure out what it will take to get there, plan how to do it, and execute it.

Expanding may also mean finding a different angle on your work. What are some obvious tangents you can follow from project A to project B? Maybe cleaning up city parks can be expanded to include streets in residential neighborhoods. If you've just gotten a student representative onto the governing body of your school, you should try to create a network through which all students can interact with her to discuss their priorities, be it a formal student government, a suggestion box in the lobby, or weekly visits to homerooms or dormitories. Think about your options: more, different projects in the same place; similar projects in different places; or both.

You might also decide to shift your focus entirely. Maybe your anti-racism work has made you aware of environmental justice issues facing your community, or maybe an unsuccessful attempt to organize an environmental rally has brought you in touch with problems of apathy among your fellow students. There's nothing wrong with shifting your focus entirely. Changes like this can sometimes be refreshing and invigorating. You can still apply the strategies you developed in your first effort to future ones in another field. If you decide to switch gears radically, think first about the resources you'll be losing out on by starting at square one with a different set of priorities.

Maintaining Momentum

However you decide to look ahead to future projects, remember that you and your volunteers need to rest, devote your energies to the other things in your life, and absorb the lessons of your success or setback. Once evaluations have been completed, take a little break—maybe a week or so—before diving headfirst into a new project. An important balance should be struck between getting rest and maintaining focus: Don't allow your group's members to lose momentum and a sense of continuity and permanence of their commitment. Only you can gauge how much rest is needed; in general, the more intense your work has been, the longer a recess you should take. But think in days, not weeks—except in situations like final exams, where large chunks of time must be given to other pursuits.

11

Media Manners: Courting the Fourth Estate

You don't need me to tell you that the media plays a central role in society and in how we think about and understand the things happening around us in the world. What we see on television and read in the papers one day affects what we're talking about and thinking about the next day, and it can often change the way we act in the long term. Look at the social impact of media coverage on drunk driving in the 1980s or at the more recent attention given to the dangers of smoking. Although legislation was passed to curtail such behavior, it was the media attention—often spurred by the efforts of grassroots activists—that kept these issues on the public agenda.

As activists, you and your group should develop the ability to harness the power of your local media for the benefit of your cause. Particularly if community education is an important element of what you're trying to do, getting and keeping the attention of local news sources will be a determining factor in your success. Likewise, the attention you get will increase your group's legitimacy in the eyes of the community, and this will improve your ability to get things done.

To some extent, working with the media involves basic talents of panache and diplomacy: cultivating friendly contacts with reporters, knowing the name of an editor sympathetic with what you're trying to do and keeping her posted on your work, or writing quality letters and columns that will be consistently published—even sought—by your local paper. More often, and especially at the outset, your ability to "get press" will depend on effective use of materials like press releases and on conveying a professional and organized image to those members of the press with whom you interact.

Before beginning, let me mention one caution. In this chapter, I make references to "using" the media. This is an easy and not unreasonable way of thinking about the issue because the media are tools you'll need to use as part of your campaign. Always remember, however, that "the media" are people—some of them with very big egos—who don't like the idea of being used. It's not their job to help you; it's their job to report the news as they see it. Your job is to do things that are newsworthy and to make sure that they know about what you're doing so they can cover it. Be gracious and respectful, try to speak their language, and demonstrate an enthusiasm about your efforts that is infectious without being overbearing.

Who's Out There?

Let's start by breaking down this monolithic idea of the media. Make a list of the local media sources where people in your community get their news. These will include local television news programs and radio stations, local daily and weekly newspapers, magazines of local interest, and specialized publications like church bulletins and periodicals produced by local businesses or ethnic communities.

In most cases, national magazines and network television news shows are beyond your reach as a local activist group. Once you've been around awhile, however, and if you feel you've created an organization with very impressive achievements and/or a very unique take on a certain situation, drop a line to the producers of some television newsmagazines. Or add them to your press mailing list. Maybe you'll get lucky and they'll be looking for a story just like yours. The legitimacy conveyed by national coverage will vastly improve your efficacy in your own community and may inspire similar efforts elsewhere.

But back to reality: local news. Think about each one on your list in the context of how and when you want to try to "reach" them with news of your efforts. The biggest thing to think about at this point is whether you want publicity *before* your event (to bring people in) or *of* your event (to let people know what happened, what your group stands for, and how to get involved later). For example, if you're organizing a community cleanup effort, you'll need to have some mention of the event in church bulletins and local newspapers ahead of time in order to get people to attend and be involved. For coverage of the event you should also approach local television news programs as well as major local papers and magazines.

The best place for precoverage of your event may be a free service offered by many local media outlets: in newspapers, the calendar or "community events" section; and on local radio and television, public service announcements or roundups of upcoming activities. Later in this chapter we'll discuss calendar entries, public service announcements, and other media advisories you should know about.

Making Contact

Your list now includes the who (local media outlets) and the when (before and/or day of coverage). Let's talk about the how: How should you contact these various outlets, and exactly whose attention are you trying to get? Get out the phone book and start dialing. You'll usually get the switchboard operator or front desk secretary. Begin by explaining who you are ("Hello. I'm calling for the youth environmental club in [your town].") and obtain answers to the following questions: When is your community events calendar deadline? To whose attention should I send a calendar submission? What is his/her fax number? Mailing address? What is the name of the editor [for print media] or producer [for television and radio] I should contact about coverage of our events? What is her fax number? How far in advance should we notify her of an event? Do you have a reporter who usually covers youth or the environment? What's his name? What's the best way to reach him? You get the idea. Use the worksheet on the following page as a guide to the information you should get; photocopy it as many times as you need and make it part of your project notebook.

Media Directory

Group Name ______________________________

Newspaper/Magazine/Station	Calendar & Other Deadlines
Contact Person & Title	
Phone	Remarks
Fax	
Address	

Newspaper/Magazine/Station	Calendar & Other Deadlines
Contact Person & Title	
Phone	Remarks
Fax	
Address	

Newspaper/Magazine/Station	Calendar & Other Deadlines
Contact Person & Title	
Phone	Remarks
Fax	
Address	

Newspaper/Magazine/Station	Calendar & Other Deadlines
Contact Person & Title	
Phone	Remarks
Fax	
Address	

If you are on such a tight schedule that you don't have time to obtain this information, or if for some reason you don't have information on a certain newspaper, you'll have to address your release to a title and hope it gets to the right person. For daily newspapers and most weeklies, address information on breaking news (events) to the City Editor or News Editor, and general profile information to the Features Editor; when in doubt, go for the City Editor. Remember, every newspaper has a "staff box," usually on page two or on the editorial page, that lists the names and titles of all editors. For television news stations, address releases to the producer of the show you want to target in care of the local news station it's on; for example, "Producer, Evening Report, WGAL-TV."

For calendar listings, write something brief that mimics the style each newspaper uses for its calendar listings. Include a contact name and telephone number and send it to the attention of "Calendar" or the name of the person who puts together the calendar each week. Always meet deadlines.

Getting Their Attention

The next question to ask is: Why do we matter? What is it about what we're doing that makes it a story? As a general principle, think of the editor you're approaching as a hardened cynic who doesn't think much of you or of what you're doing. (This is called "worst-case scenario.") Your job is to convince him your project deserves the attention of his readers. You need to give him what's called a hook or an angle—something that conveys the urgency of your effort without being sensationalistic, that shows him your group is into action and not just talk, and that tells him what makes you different from all the other groups out there. And you need to do this in about five paragraphs that fill less than one page.

Sometimes your youth alone will be enough of an angle; it allows you and the editor to debunk myths about our apathetic, do-nothing generation and to play on the guilt of our parents' generation all at once. Usually, the fact that you're *doing* rather than *saying* is a strong point in your favor. This is why you shouldn't rush right off and try to get in the papers: Going to anyone and saying, "See, we *did* this," will always be the most impressive thing you can do. It's also very important to say why you're doing something because you may be filling a need no one else has even recognized. Explain what you're doing in terms of the reason statements you composed at your first meeting (see Chapter 3). Always back up your opinions with facts.

Some examples of good hooks are the following:

- You are a group of young people organized to change the dismal environmental stance of a local congressional candidate.
- You are a multiracial coalition of students at your high school trying to combat racism among your peers by encouraging dialogue among various groups.
- You are a group of young suburbanites that feels a responsibility to assist those less fortunate and are organizing a food drive for the homeless in your community.
- Using the cutting-edge technology of the Internet, you have made contact with students in a certain country and are working with them to formalize a "sister city" relationship and create opportunities for international exchange.

You get the idea. Think of a statement like the ones above that includes both information on what you're doing and an explanation of your unique "angle." Now it's time to write your first press release.

Press Releases

A press release is designed to convey the crucial points of your action and of your group's identity. It should follow a fairly standard pattern that conveys a maximum of information in a minimum of space; of course, as you'll see from the samples in this chapter, the guidelines given below will have to be tailored to your exact needs. Keep sentences and paragraphs short and simple; try to mimic the journalistic style of a newspaper article. Always type double-spaced, indenting each paragraph about half an inch or leaving an extra line between paragraphs. If your group has a letterhead, use it consistently for all press releases. Don't use a personal letterhead even if the release is about you.

Some smaller newspapers may print press releases verbatim, and some (especially weeklies) may be willing to print several releases just prior to your event. Hence, begin advance publicity as soon as you've planned your event and are able to give all pertinent details. Also be sure to use the journalistic style when writing your release; read the newspaper and look at the samples here to get a better idea of what that means.

In the upper left corner of the page (below your letterhead, if you're using it), type the date and below that FOR IMMEDIATE RELEASE. If you don't want the information made available until a certain time, indicate that by typing (for example), EMBARGO UNTIL FRIDAY, FEBRUARY 28, 10:00 A.M. "Embargo" is the journalistic word for "hold" or "do not release." Be aware that embargoes are often broken, especially if reporters smell a scoop. (There's nothing worse for a militant effort than the campus newspaper headlining ACTIVISTS TO OCCUPY ADMINISTRATION BUILDING TOMORROW the day before your climactic event.) If the element of surprise is so important, wait until the last minute to fax your release with a cover page reading "extremely urgent," and follow it immediately with a phone call to confirm that it was received and noticed.

In the upper right corner, give the name and telephone number(s) of a contact person or two. This should be your group's spokesperson and, if a second name is indicated, either your media coordinator or the group's leader.

Always write about yourself in the third person except when it's a direct quote.

Begin with a brief, catchy headline that contains an action verb. The headline should explain the contents of the press release as completely as possible without containing more than about eight words. Center your headline above the first paragraph of your release and use all capital letters.

Your first and second paragraphs should answer the "five W's" of journalism: who, what, when, where, and why. Try to answer at least three of these questions in a two-sentence first paragraph.

The first two paragraphs should also contain your "hook." Think of editors as having a very short attention span: Your task in the first two paragraphs is to make them want to read the last three.

Follow the basic information by explaining why you're doing what you're doing. Begin with your strongest argument—the big reason that the media should pay attention and the people should get involved. State it simply and directly. Remember the difference between fact and opinion (see below) and begin opinion sentences with phrases like, "The group feels that . . ." If you have space, state your second strongest argument in the same manner.

The fourth paragraph should contain factual background information on your issue: the voting record of the legislator in question, the results of your water-quality tests at the reservoir, the number and type of bias incidents reported at your school, and so on. Refer only to verifiable facts; save interpretation and other remarks for position statements.

The last paragraph should convey the group's "first-person" viewpoint on the issue through a quote from a member. Don't feel the need to make the quote sound "talky"; make it as well stated and concise as the rest of the release. Try to avoid using a quote from your spokesperson or group leader, but be sure to get the permission of the person quoted to release the remark.

Indicate the end of the press release with "-30-" or "####," centered below the last paragraph. These are journalistic shorthand indicating the end of the release. If you prefer, you can also use "-END-."

If you must use more than one page, put "-MORE-" at the bottom of each page except the last one so that reporters know to keep reading. Remember to use the journalistic "inverted pyramid," conveying information in descending order of importance so the editor can cut from the bottom when printing an abridged version of your release. For more ideas on the structure and style of press releases, take a look at the two examples included here.

W i l l i a m s t o w n
Clean Water Coalition

P.O. Box 301
Williamstown

(123) 456-7890

Williamstown High School Environmental Club

Williamstown Vo-Tech Environmental Society

Williamstown Middle School Environmental Club

Sierra Club, Williamstown Chapter

Calavaras County Friends of the Earth

Physicians for Social Responsibility, Williamstown Chapter

For Immediate Release
September 16, 1996

Contact: David Katz
(123) 456-7890

Coalition Sponsors Riverside Cleanup Saturday

The Williamstown Clean Water Coalition will hold a cleanup on the banks of the Williams River on Saturday, September 21, at 10:00 a.m. Participants from local schools and service organizations will walk along a two-mile stretch of the river, picking up trash and exploring the river ecosystem. The public is welcome.

Following the cleanup, participants will meet at Williams Park for a picnic, sponsored by Ed's Corner Deli in Williamstown. The Williamstown High School Band will provide musical entertainment.

Organizers say the event will kick off a year of cleanup activities, including monthly river events and other projects.

The Williams River is a vital part of the local ecosystem. It feeds the reservoirs of Williamstown and several towns downstream, including Forest Park and Pine Bluff. The river ecosystem contains a number of species unique to the area. Littering by careless campers and drivers on nearby roads endangers wildlife and destroys the natural beauty of the area.

"As residents of this area, we have a civic responsibility to protect and care for the nature around us," says Robin Smither, president of the Williamstown High School Environmental Club. "If we all play our part in this project, the Williams River will be a beautiful and vital place for generations to come."

-30-

Sample press releases. Note open, "airy" layout, easy-to-read typeface, and prominent contact information.

Students for Peace

89 Berlin Road
Hometown, IL

For Immediate Release
May 1, 1996

Contact: Donald Beattie
(648) 628-6237

Students Lobby for Peace, Economic Growth

Local students are urging Congressman Jones to support the defense economic adjustment act, and asking their neighbors and classmates to do the same.

The defense economic adjustment act, first introduced in 1977 by the late Congressman Ted Weiss of New York, provides a strategic plan and government support for "building down" America's military industries by converting them to non-military applications. Backers — including the Worldwatch Institute in Washington, D.C. — say the five-year plan will actually create 400,000 more jobs each year while increasing spending on consumer-oriented high-tech industries.

"The defense economic adjustment act represents an opportunity to stop the senseless waste of trillions of dollars on unnecessary military equipment and allow us to focus America's limited funds on education, health, and the poor," says student campaign organizer Donald Beattie.

Congressman Jones has proclaimed his interest in increased spending for non-military uses, but has not yet stated his position on the defense economic adjustment act. A member of his staff said the Congressman was "waiting to hear from his constituents before making his decision."

The student committee will go door-to-door this week asking residents to contact the Congressman in support of the bill. They will also have a table at Tubig Mall every day this week between 5:00 and 9:00 p.m., where anyone can sign a letter supporting the adjustment act. Interested people can call 628-6237 for more information.

-END-

Other Types of Releases

Public service announcements are a form of free publicity offered by radio and television stations as part of their commitment to serve the community. They are ten- to thirty-second spots, usually read by the deejay, and can either promote an event or address an issue more generally. They should sum up your information as briefly as possible, repeating details like date and time of an event at least twice. Target radio stations that you think will best reach your intended audience. Call ahead to the radio station to ask if they have any special guidelines on length or format; otherwise, follow the format indicated on the sample shown here.

When figuring out the time duration of your announcement, read it aloud several times—quickly but clearly and with enunciation, as you've heard deejays read similar announcements—and time yourself with a stopwatch. Average the times you get in about half a dozen trials and round to the nearest five-second interval; this is the "time" you should indicate on the announcement.

Sometimes it pays to keep journalists informed of upcoming events through *media advisories*. A media advisory is like a press release but is less formal. It's more like giving a tip than like making a formal announcement—in fact, a media advisory can usually be replaced with a phone call or two to reporters you've met. It's not intended to be published and usually involves bullet points rather than complete sentences. Its heading follows a press release format, with MEDIA ADVISORY added above the title of the release. It then moves on to what, who, when, where, and why in that order. The "why" is optional but is usually the best place to put your group's argument or a variation on your mission statement. Take a look at the example shown here, which wisely puts the names of notable speakers in a subheading and uses member quotes heavily to convey the group's stance.

You may wish to accompany a media advisory with a short—two- to four-sentence—cover letter explaining why you think this information would be of interest to the editor. Make your argument in terms of the event's "story potential" rather than its importance to your issue; show the editor what's in it for her. If you are interested in having a feature or human-interest story written about

WC

Williamstown
Clean Water Coalition

P.O. Box 301
Williamstown

(123) 456-7890

Williamstown High School Environmental Club

Williamstown Vo-Tech Environmental Society

Williamstown Middle School Environmental Club

Sierra Club, Williamstown Chapter

Calavaras County Friends of the Earth

Physicians for Social Responsibility, Williamstown Chapter

Event Date: September 21
Start Time: 10:00 a.m.

Contact: David Katz
(123) 456-7890

Reading time: 20 seconds

The Williamstown Clean Water Coalition will hold a river cleanup on Saturday, September 21, at 10:00 a.m. at Williams Park. Come and join local students in cleaning up a vital part of our ecosystem. Protect your water supply and preserve the river for generations to come. The Williamstown High School Band will perform at a picnic following the cleanup. Come make a difference, hear the music and enjoy the food on the twenty-first at ten. For more information, call the Clean Water Coalition at 456-7890.

A public service announcement for use on radio and television. Note that time and date of the event are repeated twice; don't leave interested listeners saying, "When did they say it was?"

Student Alliance for Educational Access

MEDIA ADVISORY

Contact: 202-687-3476

Ali Carter
Chad Griffin

For Immediate Release **February 25, 1995**

STUDENTS RALLY AGAINST FINANCIAL AID CUTS:

Rep. Bonior, Rep. Schroeder, Rep. Schumer, Rep. Lowey, Rep. Woolsey Confirmed To Address March 1st Rally

(WASHINGTON, D.C.) -- The Student Alliance for Educational Access, a new District-wide movement formed by university students to combat the elimination of federal financial aid programs, will be holding a protest on Wednesday, March 1, at 12:00 noon.Students from Georgetown University, The George Washington University, The American University, Catholic University, Howard University, The University of Maryland, Trinity College, Marymount University, Mount Vernon College and Washington College will be present. The rally will be held on the south side of the Capitol, on the grassy area across from the Library of Congress and Independence Avenue.

"If you want to talk about running the government like a business, it shows real short-sightedness to cut funding for college students," said Ali Carter, a Georgetown student who, along with Chad Griffin, founded the movement. "I don't know of a single successful corporation that would sabotage its future leaders in the immediate interest of balancing its budget." Griffin added, "The proposals eliminate the in-school interest subsidy for students on federal loan programs, adding anywhere from twenty to fifty percent to students' loan debt and placing a university degree out of reach for more than four million students nationwide."

"Students have been the silent party throughout much of the debate over financial aid cuts," said Carter. "Tomorrow, we plan to show Congress that we are a powerful voice and the most sound investment America can make in its future." Griffin added, "Proposals to eliminate student aid are simply reckless attempts to cut the federal deficit. Everyone agrees that the deficit must be eliminated, but not at the expense of our education."

"I fully support the District-wide student efforts against proposed reductions in student financial aid and I am pleased Georgetown students are active in the Student Alliance for Educational Access," said Leo J. O'Donovan, S.J., President, Georgetown University. "As these proposed cuts would directly affect each and every student on financial assistance, it is important for students to take the lead in addressing this threat to their future and higher education."

1608 Leavey Center, Georgetown University
Washington, DC 20057
Phone: (202) 687-3647, (202) 687-3476; Fax: (202)687-5558; Cellular:669-0287

Although denser than a typical media advisory, this sample gets journalists' attention by featuring well-known speakers in the sub-headline and conveys strong opinions by including a lot of direct quotes from organizers.

your group, say so (again, in her terms). A feature about your group often has the advantage of being longer and allowing more space to be spent talking about why your group is doing what it is doing. Seek such opportunities, especially when your project doesn't really count as "breaking news."

Note also that a Media Advisory heading is sometimes put on press releases that announce events, the idea being that the release's only real purpose is to get a reporter out to cover the event.

Press Conferences

You're not likely to be holding a press conference anytime soon, but it is mentioned here because it can be a useful tool when you have really big news to share. Press conferences should be reserved for only the most important announcements. Editors won't send their reporters to cover a press conference that isn't "hot," and a press release or media advisory will usually suffice for most major events. Examples of reasons to hold news conferences are the arrival of an especially well-known or controversial figure ("Interior Secretary Bruce Babbitt will be speaking at Springfield High School"), to announce surprising or alarming results of some research ("Students' testing indicates high levels of lead in local playground soil"), or to announce an upcoming debate between political figures.

Press conferences should take place early in the day to make it easier for television and newspaper reporters to meet evening deadlines, and they should be held in an accessible location near media offices, if possible. The goal is to get a maximum number of journalists from all media to attend and to use the event to make personal contacts with reporters who are especially interested in the story. Send advisories to those on your contact list well in advance; try to provide enough information to provoke interest without giving your story away. Make follow-up phone calls in order to convey the news conference's importance.

A press conference should begin with a brief statement by your group's spokesperson or leader summing up the reason for the press conference and the position of your group. This is followed by a question-and-answer period; the total length of the program should not exceed half an hour unless your major speaker actually makes an appearance. Remember that a press conference is also a photo opportunity. Place your podium in front of a plain background, a wall or single-color curtains, and avoid visually "loud" backgrounds, especially those including text (besides the name of your organization if you have a professional-looking banner to hang behind the podium). Dress well. Also think about the acoustics of the room: Avoid high ceilings, tile floors, and anyplace with background noise (such as outdoors). Remember that fluorescent lights will make you look pallid and green.

Letters to the Editor

Letters to the editor offer a good opportunity to state your group's opinions and air facts on the issue with a minimum of editing. In other words, they're "pure you," while interviews and articles may not focus on the issues or concerns you desire. Letters should be timely and brief, preferably around three hundred words but never more than five hundred unless you're writing a column, which could go up to one thousand.

Discuss one issue per letter; readers should get to the end of the letter and know exactly what you talked about and what your position was. Follow the maxim, "Tell them what you're going to tell them, then tell them, then tell them what you told them." (This is a variation on what we all learned in elementary school: that a letter should have an introduction, a body, and a conclusion.) Don't repeat yourself but find a way to express the same thing in different ways. Use evocative language and action verbs. Explain in detail what readers themselves should do about the issue. Don't use many contractions. Avoid speaking negatively of your community or individuals in it without also conceding something good about them; rather than speaking poorly of the present, convey the idea of *improving* in the future. In all cases, avoid personal attacks and never use profanity.

Finally, don't submit a poorly written letter. If you don't feel you're a good writer, see if someone else in your group can carry

SUCCESS STORY

Multi-issue Organizing in Rochester

Founded in 1990, Brighton Awareness is an environmental club with plenty of extra twists. The club, based at Brighton High School in Rochester, New York, has thirteen committees that focus on such diverse and disparate issues as AIDS, race relations, recycling, and community service—committees that work alongside the more traditional fund-raising committee and group newsletter. With about twenty active participants, Brighton Awareness has been able to have a great deal of effect in the Rochester community.

Brighton Awareness started a recycling project at the high school in 1991; facing funding challenges, the group began the effort by going room to room with a big trash can, and sometimes even went through the trash for recyclables. With the passage of recycling legislation in New York later in 1991, the school built on Brighton Awareness's work by establishing an official program. That same year, in the wake of the Rodney King beating, the group worked with the Black Student Union to convene a workshop focusing on black history, racism, and role models; eighty students, faculty, and parents participated. The coalition also sponsored a series of presentations and an "Awareness Concert" that earned the group and the issue a great deal of press coverage. The concert was a full day of music from local bands, raising $5,000 for Food Link and offering attendees a chance to learn about the organization's work in Rochester.

Another Brighton Awareness committee called the Rochester Youth Awareness Network (RYAN) created a network of local student organizations in thirteen area high schools. The group, which came together through an exchange of letters, met regularly to share ideas and plan events. Through a pooling of resources, the network sponsored a "Monroe Avenue Clean-Up" in which more than thirty students picked up litter on the main street that runs through all area suburbs, then convened to celebrate. RYAN maintains communication through meetings and a newsletter called *Visions* that's distributed to students through networked organizations.

With recycling, race workshops, RYAN, and a fund-raising concert under their belts, the members of Brighton Awareness continue to look for ways to work with community members to effect change. "I wish to find a balance between corporate needs and social issues," says founder Jaime Wemett, "by establishing ethical business habits and skills and making it profitable to do good in our community."

---

that torch. There are plenty of bad letters to the editor out there; often, they do as much harm as good to the cause they're meant to advocate by confusing readers or making a movement's members look foolish.

Press Packets

At events, have a press packet available for reporters to take away with them. This packet should include a copy of the press release or media advisory announcing the event, a profile of your organization, some simple background information on the issue (this could include copies of material sent to you by national organizations as well as your own research), and a copy of relevant leaflets or information sheets. You may also want to include a black-and-white photograph relating to your issue; this could be a photograph of toxic waste barrels behind your school, the "head shot" of the well-known speaker who is headlining your event, or something similar.

If you have the resources, assemble all this information in a folder with pockets and your group's name, the event, date, and time on the front. Otherwise, staple everything together. Press packets should be handled by your spokesperson, media coordinator, or an assistant, and should be provided only to members of the press.

Misrepresentation

One risk you'll face when speaking to the media is what I call selective quoting. This is when your three-second sound bite is cut from the wrong part of your statement. It is particularly likely to occur if the editor or reporter is unfriendly to your cause. For example, if you say, "It may be true that ACME Strip-Mining Corporation will provide an economic boon to our town, but the environmental dangers outweigh those potential benefits," the television clip may have you saying, "It may be true that ACME Strip-Mining Corporation will provide an economic boon to our town." Yes, you said it, but that wasn't your point. Congratulations, you've just been misrepresented. (This can happen in the newspaper as well, although the ability of print journalists to include more information usually means they quote you completely.)

There is no sure way to prevent this from happening, but there are ways to structure your speaking so that it is less likely to happen. In the example given above, the following phrasing would have made it very difficult for a television station to misrepresent your message: "The environmental dangers of ACME Strip-Mining's methods seriously outweigh any possible economic benefits." (Note that this is also more concise.) The night before an event, think about what you're going to say to the media. Plan a few strong "sound bites" and think about how to structure them concisely, to avoid selective quoting. You may even find it useful to write out these quotes and read them over several times before your event. (Never read from paper or cards when standing in front of the camera, however, unless it's a news conference, rally, or other appropriate speaking situation.)

If you've been misrepresented in the media, let them know it. Tell them about their mistake. If it's something minor—a description of your organization or action that's inaccurate but still in the right ballpark—a phone call to the reporter or editor "just to clarify the facts for next time" is in order. If they've made a serious error—particularly in a direct quote or by incorrectly identifying a speaker—call the editor, explain the mistake, and ask him to print a correction. If you want a chance to clarify things and to restate your position in your own words, a letter of response (to be published as a letter to the editor) may be a better bet. Likewise, if you want to take issue with an editorial opinion about what you're doing, write a letter. Letters to the editor of local papers to correct an error made in television coverage would also be appropriate since there's no effective way to get a television station to run a major correction.

Become a Source

As your group develops and conducts more projects and events, make an effort to stay in touch with the same reporters. Always thank them for covering your work, compliment them on good stories, and give suggestions for other angles of your issue they could cover. While objectivity is ostensibly the goal of every good journalist, many reporters become sympathetic with the causes they are covering; encourage this among your media contacts because it will be to your advantage in the long run. (Remember, however, that you can never count on this; if your effort isn't real news, it won't be covered.)

By knowing your issue, you can become a source—someone the reporter comes to when he needs information on a certain topic. Even if you don't know the answer to his question, try pointing him in the right direction or referring him to another knowledgeable individual. When your group brings a big-name speaker to town, try to provide your "ally reporters" a special opportunity to meet and interview her.

Make an effort to anticipate interesting developments in your field. Telephone reporters when a major new study is being released on your issue; let them know what it means to your community and how your group feels about it. These things will become the seeds of stories that keep your issue in the public eye.

If you don't want to be quoted or mentioned, or if you're passing along a hunch rather than a known fact, go "off the record" and offer tips to your reporters. For example, you're looking into the environmental practice of local businesses, and you think one of them is violating hazardous materials laws by, say, pouring photographic chemicals down the sink. You may not have the capacity to investigate this allegation, but a reporter could. In the course of discussing your issue with an ally journalist, you might say, "Off the record, we have reason to believe that Joe's Photo Express is dumping its hazardous materials in violation of clean water laws." This tip offers your reporter the opportunity to investigate and possibly to break a real story; in the process, he'll do a lot of your investigative legwork for you. *Always* clearly state that you're going "off the record" *before* giving uncorroborated tips like that; otherwise, you could find yourself facing a libel suit or, at the very least, public embarrassment if the reporter goes to press with an unfounded allegation from you.

Fact and Opinion

Always remember that facts (the "truth," what everyone should be able to agree on) can be written as statements, while opinions (your "take" or your group's on the facts) must be preceded by an indication of whose opinion it is ("We feel that . . .") or written as a direct quote attributed to a group member. The exception is in a letter to the editor where, because it's in the first person, opinions and facts can be conveyed in the same manner.

One thing to think about is the question of "recognized fact," what you might call "common knowledge" or "what everyone knows." For example: Smoking is bad for you. This fact is recognized by everyone but the tobbacco lobby, which in some cases continues to insist on the social and health benefits of smoking. So while the word "bad" implies an opinion statement, it's something everyone knows and so can be used as fact in the context of a press release. If you're planning to use a recognized fact in your press materials, first think hard about who recognizes it and who is going to take issue with it. When in doubt, frame it as an opinion or a "general consensus" in society.

Advertisements

In all likelihood, buying advertising space in the newspaper or on television will be beyond your group's budget. If you are able to run a print ad, follow the same guidelines given above for the materials: Keep it simple and eye-catching, and include your group's name and contact information as well as the "five w's" about your event or project. If you have "camera-ready" material, tell the newspaper; otherwise, ask them to lay out the ad for you. If you're going to include a photograph, tell them so; they'll probably need to process it for publication. If you're going to run a television advertisement or produce your own radio advertisement (instead of just providing copy for the deejay to read), talk to the television or radio station about how to do it.

Working with the media is a practiced art; don't worry if things start off slowly. You'll develop a knack for appealing to reporters and packaging yourself effectively. The media isn't everything. Sound bites are useful for publicizing your issue, but they also oversimplify things. (This is why I prefer writing my own opinions for the editorial page over straight news coverage.) The issues surrounding your work probably don't fit into three-second quips. Consider this a credit to your work: Nothing that really matters should be able to fit into three seconds. Don't devote energy to the media that would be better directed toward effecting real change. In the end, what you're doing is more important than who's watching.

12

Strategies for Raising Funds in Your Community and Beyond

There's only so much that enthusiasm and person-power can do for you. When it comes to producing materials, covering your phone and fax expenses, getting your group from place to place, and making accommodations for events, you need financial support—in short, money. Budgeting is more than half the battle. Much as we'd like to have the kind of money that corporations and politicians have to throw around, most student activists have to make do and cut corners. (I prefer to call it creativity!) But there's still plenty of support out there.

Fund-raising is a huge field that runs the gamut from bake sales to foundation grants with great variety in between—cash contributions, in-kind donations, special events, merchandise sales, membership dues, and more. You'll have to find the right combination for your group. Always remember that time is money. You should keep in mind how much time and effort you are expending to raise each dollar. For example, ten people working for six weeks to plan a spaghetti dinner that raises $150 could instead have worked just three hours each at a fast food restaurant and donated their pay to raise the same amount of money.

This doesn't mean you should go out and get a job to support your organizing efforts. It *does* mean that there are two sides on your fund-raising "balance sheet." You'll waste a lot of time and not make as much money if you don't plan ahead and figure out the best ways to get what you need.

The real work of fund-raising occurs before you even make your first request. This means creating your budget, line item by line item, and figuring out the best way to get support for each, then drafting a simple proposal that outlines your project in terms that appeal to potential supporters.

Two thoughts should underlie all your efforts: salesmanship and persistence. Salesmanship simply means how you present yourself. The arguments you make and the way in which you phrase your requests will determine your success.

Remember that there are a lot of groups out there looking for funding, even in your own community. You are competing for support, and the winners will be those who convince potential donors that their money is needed, deserved, and appreciated. There's an advertising term called USP—"unique selling point"—that's useful in thinking about how to sell your project as the best possible recipient for donors' support. Think about what makes your project different from every other one out there and why that also makes your project the best solution to the problem at hand. You need the USP to prove to potential sponsors that you will give them the most "bang" for their philanthropic "buck."

Persistence is key. Expect rejections and bounce right back when they happen. Somewhere there is someone who will help you. As a friend of mine who is a professional fund-raiser likes to say, "If you don't ask, the answer is always no."

In-kind Donations

In this chapter, I'll talk about the terms "fund-raising," "money," and "resource" interchangeably. There's a reason for this. Many times you will be seeking actual financial assistance to offset various expenses. As a young activist, however, you will almost certainly be most successful in getting what's called in-kind donations. As contributions go, they are the backbone of student organizing. In-kind donations are contributions of goods and services that businesses or individuals are able to provide and that they often prefer to give because it makes them feel more a part of the project. For example, a restaurant is more likely to give you dinner for two to use as a raffle prize than give you $50 in cash, even though that may be the value of the meal. The same goes for everything from the corner copy store—which will probably let you make some copies for free but almost certainly won't give you cash—to the local garden center giving trees or a parent's business letting you use their fax machine. When you're planning your fund-raising efforts, think most often in these terms.

Outcome They Can See

The first principle of effective fund-raising is to have a visible product. People want to see the results of their donations. They are more compelled to support something they can see, hear, or touch—a tree-planting, a special event, or a station on an educational nature walk—than to finance a percentage of your total budget or a concept like the "racial atmosphere" in your school or community.

Make sure that your appeal for support focuses on outcome. What will there be to show for your work (and for their donation), and how long will it last? If you're putting together a one-day conference, divide the total budget by the number of participants and ask a business to sponsor *one child.* Not "Could you please give us $278" but "Would you sponsor one young person from our community to participate in this important event?"

Even when the physical outcome of a project is apparent—like the nature walk example given above—you should approach donors to give a *particular* station, a *particular* planting, or even a *particular* section of the path.

When a friend of mine was raising money for herself to participate in a one-month international student exchange program, she divided the total cost by thirty and asked thirty people each to sponsor a day of her trip. This didn't just reduce an intimidating number to a more manageable sum; like the "one child" example above, it gave each person a connection to some unique part of the experience. When they received a postcard talking about what she did on July 9, they knew it was their day. A sense of personal connection between donor and benefactor is also an important emotional factor in charitable giving.

The challenge of the "visible product" strategy is translating general operating expenses into a donor-palatable item. General operating expenses (GOE) are the day-to-day costs of keeping your group going, like copying and fax charges, phone bills, and so on. Most organizations find that GOE are more difficult to raise than funds for a specific project or program.

General operating expenses make a great in-kind donation. Get your school to let you use their phone for an occasional long-distance call, ask a member's parent who owns her own business for phone and fax privileges, or approach your local copy shop to subsidize your posters in exchange for its logo appearing in the corner or favorable mention when events roll around.

Furthermore, you can use your special events as fund-raising vehicles by offering sponsorships that will raise more than the cost of the event. (For instance, you can set out to raise $1,000 for a $500 educational project. The "extra" money can then subsidize your GOE before and after the project—the work that makes the project itself possible!) GOE for long-running programs can be translated into visible products by illustrating your mission as tangible products: "Your contribution will help thirty low-income elementary students attend after-school tutoring each week."

Demonstrate Feasibility

Principle number two is demonstrating the feasibility of your proposed project. Before you begin fund-raising, write a detailed plan for your event. Start with the reasoning behind what you're doing—the "why"—and a discussion of what makes it appropriate to the community being served. Also include information on why your group is best able to carry it out. Follow this with additional information such as a complete schedule, line item budget, directory of your staff with short biographies, and mention of any support that you already have. Letters of endorsement from appropriate individuals and letters of commitment from speakers are extremely helpful in demonstrating that what you're doing is for real. Exactly what is included in this proposal will depend on what you're trying to do: For a small direct-action project, less than a page may do it, but if you're planning a major conference, you'll need a professional-looking ten- to twenty-page proposal to take to major corporations and foundations.

Assemble this information into a packet that begins with a one-page "executive summary" of the proposed project. Include copies of press clippings about your group or about similar projects on which your program is modeled. Carry this "flashbook" with you as you pound the pavement looking for support, and include the executive summary with any solicitation letters you mail or fax. Make more detailed information available upon request.

Of course, any discussion of a word like "feasibility" will inevitably bring your age into question. Potential backers will be thinking, "Can these kids do it?" The best way to prove that you can is to have a track record—a series of successful smaller events that demonstrate your abilities to organize effectively, succeed, and get press. Lacking a track record, you can present your members' individual experience and talents as a point in your favor. Also, once you have one sponsor, mention it to all other potential sponsors in hopes of generating a bandwagon effect. A well-presented proposal, demonstrating organization, is your strongest weapon against this kind of ageism. For larger projects, supportive letters from adults who will participate are very important. See if you can get your advisor or a school official to write a letter of support or to help you make the initial contact with a potential funder.

There are also times when your age can be an advantage. There is a great appeal to helping young people, the rising generation, future leaders of our country, that whole thing. You've heard all these phrases in the rhetoric of politicians and educators. Don't be afraid to use this appeal by speaking in terms that connote innocence, bright-eyed hope, and other images that older people want to see in contemporary youth. Remember that these Rockwellian images are how many adults today characterize their own youth. At the same time, don't pander and don't use statements that ring false. The appearance of dishonesty will sink any fund-raising campaign. Likewise, if people ask questions about your project and you don't know exactly how to respond, don't be evasive. Give a confident but general answer and promise more specifics in a follow-up communication; you can inconspicuously use a phrase like "I think" or "as I understand it," or just say you're not sure.

Donor Acknowledgment

Principle number three is to show what's in it for the donor. Most individuals and firms who give assistance to your project will want some kind of recognition, although private donors may wish to remain anonymous. Mention sponsors in the last paragraph of your press release (either alphabetically or in descending order of contribution), thank them in your remarks at the event, and when appropriate have their names or logos appear on materials. (Be sure you have their explicit permission, preferably in writing, to place their logo on your materials.) Keep in mind that including their logos on your materials could increase production costs. If you do offer advertisements or the appearance of their logo, be sure to request from the donor camera-ready artwork, specifying black-and-white or color separation.

Many of us in the not-for-profit sector find fund-raising uncomfortable and unseemly. Avoid letting these feelings show, particularly with donors themselves. Also, don't let the public visibility you're giving donors overshadow the work put in by members of your group; they didn't come up with or carry out the project. Strike a balance that gives due credit to those who endowed your work. On a poster, make sure your group gets top billing and never forget to acknowledge the hard work of all your fellow volunteers.

When receiving sponsorship from powerful corporations, beware of attempts to co-opt the event by making it a pure publicity vehicle, thus curtailing its effectiveness or subsuming its message in a barrage of hype. Outline on paper what sponsors will and will not receive in exchange for their contribution. If you are uncomfortable with a sponsorship situation, you can decline or return their contribution—as a major women's organization recently did to a five-digit offer from *Playboy* magazine.

Part of what's in it for the donor from the standpoint of self-interest is what the project brings back to the community at large

SUCCESS STORY

Making the Links, Sharing the Profits

An innovative program in Toronto links up-and-coming student organizations with up-and-coming small businesses in projects of mutual benefit. Developed under the aegis of the Toronto-based Youth Action Network, the Community Connections Service "increases the economic viability of small businesses while at the same time establishing a dependable source of non-government funding for youth-run projects," says its founder Fahim Hussain Ali. By convincing both sides that their involvement would be beneficial to their own objectives—no easy task—the CCS has begun creating partnerships that foster economic development and student action.

CCS is designed to meet business needs for visibility and for a way to attract customers. Working with a small committee of Network organizers, Ali directed his appeal to small businesses demonstrating a genuine concern for environmental and social justice issues. At the same time he went to high school groups working on similar issues. With a database of information established, CCS began proposing link-ups between the groups based on the needs of both. CCS also offered advice for the student organizations, help with publicity, and a little seed money.

"We are looking for innovative partnerships," says Ali, such as "a new restaurant that can team up with a local women's shelter for a 'free food day.' The shelter would be responsible for generating media coverage and distributing flyers and posters, and the restaurant would offer 'free food' to customers—hopefully a new loyal clientele—in exchange for a donation to the shelter. The shelter would help run the restaurant that day to keep costs down. The same kind of project could work at a local video store on a slow night like Wednesday, or with an equipment raffle at a new sporting goods store. Or how about aspiring musicians from African or Asian traditions teaming up with a high school anti-racism group, or young feminist singers with a university women's center? The artists would donate their time, and the students would be in charge of the venue, selling tickets, and promoting both the concert and the cause. The possibilities are endless."

With support coming in for CCS, the Youth Action Network itself has discovered new avenues in the "business" of fund-raising—working with a local recycled products company to promote their wares in exchange for a percentage of income, and having Network members who are trained CPR instructors give lessons at the going rate and contributing the proceeds to the Network. Programs like CCS show that fund-raising doesn't need to look or feel like begging.

---

or even to their neighborhood or ethnic or religious community. Remind potential sponsors of how your efforts will reach those communities. Also, the project's benefit will be a positive reflection on the sponsor.

Avoid overusing certain donors. Family members and friends are especially easy to keep going back to, and they often have trouble saying no. Using the "personal angle"—asking friends, family, and businesses that you patronize to support something because of your affiliation with it—is reasonable, and people will often be willing to help you. But if you find yourself going repeatedly to the same persons and businesses for cash or in-kind contributions, you may wear out your welcome. Diversify.

Cultivating relationships with donors, on the other hand, will enable you to go back every few months. Donor cultivation includes education about your mission, goals, and successes; prompt thank-yous and acknowledgments of all contributions; and open communication about how your relationship can continue to evolve. Through cultivation the personal angle falls away as the individual, business, or foundation becomes a champion of your cause. A good example is Reebok's support of Amnesty International; what began as one grant has developed into ongoing support and the creation of the Reebok Human Rights Award.

Service Fund-raisers

Fund-raisers that offer products or services to members of the community in exchange for a donation can be an effective way of raising funds as long as your up-front investment is minimal. Food-oriented events like bake sales, pancake breakfasts, and spaghetti dinners can raise several hundred dollars if all your materials and labor are donated. A bake sale is the best example: Each person's contribution is minimal (a plate of brownies, for example), but the assembled goods become worth a lot to your organization. For food events like special dinners, you'll also need facilities contributed. Be sure to check local and state regulations or prohibitions on food service and raffles in order to avoid trouble later.

Events like this can be a great opportunity to get your message across to a receptive (and often captive) audience. People also love to see their children and friends in the spotlight, so try to create an entertaining atmosphere at your event. Bring in student bands, amateur stand-up comedians, and the like. Take a creative or artsy step away from the traditional event: Host a coffeehouse with student performances and artwork, or give the event a theme like "around the world in eighty minutes." Or incorporate a raffle into your ticket sales—again, making sure prizes are donated and don't come out of your own pocket!

Try to engage in fund-raising that also serves your group's purposes. An environmental organization can raise a lot through recycling. Some places still pay for recyclable materials, and members of your community should be willing to bring you their recyclables. (It's only trash, after all.) Or sell environmentally themed products like clothing from Human-i-tees, a New York–based firm that not only provides beautiful T-shirts on consignment but also gives good tips on marketing them in your community.

Support from Organizations

Sponsorship from local businesses can also take the form of a "merchant-of-the-month" project, where in the course of your own publicity, your group encourages local residents to patronize a store that is giving you a percentage of its receipts for a week or a month. Community service organizations like the Rotary Club and Kiwanis Club often have funds available for local students to participate in events like conferences and international exchange programs. Find out who the president and scheduling coordinator are for these groups and write a letter or call them to schedule a presentation about your project. Having made this contact, you could ask either for official sponsorship from the organization or simply for the chance to "pass the hat" when you give your presentation. Request the former but settle for the latter if that's all you can get; also, offer a presentation after your return from the sponsored event to "bring your experience back to the community."

Nonprofit Status

Many corporations and foundations require that grant recipients have nonprofit status; in other words, that they be registered as an educational or service organization with the federal and state governments. The process of applying for consideration as a nonprofit organization under section 501(c) of the United States Internal Revenue Code is long and complex, and you should think hard about whether it's worth it for your organization. Most student organizations can get by with the small donations that come with the kind of fund-raising discussed above.

On the other hand, "having your 501(c)(3)"—or 501(c)(4) for political lobbying organizations—makes such things as grant writing a lot easier. If your group has been around for a while and wants to create large-scale projects requiring a great deal of money, you should consider putting in the time and money that nonprofit status entails. Start by taking the time to learn what's involved and how best to go about it. Consult other people who have founded non-profit organizations, look through the resources of The Foundation Center or your local library, and call the IRS to receive all the necessary forms and instructions.

A more accessible alternative for most groups, including younger ones who would just like their backers to be able to collect the tax deduction for their contribution, is to affiliate with an organization that has its 501(c)(3). Schools and universities are usually considered non-profit entities, so if you're an official student organization, you may be able to receive tax-deductible contributions under those auspices. Sometimes non-profit status is conveyed by being a chapter of a national non-profit organization. If neither of these applies to you, you may still be able to find a local 501(c)(3) organization that will take you under its wing for purposes of grant applications.

Grant Writing

Major corporate giving programs and foundation grants are out of reach for most student activists because the amount of money in question is far larger than you'll need and the process of applying for the grant can last up to two years. Also, such organizations are more likely to give money to programs that have a five- to ten-year track record and older leadership. When foundations are willing to take a chance on you, however, they can be a good source of funding for larger projects—in such philanthropic circles, a "small grant" is anything under $5,000!—if you take the time to write a solid proposal and send it to the right places.

Corporations and foundations often put geographic limitations on their giving programs. Corporate giving programs usually have a focus in the corporation's home community—Eastman Kodak's extensive donations within Rochester, New York, for example. Another factor to consider when approaching corporations is that even corporations with separate foundations often make additional contributions on a less formal basis through their public affairs department. A few phone calls can often uncover a few hundred or a few thousand dollars.

Almost always, both corporate foundations and private foundations—from giants like The MacArthur Foundation and The Pew Charitable Trusts to local foundations and those with small grants programs—have certain issues on which they prefer to spend their money. Therefore, the first guideline for a prospective foundation grant seeker is this: Do your homework. Don't waste your time and theirs submitting a proposal that doesn't fit with their area of interest. For basic information on grant-making organizations, look at *The Foundation Directory* in the reference section of your local library. If you're near a major American city, find The Foundation Center (which publishes the directory) and go there to use their resources; ask the Center's knowledgeable librarians to point you in the right direction.

Once you have chosen a few foundations that you think might be interested in your project, pick up the phone or drop them a postcard to ask to whom a proposal like yours should be directed. If you've done your homework, this question should sound like, "Who is the director of your Environmental Grants Section?" instead of: "Umm, hi. I'm looking for funding for an environmental project. Can you help me?"

If you're comfortable giving a short pitch for your program over the phone, ask to talk to that person. He will often be willing to give advice on writing your application and offer hints as to what kind of proposal the foundation would like to receive. Think twice before you change your program to fit a foundation's guidelines for funding, but there's nothing wrong with tailoring your proposal to foundation guidelines. With some "spin doctoring," virtually any program that generally fits a foundation's guidelines can have the appearance of being an exact match. A good pilot program will already include the major components of a good grant proposal: demonstrated need, quantifiable goals, evaluation methods, and plans for the future. Thus, making a project match grant guidelines really becomes a choice of language and tone.

The toughest grant to get is the first one. Foundations are much more likely to give money to groups with whom they have already worked successfully. Each grant you receive makes you more likely to receive another one.

What Foundations Are Looking for

Even more than local firms, foundations want to see something unique. They love to give start-up grants for "pilot programs" that can provide a model for service in other communities. They'll want to see a program that is reaching a lot of people and offering some tangible outcome for all those involved, particularly disadvantaged groups.

A foundation grant proposal is usually divided into several sections: an introduction and executive summary that explains the project briefly, using your strongest pitch and sums up the information contained in the proposal; an introduction, background, and problem statement section explaining why the proposed project is important; "program goals and objectives" that describes the logic behind your project, intended outcomes, and a well-considered explanation of why your group is best suited to try to meet the need you have identified; a project description including a detailed time line and realistic work plan; an evaluation section that explains how you will measure your impact, how that will affect current and future projects, and how you will convey this information to the foundation; and a detailed, realistic budget.

Seeking funds is one of the most difficult parts of your job and one of the most frustrating because it takes you away from the people and places that are the focus of your concern and into the game of getting and keeping money. But it's also what can help you be much more effective as an organization, with better materials, a wider area of effect, and greater visibility. As long as you don't become an organization that spends as much on keeping itself afloat as it spends on its good works, the time expended in raising funds effectively is worth it.

13

Passing the Torch: After You, Who?

It's been said that the greatest challenge a group will ever face is surviving the departure of its founding leader. Groups able to continue effecting change for a long period of time are those that can maintain their organization and activities during and after the transition to new leadership. This challenge has special meaning for students whose time in any one place is often limited to just a few years.

One of the biggest challenges student movements face is "institutional memory," the tendency of a student body to "forget" what has happened in the past because there is no one besides the faculty and administration who has been around long enough to remember. I once spent a long Sunday afternoon flipping through past years of my college newspaper, and I discovered that most issues popped up again about every six or eight years, with very little progress visible. For example, students staged walkouts in protest of inadequate admission and financial aid for students of color in 1968 and 1975, held similar protests in 1980 and 1986, and took over a university building in 1992 for the same reason. If history holds true, the same issue will probably come up again shortly before the turn of the century. The same is true for a variety of other issues; they turn up every few years as students become dissatisfied with *the very same problems* that frustrated their predecessors.

All this occurs because students generally spend about four years in high school and another four in college. The five-year gap between, say, the classes of 1995 and 2000 might as well be an eternity because the two have no direct contact. This can be an advantage to school administrators. If they don't want to fulfill student demands, they need only drag out the process for a few years and the issue will again be forgotten. I even overheard a high school administrator say, "Students come and go. It's the faculty I'm here to please."

The challenge for students, then, is to see to it that there is continuity between their work and that of younger students. This can seem challenging since many student organizations begin as a group of friends about the same age. When they all graduate together, the organization will disappear unless measures have been taken to keep the group alive for future participants. Maintaining such continuity is actually fairly simple, and most of the strategies outlined below will strengthen your organization even if succession is not a major concern.

The most obvious first step is to see to it that younger students are always becoming involved in the group. Put posters advertising your group's first meeting—maybe a "welcome, freshmen" mixer—around the campus at the beginning of each semester. Word of mouth is your most powerful tool: Have each current member talk about the group to new students with the goal of each one bringing two new members to the first meeting. If you have the chance, talk about your group in freshman class meetings or homerooms.

Another excellent opportunity to get the news about your organization out to a large group of incoming students is through a school activity fair. Most colleges and many high schools have these fairs at the beginning of each school year. If yours doesn't, maybe you should think about starting one; this is an excellent opportunity for all the student organizations in your school to work together on a project of mutual benefit. Bring together the leaders of other campus groups and air your proposal. By dividing the responsibilities among a number of groups, no one will have to do much work, and the event will be good for everyone involved.

Another multigroup project could be putting together an orientation and welcoming packet for incoming students. The packet could contain information about each organization, including the names of its current leadership, and also "fun stuff"

SUCCESS STORY

Planting Trees, Sowing Peace

In the central African nation of Burundi, rent by ethnic violence between the Hutu and Tutsi tribes since 1994, one young man started a program that brought together local youth against a common enemy: deforestation and the loss of valuable crop land that accompanied it.

Richard Barahoga, who had worked with a campus environmental organization as a student at the University of Burundi, was one of hundreds of students forced by violence in the capital to return to their native villages. Barahoga was unwilling to abandon his environmental goals, however, and began organizing students in his village. Working with people of all ages, the group planted more than 2,500 trees, all grown from seed by Barahoga and his family. The trees began an important process of reclaiming soil ravaged by erosion and overcultivation, and the more than 100 banana trees among them have already provided the village with much-needed food. Moreover, Barahoga's project brought together Hutu and Tutsi villagers in a common cause.

The program also bridged another important gap in Burundi society: the social divide between students and the large number of illiterate people of all ages that live in rural Burundi. Environmental education for illiterate rural dwellers in the Third World will be an important part of resuscitating the region's struggling environment, and such hands-on projects are an important educational tool.

"I am an optimist," says Barahoga, who wishes to create a national network to coordinate more rural projects by student environmental clubs in Burundi's high schools and university. "Burundis are historically one people. Recognizing this common enemy will bring us back together."

---

like short articles about school lore and giveaways like a school bumper sticker or pennant. You should be able to get your school to foot the bill for copying and distributing the guide.

Once you have a group that represents a wide age range within the student body, there are ways you can organize the structure of your group so that younger members are preparing to cycle into leadership roles in future years. The first is something mentioned at the very beginning of this book: *delegate.* It's always tempting to try to do everything yourself—it's certainly the safest way to make sure things get done—but it's also a surefire way to make your group disappear after your departure. When you place the burden of organizing and executing projects on just a few shoulders, you aren't giving younger students the chance to develop the skills they'll need to lead the group effectively.

Ease new members into the group with small, simple tasks, building responsibility as you deem appropriate for each individual. When younger students have developed their abilities and increased their commitment to the group, you may want to lead them in a particular direction. As with your leadership, you'll have a small group of planners, of publicity people, of organizers, and so on. Once your group is well established, try to have several different classes represented in its leadership. This will strengthen the group by encouraging more students from each grade level to join and by incorporating the perspectives of different ages into the group's decision-making process.

When the time comes to begin planning a transfer of power to the younger generation, make an effort to speak to each one about what role he or she would like to play next year. Often, you'll have a pretty good idea of who you think will be next year's leaders; it's important to make sure, however, that your plans and their interests coincide. Be frank, and try to explore a variety of options for each of the up-and-coming.

After you've discussed and defined the goals and interests of rising leaders, encourage them to talk about their ideas among themselves and with others in the group. If your group is large enough that it represents a substantial "constituency," this will help potential leaders express their intentions in concrete, well-considered terms and will steer the election of next year's leadership away from being a popularity contest. Tempted as you may be to ease your personal protégé into a top post, realize that in a large group only democratic selection can convey legitimacy—

and, if conducted within the above framework, should result in the choosing of the best leader. Even if yours is a small task force where such a decision will be made by consensus (or by default), discussing and defining goals will help future leaders develop a vision to guide them through the challenges they will face.

If your group has a large number of rising leaders, be glad. This is a group that will live on. But be aware that in making decisions about future positions, you may lose some of these members. If a member doesn't get the future post he wants or if he doesn't get a post at all, he may want to leave because he's "gone as far as he can" in the group. Try to avoid this development by offering reasonable alternatives, but accept that the process of grooming a successor sometimes means leaving someone out in the cold.

When next year's organization has been determined, pair each rising leader with the corresponding current leader—sort of an apprenticeship. Have the older individuals describe their experiences in the post and answer questions for the younger ones. Suggest that the two begin alternating in fulfilling the post's responsibilities. (The current president leads a meeting, then the incoming president leads one, then the current president, and so on.) This is a chance for new leaders to be phased in while their predecessors are still around to offer guidance, and it offers current leaders the chance to turn their focus to other concerns—like graduation.

Many organizations find it advantageous for leaders to hold one-year terms that begin in January. This is an ideal arrangement not only because it gives outgoing leaders the chance to focus on other things during their last few months in school but also because it avoids a major discontinuity over the long summer recess. Summer is almost always a lull period for school-based organizations, and it is very often the cause of a group's demise as members find other interests and last year's issues are forgotten. January-to-December leadership terms help mitigate this effect.

Another crucial element in a smooth succession is good recordkeeping. By the end of your term you should have accumulated a file of notes, resources, and contacts. Make sure these are comprehensive. It will be most helpful if you have kept detailed notes on your experiences and impressions throughout your term. Go through these records with your successor, allowing her to copy or take any important information. If appropriate, take the time to introduce your successor to those individuals who have played a large role in your efforts: the principal, past contributors of funding or assistance, other student leaders, the school janitor, and so on. This will make her job much easier and enable her to build on your successes rather than have to begin from scratch.

A series of smooth leadership transitions will strengthen your group, and its long life will give it added legitimacy in the school and community. It will also enable you to return as an alum and proudly say, "I started that group way back in 199-." (After the year 2000, this will sound really impressive!)

Don't expect your group to maintain exactly the same "mission." New leaders and new issues will change the goals and tactics of the organization. But by their very nature a few things will remain the same: a commitment to the future, a belief in the leading role students can play in social change and environmental advocacy, and an undying faith in leaving the world a better place than we entered.

14

Always New Horizons

So there you have it, the basic tools of student organizing—or at least my version. That's the important thing to remember: All I've given you is a road map, a set of guidelines and advice based on my own travels in activism. You will blaze your own trails, as you should.

In making activism part of your life, don't exclude the rest. Give yourself the time needed to be a good student, friend, son or daughter, classmate, and participant in other things that matter to you. We don't have the person power to suffer too many burnouts; find your level of commitment and maintain it. Keep yourself strong so that your flame, while perhaps not so bright, burns long and provides more than fleeting warmth.

I'd like to offer you some thoughts and suggestions about how to relate your life to your activism. I'm talking about personal choices, about how those choices will reflect on your work (and vice versa), and about having a vivid vision of what you're striving for.

There's a link that needs to be made—a link between what you're trying to do and how you're trying to do it. In your organizing, think about the environmental aspects of what you're doing and what that represents to the people around you. If you're a student group in Phoenix, for example, a car wash is not a good fundraiser for environmental projects. Your city is already depleting the Colorado and Ogalala aquifers; raising "green" money by adding to the problem is hypocritical at best. In addition to *being* action, your efforts should *represent* the cause and goals you're after.

This goes for personal choices as well. Like it or not, we are sometimes judged by others on matters that we don't see as applying to the issue at hand. For instance, smoking pollutes and supports an industry with some pretty nasty agricultural and business practices. Does that mean that you, as an activist, shouldn't smoke? I think so, and perhaps more important, so will the people around you. It's tough to preach environmentalism with a tube of burning tobacco hanging from the corner of your mouth. People may listen, but they'll absorb your words through a filter of disbelief. (No pun intended.)

When organizing in this Puritanical country of ours, even questions of personal appearance come into play. Right or wrong, my own fairly conservative appearance has helped me work my way through this publishing business and even into the halls of power. I'm not saying that we should all cut our hair short and wear basic blue, but realize that you will be judged by your appearance and your speech and even how you walk. Sometimes not "measuring up" can damage your ability to get things done—not irreparably, but slightly, and probably nothing that a little perseverance can't overcome. But make these choices based on a holistic view of what your priorities are.

This also points to a moral decision: Walk your talk. If you call yourself an environmentalist, don't eat meat. If you do anti-prejudice work, keep even the funny off-color jokes to yourself. Not because of what people will think but because a life without contradictions is better and happier.

As a young person, you have not yet learned artifice. Fight it at every turn. Hold on to your honesty and your integrity. Frail as they sometimes seem in this material world, there is power in moral victories. If you can sleep soundly every night of your life based on the ideals you hold *right now*—not the little excuses and self-justifications that we've watched our elders build into their thought processes over the years—well, my friend, *that* is something to be proud of.

Read a lot. Travel as much as you can. Meet—really *meet*—every person who passes through your life. Take the time to ponder what you know and feel about us and our relationship to the Earth and to each other, about God and Gaia, about your little place in the universe and how you can shine brightly in it. Know not just

WORDS OF WISDOM

We Must Be the Change

This life change has caused me to become increasingly impatient with the status quo, with conventional wisdom, with the lazy assumption that we can always muddle through. Such complacency has allowed many kinds of different problems to breed and grow, but now, facing a rapidly deteriorating global environment, it threatens absolute disaster. Now no one can afford to assume that the world will somehow solve its problems. We must all become partners in a bold effort to change the very foundation of our civilization.

But I believe deeply that true change is possible only when it begins inside the person who is advocating it. Mahatma Gandhi said it well: "We must be the change we wish to see in the world." And a story about Gandhi—recounted by Craig Schindler and Gary Lapid—provides a good illustration of how hard it is to "be the change." Gandhi, we are told, was approached one day by a woman who was deeply concerned that her son ate too much sugar. "I am worried about his health," she said. "He respects you very much. Would you be willing to tell him about its harmful effects and suggest he stop eating it?" After reflecting on the request, Gandhi told the woman that he would do as she requested but asked that she bring her son back in two weeks, no sooner. In two weeks, when the boy and his mother returned, Gandhi spoke with him and suggested that he stop eating sugar. When the boy complied with Gandhi's suggestion, his mother thanked Gandhi extravagantly—but asked him why he had insisted on the two-week interval. "Because," he replied, "I needed the two weeks to stop eating sugar myself."

—Al Gore,
Earth in the Balance

---

what you're against but what you're *for*, and see everything you do as a piece in that puzzle, a stone on that path to the world we want to create for *our* children.

As you travel this high road of activism, always seek the new horizon—the creative approach to a problem, the unlikely alliance that strengthens everyone, the turn of phrase that makes your whole vision understood. "Seek and ye shall find." That's true. But then seek again. And again.

Keep faith in yourself. By rising to the challenges of activism, you also take on new risks. By trying, you accept the possibility of failure. But that's okay, because in "failure" there is learning; and in learning, growing; and in growing, the chance to try again. Don't lower your head in defeat; hold it up, look around, and figure out how to win.

Know that in working for right, you are doing more for this world than will ever be acknowledged. Feel good about that. With this book you have the tools—or at least the beginnings of them. Use them, adjust them, even ignore some of them if you must.

Tell me what you think. More than that, tell me what you're doing so that I can know and walk proudly beside you on this path we've chosen.

Part Two

Young Activists Speak from Experience

15

Activism and the Internet: A Beginner's Guide

JOSH KNAUER AND GWEN GARRISON

Josh Knauer, twenty-three, is executive director of the EnviroLink Network and founder of E-Link Interactive, a for-profit environmental information provider. Gwen Garrison is an independent computer consultant.

The Internet will soon be an environmentalist's most important tool. Where grassroots activism fostered the majority of environmental gains throughout the 1980s, the instant global communication of the Internet can help environmentalists excel throughout the 1990s by enabling us to spread information to the ends of the earth and focus global attention on what would otherwise be local injustices. Isolated activists can find others working in their field for insight, successful strategies, and support. Organizations can concentrate on new aspirations—and stop reinventing the wheel—by drawing on others' experience.

In order to take advantage of this new medium as student activists, we need to stake our claim on it now. Anti-environmental forces, such as timber and chemical companies, saw the Internet's potential years ago. They are well organized and can vastly outspend us on computer equipment, network development, and user attractiveness to "greenwash" their products and services. These advantages can be counteracted by deeper understanding and harder work on activists' part—but we must begin now. We must remain focused on our goals. It is easy to be drawn into unproductive battles and lose sight of our purpose. A war of words alone does not win any environmental progress.

This chapter will detail the various components of the Internet, including e-mail, mailing lists, Usenet newsgroups, chat areas, gopher holes, and the World Wide Web, and it will describe how each can be used to further environmental goals. It will also outline "nettiquette," standard acceptable behavior to be observed to avoid alienating other users. Since all computer systems and online services operate a little bit differently, you should consult your manuals and talk to your system administrator—the person who runs your local service provider—for specific instructions.

Getting Online

To get onto the Internet, you need only a computer, a modem, a phone line, and a service provider. Older computers and modems can get you access to all of the Internet but are often irritatingly slow. Also, a large part of the excitement of the World Wide Web is its colorful pictures, so it can be very boring with a non-graphics computer.

Look in your phone book under "Computer Services" or "Internet Services" for a local Internet service provider. Also be sure to ask around to get a sense of local providers' reputations. You don't want to find your service interrupted in the middle of an important conversation because your provider is not reliable. Small local providers are the cheapest and usually the best way to get onto the Internet since they do not have the huge advertising overhead or distant customer support of many larger online services. Heavily advertised, commercially oriented large services are very easy for beginners to use, but they charge excessive rates, often do not have the full Internet access they advertise, and have a poor reputation on the Internet in general. Remember, you are what you write, and you're also where you're writing from.

See if your school or a local college will let you have an account for free or at a reduced cost. Educational institutions are historically a cornerstone of Internet use, and most have excellent systems available for student use.

You will be looking for a shell account (a "bare bones," text-only link) if you want only e-mail and mailing lists, or a SLIP/PPP account (full access to everything that's out there) if you want access to the whole Internet. Look for a deal where you do not have to pay hourly online charges or where the first several dozen hours are included in the monthly cost. Otherwise, you could receive an unpleasant and costly surprise at the end of the month.

Once you're on the Internet, most providers will include a "beginner's guide to the Internet" or be able to suggest several to get you started. Good books to read are *The Internet for Dummies* (the book, not the CD-ROM package) by John R. Levine and Carol Baroudi, and *Navigating the Internet* by Mark Gibbs.

As you get started, take the time to get acquainted with your surroundings. We will tell you what you can find and how it may be useful to you as an activist, but don't assume that this is all you need to know. Finding your way around the Internet will take a while, and the ideas we offer here will become much more useful once you are comfortable negotiating the territory of cyberspace.

Electronic Mail

Electronic mail, or e-mail, provides almost instantaneous communication and transmission of files from place to place. Large quantities of information, especially numerical information, can be accurately transmitted at a very low cost and a very high speed. Environmental groups who deal with international affiliates and colleagues prefer to send e-mail and faxes because it's cheaper to transmit now and translate later than to stumble through a costly phone conversation. E-mail also allows many people to receive copies of your correspondence and be part of your dialogue.

The Pittsburgh chapter of the Student Environmental Action Coalition (SEAC) started planning a bicycle ride to discourage automobile use and encourage biking and use of mass transit, but the group had no experience with this type of organizing. Through e-mail they contacted a student in Philadelphia who had organized a similar event and was able to provide tips and useful suggestions. She also sent contact information for the national organization Critical Mass, which helps coordinate biking education events. On the day of the event, fifty activists were able to educate thousands of motorists on alternative methods of transportation.

Nettiquette for e-mail:

- E-mail can be expensive to the recipient. Make sure it goes to the appropriate destination and stay to the point.
- Be sure to never say anything in e-mail that you would not wish to say in public. It's easy to be embarrassed when your "private" message gets passed on to hundreds of other users.
- Forwarding or reprinting private e-mail to the public without the writer's permission is very rude and will lower others' opinion of you.
- Don't send unsolicited, obnoxious e-mail. In some cases it can get your account revoked and it will definitely annoy the recipient.

Mailing Lists

Mailing lists are like a series of inter-office memos, all distributed to the same group of people via e-mail. Although you can do this manually, it is sometimes more convenient to create a special program called a mailing list. Once you've set it up, you address your e-mail to the list, and it forwards everything it receives to all the people on the list.

Mailing lists are easy for a system administrator to set up at your request and can be for a temporary purpose or permanent discussion. Usually there is a single distinct topic for discussion. One of the most popular mailing lists is the EnviroNews service which provides the latest legislative and activist news to thousands of subscribers each day. Interactive lists, such as the Recycle list, allow all subscribers to discuss issues and post new questions.

The EnviroNews mailing list began when about twenty students were looking for up-to-date environmental information. Within one month of its creation, 100,000 readers had subscribed to the list, and it has continued to grow. EnviroNews reports have featured such efforts as those of the Mt. Graham Coalition, an alliance of environmental and cultural rights organizations trying to prevent construction of an Arizona observatory that would destroy the habitat of the Mt. Graham red squirrel and desecrate Native American tribal land. U.S. backers had already pulled out of the Mt. Graham project, and the coalition's news and action alerts attracted European and Japanese activists to the effort. With the help of EnviroNews, activists won adherence to environmental laws and convinced many universities to withdraw their support for the project.

Nettiquette for mailing lists:

- Basically, follow the rules of e-mail.
- Again, receiving mail is sometimes expensive. Stay on the topic and avoid being rude because you may be sending mail to hundreds of people and wasting their disk space.
- Avoid quoting pages of material only to follow it with an "I agree" or "I disagree."
- Quoting a few lines of the message that you are responding to will allow readers to better understand your argument.
- If you mean to reply with private e-mail, make sure you're doing so and not sending it to the entire list.
- Mailing lists don't notice state or national boundaries, so allow for variations in culture. Complaining "but the Bill of Rights says . . ." won't help a person in France.
- If someone does post something stupid, off the topic, or intentionally rude, you may send them private e-mail explaining their error. Posting a response on the list wastes further time and energy for everyone.

Newsgroups

Usenet newsgroups are a series of conferences where people can discuss any issue of interest. It is easiest to think of newsgroups as very large mailing lists where the messages do not come to your e-mail mailbox and will disappear within a few days even if you don't read them. Newsgroups should be accessible through your local service provider, who can supply the software to access them.

In addition to Usenet, many major servers maintain their own discussion groups on a variety of topics. EnviroLink and EcoNet both have localized conferences that can be read only by users of their services. These are similar to conferences on America Online and Prodigy, in that all messages stay in the home system. The Usenet, on the other hand, is available to thousands of systems, and your message will be sent to millions of people.

The names of Usenet groups are determined by a predictable system. Each part of the name is separated by a period, starting with a general category and growing more specific. Therefore, the name *talk.politics.animals* implies that it is a discussion group, a political discussion group, and a political discussion group about animals. Some sites do not carry all groups. If you want to read one that your site does not receive, ask your system administrator to subscribe to it.

Environmental newsgroups tend to be overrun by anti-environmentalists, and thoughtful discussions can be drowned out by users simply trying to offend. On the other hand, Usenet groups are a quick way to disseminate information to a great many people. The Gorton Salvage Timber Rider is legislation that would require the Forest Service to sell timber rights for 100 million acres of forest, no matter how low the timber companies' offer, and waive environmental and labor laws in effect in those forests. News about the Gorton Salvage Timber Rider has generated tens of thousands of phone calls to members of Congress and the White House, largely due to massive coverage in appropriate newsgroups.

Nettiquette for newsgroups:

- Follow the rules for e-mail and mailing lists.
- Every newsgroup has its own type of interaction. "Lurk"—just read and don't post anything—until you are positive you understand and can follow this flavor. Many groups have a FAQ—a list of Frequently Asked Questions—posted once a month or so to give a primer on the newsgroup's mission and style and to avoid rehashing the same issues over and over.
- Be careful to stay on the topic and be careful about cross-posting, where a message is sent to more than one newsgroup. Nasty arguments on *talk.politics.animals,* for example, repeat-

edly spill onto *rec.food.veg* and have made it virtually unreadable.

Chat Areas

Chat areas are sites where others can read your messages as you type them, simulating a live conversation. This is immensely useful for meeting activists from around the world on a less formal basis than e-mail. Connections like these can give you a better understanding of global issues and help you learn about issues other activists are dealing with around the world.

The EnviroChat is specifically designed for environmental activists to network and discuss current and upcoming campaigns. One EnviroChat user in California was able to use tips and support from a student in Massachusetts to relax university administration resistance to a school-wide recycling program, and was able to help speed its introduction.

Nettiquette for chat areas:

- Chat areas for a specific purpose must be used for that purpose. Inquiring after someone's health is a good thing, but talking about your recent breakup has no place on a chat designed to discuss biological engineering ethics.
- If off-topic conversation gets out of hand, don't hesitate to tell the chat area's administrator about people who ignore the above rule. Administrators can't be everywhere, and people who can't follow the rules should not be allowed to ruin it for everyone else.

Gopher Holes

Gopher holes are read-only areas of information. While the World Wide Web is fast eclipsing gopher sites as the source of choice, a number of older documents are accessible through this format. The term "gopher hole" comes from the name of the program originally used to access them—Gopher. But it's also very appropriate because you really can go down a "hole" at the University of Utah, wander down several byways, and surface in New York.

When navigating through a gopher hole, you will choose one menu option after another—each menu leading you to the next—until the desired document is reached. You can get to gopher holes through your server or via the World Wide Web.

Useful information is fairly simple to find, if often a bit dated. Toby Scott's Political Gopher, for instance, can provide names and contact information for members of Congress as well as some links to information on state and local governments.

Nettiquette for gopher holes:

- Since peak load hours are from 9:00 A.M. to 9:00 P.M. Eastern time, try to avoid adding to the system load by accessing gopher holes during this time.
- There's not much you can do to a gopher hole, so don't worry about "hurting" it.

World Wide Web

The World Wide Web ("WWW" or "the Web") is a series of documents, called pages, that link to each other in a treelike structure. Each page gives you options of where to go next, which makes it a great place for research because related pages are usually linked to one another and the click of a mouse can take you from UCLA to Johannesburg and everywhere in between. The Web can show graphics, sound files, and even short movies. Even though it's barely two years old, the Web is huge and growing by thousands of sites each day. You've probably heard people talking about it as the mall of the future, and the same goes for activism. The Web is quickly becoming one of the best information resources available.

To get to a particular Web site, you need to know its address, which is why you'll usually hear people talk about "pointing to" a certain site (called a "hostname"). To point to a Web site, type *http://<hostname>*. To use the Web to access a gopher hole, that becomes: *gopher://<hostname>*.

Here's a story that illustrates the large and growing influence of the World Wide Web. The Headwaters Forest in northern California is a remote old-growth area in danger of being cut by Pacific Lumber, which is owned by MAXXAM. The Headwaters page, after being listed as the "pointer of the week" on the EnviroWeb, generated thousands of phone calls and letters from all over the country. This let the timber company know that they would not be able to hide the cut and treat resistance to it as local and minimal. The cut was postponed, giving local activists time to file an injunction against the cut.

It takes a while to become familiar with the Web, and sometimes it can be confusing to navigate. Try starting off at the Yahoo search page, a sort of yellow pages that lists tens of thousands of Internet sites by topic. You can find pages all over the Web just by typing in what you're looking for. (That's called a "keyword search.") The EnviroWeb either hosts or points to almost every environmental site on the Web and also offers a keyword search. The addresses for these and other useful Web sites appear in the Resource Directory.

Nettiquette for the World Wide Web:

- Avoid peak hours—from 9:00 A.M. to 9:00 P.M. Eastern time—because that's when the largest number of people are accessing the Web. More people slows things down for everyone, and you will save yourself a lot of time by working late at night or early in the morning.
- If you're interested in writing Web pages, a good introduction to this kind of programming is *The Definitive Guide to HTML* by Dave Raggett.

The Internet offers a huge opportunity for environmental activists to meet, organize, and speak out for their goals. Small organizations can be as effective as larger ones in this new medium, and imaginative effort can overpower large financial expenditures. Making use of this opportunity requires a little background, a little cash, and a lot of imagination. Good luck, and have fun!

Glossary

Cross-posting: sending the same message to more than one mailing list or Usenet newsgroup. In general, it's best to avoid doing this because inevitably discussions on the topic will digress. What's appropriate on rec.hiking will not be appropriate on alt.save.the.earth.

FAQ: the Frequently Asked Questions posting. This contains the basic information about a newsgroup or mailing list, material that moderators are tired of repeating every week. This introductory document is usually posted at least once a month or so. Try to read the FAQ before you post anything.

Forwarding: passing a piece of mail or a Usenet message to another recipient. It's frequently very useful, but it's best to ask permission of the original author first, especially if the material is private or sensitive. Check your manual or ask your system administrator about forwarding on your system.

Lurking: reading a mailing list or Usenet newsgroup but not contributing to it. Since no one knows you're there until you say something, lurking for a few weeks or months is a good way to figure out the dynamics of the group before taking part. It gives you time to read the FAQ, figure out who the major contributors are, what topics to avoid, and whether you want to "join" the group at all.

Posting: sending a message to a Usenet newsgroup, making it available to everyone on the Internet. Think of it as putting up a billboard with your personal beliefs. It is fun and useful, but unnerving at the outset. Share your convictions and prepare to be challenged as well as praised.

Service provider: the company you dial with your modem to gain access to the Internet. As stated above, we recommend small local providers with flat-rate charges. (Two dollars an hour may not seem like too much, but if you use e-mail for an hour every day, that's sixty hard-earned dollars, and you haven't even had time to explore the Internet!)

Shell: a text-based connection to the Internet. Usually it runs on UNIX, the operating system of most large computers; it's not very user-friendly, but it gets the job done. Because this account is text-only, exploring the Web loses most of its appeal, and many shell accounts limit you to e-mail and Usenet. This is the cheapest way to the Internet, however, and you may want to learn the basics here.

SLIP/PPP: an Internet connection that shows graphics. It is recommended if you want to access the World Wide Web. Often more user-friendly (and more expensive) than a shell connection, it may even be icon-driven. Use a fast modem for this because graphics take much longer to download than text.

System administrator: the "sysadmin" or "sysop" is the person running your service provider's computers. If you don't know how to do something, e-mail or call the sysadmin and ask. It's your responsibility to learn the basics on your own, and it's his job to help when they aren't enough. Keep on good terms and follow the rules, and you'll both be happy.

Telnet: a way of logging into a system that you are not directly calling to. For instance, if you have a local account and want to access your EnviroLink account, you would type something like *telnet envirolink.org*, then log in as if you were dialing directly.

Web page: a single document that can be viewed on the World Wide Web.

Web site: a collection of Web pages run on the same computer or by the same organization.

16

Communities Rising Up for Environmental Justice

ABDI SOLTANI

Abdi Soltani, twenty-three, is a member of the People of Color Caucus of the Student Environmental Action Coalition (SEAC) and an organizer at the Center for Third World Organizing in Oakland, California. In 1994 he helped found Youth for Community Action, a SEAC project that places California youth of color with community-based environmental justice organizations.

Most people know Kettleman City as the intersection of Highway 41 and Highway 5, halfway between San Francisco and Los Angeles in California's Central Valley. To the travelers who pull off the highway it is nothing more than a small, hot island of gas stations and fast-food joints in what appears to be endless, unpopulated stretches of hazy agricultural land. What most people don't realize is that the Latina and Latino farmworkers who live in Kettleman City earned one of the major victories in a growing movement led by communities of low-income people of color, to protect the health of people and the environment. This is the emerging movement for environmental justice.

In 1993, Chemical Waste Management (ChemWaste)—a subsidiary of WMX Technologies, the world's largest hazardous waste disposal and incineration company—withdrew its application to build a toxic waste incinerator in Kettleman City. If the application had been accepted, tons of toxic and hazardous waste from throughout the western United States would have been shipped to Kettleman City and burned. The resulting fumes and ashes would have exposed the community to potential health threats such as cancer, sterility, and birth defects, and could have contaminated water and food throughout California.

After six years of struggle, El Pueblo para Aire y Agua Limpio, a group of Kettleman residents, won their own version of a David-and-Goliath struggle, except this time the Goliath was WMX, one of the world's most powerful multinational corporations with annual revenues of $6 billion. And the people of Kettleman, many of whom don't speak English and many of them women, were David. So when ChemWaste withdrew its application, Mary Lou Mares, one of the organizers of El Pueblo, was not exaggerating when she rejoiced, "This is a *grande, grande, grandisima* victory."

An Emerging Movement

Mares is one of many leaders of a growing movement for environmental justice, ordinary people who have come together to fight for the survival of their families, their communities, and the planet. In the past few years this movement has been galvanized by the efforts of thousands of people across the United States.

It is not hard to see what goes on every day in this country. We live in a society where government and corporate policies have allowed the rich to get richer and forced the poor into even deeper poverty. Many of the poor—far beyond their proportion in society—are children, women, and people of color. The environmental justice movement recognizes that environmental issues fit into this social context. Across the board, proven by studies and by the experiences of communities, these groups pay the price for others' privileges.

This analysis—that communities of color and the poor bear the brunt of environmental destruction and that they have now risen up to fight for their rights—runs counter to many people's perceptions of environmental issues and environmentalists. After all, some people say, people of color don't care about the environment. They drive old gas-guzzling cars, pollute, and have lots of babies, contributing to overpopulation. And, they say, people of color aren't part of the major environmental organizations such as the Sierra Club or the National Wildlife Federation. After all, developing countries generally have terrible environmental conditions and don't even have laws to deal with it.

Many people, both whites and people of color, believe these mistaken assumptions. The truth is that communities of color and "developing" countries often don't have access to environmental technologies. But a deeper perspective requires that we analyze what we consider "environment" and the source of environmental problems.

Members of the environmental justice movement consider themselves environmentalists, but "the environment" isn't usually the first thing they talk about. They are motivated by questions of community health and safety, economic development, and ongoing efforts to combat institutionalized racism and sexism. Kettleman City's mobilization was based on presenting the incinerator as more than just an "environmental" issue; it was about the community's health, corporate racism, and short-sighted government agencies. And it was about the economic future of the community's jobs and livelihood.

It is time to broaden our definition of the environment to include, in addition to open spaces, the places where we live, work, and play. The concept of environment is wrapped up in issues of daily life—and survival—for victims of environmental racism.

Models of Sustainability

Sustainability refers to the survival of communities as well as the preservation of resources for future generations. If we look at how poor communities and communities of color live, work, and play, we can see models of sustainability far ahead of mainstream society. The Laotian community in Richmond, California, a newly established immigrant community, brings traditional cultural practices into play as an environmental model.

With 350 industrial facilities, including waste incinerators, oil refineries, and pesticide plants, Richmond is a hot spot of toxics and environmental hazards. The Laotian community faces myriad issues, including poverty (70 percent receive government assis-

WORDS OF WISDOM
Right to Know

There is still very limited awareness of the nature of the threat [of chemical pollution]. This is an era of specialists, each of whom sees his own problem and is unaware of or intolerant of the larger frame into which it fits. It is also an era dominated by industry, in which the right to make a dollar at whatever cost is seldom challenged. When the public protests, confronted with some obvious evidence of damaging results of pesticide applications, it is fed little tranquilizing pills of half truth. We urgently need an end to these false assurances, to the sugar coating of unpalatable facts. It is the public that is being asked to assume the risks that the insect controllers calculate. The public must decide whether it wishes to continue on the present road, and it can do so only when in full possession of the facts. In the words of Jean Rostand, "The obligation to endure gives us the right to know."

—Rachel Carson,
Silent Spring

tance) and isolation (many families don't speak English). Yet by using few resources and growing much of their own food—even fishing in Richmond's polluted waterways—they maintain model lifestyles. While gardening and fishing in communities like Richmond can expose community members to toxins, these practices are central to the economic and cultural survival for many people. The focus of community efforts like APEN's is to educate community members on safe practices and to ensure a clean community where all people can thrive. In the words of Boupha Toommaly, a young Laotian woman, "Don't overlook us. We have lived off the land for hundreds of years. We know some things about taking care of the land. Richmond should be clean enough so we can continue to think of the land and water as good things, not poisonous things."

Similar examples abound. In New York, Los Angeles, Philadelphia, and other major cities throughout the United States, poor people use buses as a matter of necessity, thereby reducing traffic and air pollution, while wealthy suburbanites clog highways and promote large-scale environmental damage through their "conspicuous consumption." Poor communities live simply as a matter of survival. Traditional and indigenous cultures live with the land as a matter of culture. But these communities often pay the price for the excess of others.

Roots Run Deep

While "environmental justice" is a new term, the struggle that sustains it is not. Environmental justice is rooted in African-American churches, Native American nations, Chicano organizations, and Asian community and labor groups. Since the mid-1960s, when César Chavez and the United Farm Workers started the grape boycotts and strikes over worker rights, the intersection between environmental and social justice issues has been clear.

But looking further back, the struggle for environmental justice in this country was touched off at Plymouth Rock. European settlers conquered North America by stealing land from Native Americans and exploiting the labor of slaves brought from Africa. As a result, many traditional forms of knowledge and sustainable practice have been lost. Public and corporate institutions still with us today were created to carry out and maintain this conquest. These destructive, materialistic traditions still run deep in the veins of American culture and government.

The catalyst for the current movement for environmental justice came in 1982 when the state of North Carolina decided to place a PCB dump in Warren County, a primarily African-American and Native American community and one of the poorest in the state. Drawing on the tradition of the South's civil rights movement, religious leaders, farmers, and citizens came together to organize against the dump, leading to the mass arrest of five hundred people. While the community did not succeed in blocking the dump, its activity brought national attention to environmental conditions in communities of color and coined the term "environmental racism."

In the years that followed, academic studies and personal testimonies bore out the same message: Poor communities and communities of color from Houston to Chicago to Emelle, Alabama (site of the country's largest hazardous waste landfill, in a community that's 79 percent black), are disproportionately the victims of a pollution policy supporting the wealthy and white at their expense.

In 1991, the First People of Color Environmental Leadership Summit convened six hundred grassroots activists and national leaders from all fifty states, Puerto Rico, Chile, Mexico, and the Marshall Islands. Summit attendees drafted and adopted seventeen "Principles of Environmental Justice" upon which regional and local networks and organizations now base their work.

Holding Institutions Accountable

At the same time that much of the environmental justice movement focused on building a powerful movement from the ground up, it also tried to hold people with power directly accountable to the communities most impacted by environmental injustice. Major environmental organizations, government agencies, and corporations all bear the responsibility for not only ignoring but also actively hurting communities of color.

Often, the very corporations that are responsible for large-scale pollution are funders of some environmental organizations. Across the board, people of color are underrepresented among the staff and boards of directors of the "big ten" environmental groups in America. In a 1990 letter to ten of the largest environmental organizations in the United States, the Southwest Organizing Project, a community organization in Albuquerque, New Mexico, charged that "although [you] often claim to represent our interests, in observing your activities it has become clear to us that your organizations play an equal role in the disruption of our communities." Although some of these organizations have since taken steps to recognize the importance of environmental justice issues in their agendas, they need to do much more to be relevant and accountable to communities of color. It is the responsibility of all environmental activists to continue and accelerate this process.

Given the fact that the poor and people of color wield relatively little power in our country's political institutions, it's not surprising to find that environmental justice issues get short shrift there as well. Institutional racism cripples the "justice" meted out by U.S. government agencies, particularly the Environmental Protection Agency. For example, while 50 percent of children suffering from lead poisoning are African American, the EPA took no action on the lead hazard until 1984 when the effects of lead poisoning were shown—at lower levels—in suburban children. In Warren County, the EPA fought against the community group, while in Kettleman City, the EPA encouraged ChemWaste to build its incinerator.

Even with the steps toward reform recently taken by the "big ten" and government agencies, corporations continue to drive the engine of environmental injustice while portraying themselves as environmental leaders. Corporate environmental racism is not an accident; it is a product of profit. A 1984 report commissioned by ChemWaste recommends that the company target "lower socioeconomic neighborhoods" for toxic sites in order to avoid political opposition.

Building Our Bridges

It's not a pretty picture I've drawn, is it? But now it's time to talk about what we can do. And that's plenty.

Environmental justice organizing involves building power among those people most affected by social and environmental disadvantages. Divisions within these communities themselves—racial divides between low-income whites and communities of color, for example, or divisions created between men and women by sexism in our society—are the first obstacle. When organizing on an environmental justice issue, you must begin with extensive dialogue that brings in the disparate parts of your community with a focus on the desired outcome. For more details on establishing this kind of dialogue, turn to Chapter 23, Malik Yoba's discussion concerning the building of coalitions in diverse communities.

When bringing the community together on environmental justice issues, it's particularly useful to begin by establishing "common knowledge" on what the problems are. Take community leaders on a tour of your community and talk together about what was seen—potential strengths as well as problems. Identify the barriers to collective action in your community, and talk about how they can be overcome.

Focus on empowerment. Environmental justice often looks complicated, as if somehow it is more about chemistry and statistics than about the community. The key for you as an organizer is to balance these issues. Conduct a survey that asks people what the problems are (your "statistics") and how they should be solved (the moral imperatives to which you can appeal when organizing). Find out what people are willing to do. Would they spend two hours a week on a project? Would they attend and speak at hearings? What can each individual contribute to a collective organization?

Talk to a cross-section of the community—students and elders, workers and the unemployed, women and men—and use the resources of your (hopefully) diverse group to overcome linguistic and cultural barriers. Remember that the survey itself is not a goal but a step toward building effective and well-informed opposition to acts of environmental injustice. Use the information you gather to develop your priorities, action agenda, and a proposal to take back to the community outlining how everyone can (and should) be involved.

Between the Lines

A great deal of environmental injustice is rooted in how we look at racial and economic issues in our country, and this comes straight out of our textbooks beginning in the first grade. Part of an effective environmental justice campaign is to question the assumptions that we were never told to question. Look at the way relevant information is conveyed in your school. How do textbooks present people of color? Are the contributions of women and people of color throughout history a central part of what you're learning? Are biology and environmental science classes just about

SUCCESS STORY

Educating on the Dangers of Lead

Latoya Connors lives in a working-class neighborhood in Milwaukee, Wisconsin—"some people call it the ghetto"—where environmental issues don't often get much attention. Because the neighborhood included many old houses with lead-based paint, Latoya was concerned about the danger of lead poisoning in young children. In 1993, at the age of seventeen, she obtained more information about the issue from the Lead Poisoning Awareness Project of the Sierra Student Coalition (SSC). But there wasn't much interest in her community—until kids started getting sick.

Then Latoya found local schools very enthusiastic about her information. Because she came from within the community, Latoya was able to put a human face on an educational campaign that had been confined to milk cartons and billboards. She went to several high school principals to discuss getting lead information to students, and she met with an official from the Department of Health in Milwaukee, who provided her with more information on the problem and contacts with everyone from public librarians to health-mobile services. Building on these contacts, Latoya offered high school presentations based on the educational materials being developed by the SSC. "People were interested, and not a lot of people had thought about the issue before," says Latoya, "but the problem was that our materials were geared only toward younger kids, the ones actually at risk."

When the SSC put the Lead Poisoning Awareness Project on the back burner, Latoya made the difficult decision to stop the outreaches and focus first on developing materials for a wider audience. Amassing information and preparing educational materials for students aged four to adult, Latoya stayed active "on the ground" with waterway cleanliness campaigns in Wisconsin.

On the difficult decision to set aside the outreaches, Latoya remarks, "You can't just do a campaign where you go out and give people a coloring book . . . and say, 'Okay, we did a lead poisoning education campaign.' It needs to be better developed than that." With the SSC bringing lead poisoning back onto its primary agenda in 1996 and 1997, Latoya is poised to continue improving her materials and perhaps even make them available across the country.

---

bugs and birds? Do they adequately address questions of community health? If you don't like the answers, approach teachers and administrators about developing lessons that better address your concerns; offer to work with them and even do some of the teaching. Take a look at the fall 1994 issue of *California Tomorrow* and ask organizations such as the Center for Third World Organizing and the Three Circles Center for Multicultural Environmental Education for guidance on what you should be looking for and information on alternatives to traditional textbooks and teaching manuals.

A major success in this area was won by young people involved in All Youth, part of the Direct Action for Rights and Equality (DARE) organization in Providence, Rhode Island. Here students worked with teachers and other allies to develop and implement "$E = MC^2$": Education = Multicultural Core Curriculum. They outlined specific areas in the sciences (looking at scientific contributions of different cultures), literature (looking at the history of writing and language as well as contributions from writers of diverse backgrounds), and history (internationalizing the curriculum and taking a better look at minority cultures within the United States) where the curriculum could be changed, and they worked with faculty to effect the changes.

Here's one more question for you to ask: Are corporations telling you in the classroom what to learn or buy? For example, the national "classroom news service" Channel One has targeted low-income schools with offers of free video equipment in return for having students watch corporate advertisements. There should be no place in the classroom for encouraging mindless consumption, especially when it targets poor students who are least able to keep buying the latest acne medicine or high-top sneaker. Every school needs support beyond the public funding it receives, so when you're thinking about these issues, look at corporate "contributions" and ask yourself these three questions: Is it really needed? What are other ways to get the same thing? Do the benefits outweigh the costs? The answers to these questions will determine your support or opposition to the contribution. Contact organizations such as UNPLUG, which works with high school students to keep Channel One out of the classroom, to fight advertisement-driven education in your school.

Transform Your Whole School

Most schools, especially colleges, are big organizations. Their potential impact on environmental justice issues goes beyond what is taught in the classroom. Schools spend millions of dollars each year on products and services. In addition, universities invest millions of dollars in corporations worldwide. These companies often pollute in U.S. communities and export military hardware and toxic chemicals abroad. More often they take away resources from local people and increase poverty. As a student you have the power to face this problem head-on.

At Colorado University in Boulder, members of the Student Environmental Action Coalition (SEAC) have started a campaign to get the university to divest its $1.1 million holding in the World Bank, whose development projects have created poverty and environmental destruction worldwide. Take a look at your own school. Where is its money going, and where should it go? Do some research on the companies they invest in and buy from; environmental justice organizations and student groups like SEAC can help you with this research. Educate faculty, staff, and students about the connections between school action and environmental justice worldwide.

Join with Workers

Many of the primary victims of environmental injustice have been "blue-collar" workers. Workers' organizations are also some of the strongest and most outspoken fighters on the issues. At your school these may include the custodians and groundskeepers as well as teachers and administrators. In your community these include assembly-line employees and those who labor away in garment sweatshops. Globally, they are the children and women trapped in slavelike conditions to feed the needs of the discount and retail stores of this world. Many of these workers face dangerous work conditions. They often work for low wages, little job security, and no benefits. Many are people of color and immigrants.

With the passage of laws and agreements like the North American Free Trade Agreement (NAFTA), corporations can go abroad to avoid the United States' relatively strict environmental and labor laws by exploiting the low wages and weak protections in other countries. That means workers, communities, and the environment on both sides of the border are most vulnerable. Companies' newfound "freedom" has meant the opposite for American workers: Each one now faces the possibility of her job "moving south." Talk about a trump card for the executive class!

Contact existing labor groups in your community, local chapters of the Service Employees International Union (SEIU), or national networks such as Asian Immigrant Women Advocates (AIWA) and Justice For Janitors, and find out how you can support them. Talk to workers at your own school to find out what issues are affecting them and how you can help. Demonstrate solidarity with workers' struggles, and you will make loyal allies. Join efforts against unregulated global free trade, which gives corporations more power and communities even less.

Five Hundred and Four Years and Counting

Find similar ways to support our continent's native peoples in their continuing struggle for land and cultural sovereignty. Oppose oil drilling on Gwichi'in land in the Arctic National Wildlife Refuge, the theft of land and water rights in Hawaii, and the testing of atomic weapons by the French in the Pacific and by the United States on Shoshone land in Nevada.

Indigenous youth can come together to preserve their culture and act in tandem with their elders. Others can join in solidarity with these groups' political efforts. A good example is the campaign against the Mt. Graham telescope project, which would have seen Apache tribal land in Arizona crushed beneath a giant new observatory. Working with the Apache, students at the University of Arizona have pressured their own school to abandon the project. Contact such groups as the Seventh Generation Fund, Indigenous Environmental Network, or American Indian Movement to find out what's going on and how you can be involved. Organize in your own community when possible and work with those defending other communities.

Network, Network, Network

As environmental justice activists, we face a global challenge. Analysis has shown that when we win a campaign in one place, the problem is often displaced to another community. Global trade agreements don't make this problem any easier; they allow corporations to "hide" pollution and poor working conditions "across the border." SEAC is a good place to start for contacts and campaigns in your city, throughout the United States, and abroad. Join and stay in touch with a network. Exchange information and join forces with others.

We Speak for Ourselves

Environmental justice is about people defining their own issues and building grassroots power within their communities. In the words of the Principles adopted in 1991, "Environmental justice affirms the fundamental right to political, economic, cultural, and environmental self-determination of all peoples." We must all speak for ourselves and help amplify the voices of others who are doing the same.

These campaigns are as much about reversing inequalities of power as they are about reducing pollution and protecting community health. With the late start of even the "better" environmental organizations and government agencies, environmental justice demands effective grassroots organizing. Use your own powers and strengths to go to the people with the "official" power and demand your share. The patterns of institutional and environmental discrimination we're up against are not only unjust but also unsustainable. The call of environmental justice gives us a historic opportunity to turn the tide of historic oppressions. Seize it.

17

A Broader View for the Feminist Movement

STEPHANIE CREATURO

Stephanie Creaturo, twenty-five, was program director at the National Abortion and Reproductive Rights Action League of New York (NARAL/NY) from 1993 to 1995. She is currently a graduate student at New York University's Wagner School of Public Service.

One quick glance at the current political climate and the ways in which women are treated and viewed will make you realize how important it is to speak up, speak out, and organize. To say things are bad for women right now is, at best, an understatement. "Bad" is in itself complicated, with many contributing factors. Historically, women have not been entitled to the same economic and social opportunities as men. This discrimination still manifests itself in both subtle and overt ways—sexual harassment in the workplace and restrictions on reproductive rights, to name just two. These issues shape the way in which women are viewed in society, and as a result many people still have a hard time talking about women's health and sexuality. But this is changing, albeit slowly, because of activists working toward equality for women.

Young people are some of the most important activists in the struggle for reproductive rights and gender equality. We infuse tired organizations with much-needed enthusiasm and serve as an inspiration and a reminder to older activists. In working with these experienced activists, we can learn more about the origins of what is still a very young movement.

Young people are the group most impacted by the current erosion of abortion rights, through laws requiring young women to receive parental consent before having an abortion. Restricting minors' access to abortion has become an easy political compromise because it allows politicians to walk the fine line between anti-choice and moderate pro-choice camps. Judicial bypass—where a young woman must petition the court to waive the parental involvement requirement—has provided an easy out for even those lawmakers who are uncomfortable with restricting young women's access to abortion. Forty-five states have parental consent laws on the books, and they have been upheld by the U.S. Supreme Court. Such laws, and the attitudes that allow the chipping away of abortion rights, put our lives and the lives of our friends in danger.

All women's issues are not as "sexy" as the pro-choice/anti-choice fervor of the abortion debate. Women are organizing around a wide range of issues that are less obvious but equally important: welfare reform, accessible low-cost quality health care, and violence against lesbians and gays, for example.

Women's issues affect the whole society and encourage us to question some of the fundamental tenets by which we live, assumptions that keep us silent and therefore buttress patriarchal power structures and perpetuate Victorian attitudes toward women and sexuality. By getting involved in "women's issues," you can find yourself confronting any number of related issues.

Their breadth might make these issues seem daunting, but reproductive rights activism alone provides unlimited opportunities for involvement—from lobbying and clinic escorting to pushing for public funding of child care and safer sex education. Because of my background as a member of the National Abortion and Reproductive Rights Action League (NARAL), I will focus primarily on issues of reproductive choice. Founded in the late 1960s as the National Association to Repeal Abortion Laws, NARAL trains people to become activists at the grassroots level. We use the legislative and electoral arenas to keep abortion safe, legal, and accessible, as well as expanding the full range of reproductive rights available to all women, regardless of age or income. NARAL/NY high school projects educate young women to make safe and informed decisions about their reproductive health care, while also encouraging them to stand up for their rights.

Getting Organized

The reproductive rights movement is a proactive movement that seeks to change how people deal with sex, sexuality, and issues of family planning. Organizations and activists involved in this movement take into consideration everything that affects a woman's ability to make valid reproductive choices. Issues such as income, access to medical care, employment status, education, community, and physical safety are critical to reproductive choice.

Young activists are in an ideal position to incorporate important consciousness-raising work into their political organizing. We have direct access to the group of people—young men and women, our peers—that most need to learn the facts about the legal and medical issues surrounding sexuality and women's rights. If you have the facts and can find a way to convey them effectively, you will often be your peers' only accurate source of this kind of information.

One of the best examples of this type of organizing occurred in New York City in 1994 when, after three years of debate, the Board of Education devised an "opt-out" policy. "Opt-out" gives parents the power to put their children's names on a list that would prohibit them from getting condoms, which have been distributed in the system since 1992. This move was designed to appease conservative forces on the Board and in the community who had finally gained control of enough votes to go up against school HIV-prevention measures, including the condom initiative. With the sobering number of teens infected with HIV or pregnant in New York City (New York accounts for 20 percent of the nation's teen AIDS cases), NARAL/NY student activists had attended many Board meetings urging the accessibility of condoms and confidential counseling to all students. We worked with New York chapters of the AIDS Coalition to Unleash Power (ACT-UP, a direct action and educational organization) and its Youth Education Life-Line (YELL) program, Mothers' Voices, and other concerned students and parents.

The Board still passed the opt-out measure. Infuriated by the outcome, we took our efforts to the streets. Every morning before school we handed out condoms along with a detailed information pamphlet about their correct use and the importance of using them to prevent pregnancy and the spread of sexually transmitted diseases. This was an effective and satisfying way to solve temporarily the practical problem of getting condoms and information into students' hands, and it helped raise their political awareness of the current public health situation. It also showed the Board of Education that people who disagree with their decision were going to do something to solve the problem—that "opt-out" was not just bad policy, but it was potentially deadly to New York high school students. Since then, the condom distribution has continued through the work of the AIDS and Adolescents Network and other groups. But the school situation has become even worse, with right-wing school officials in charge of carrying out the distribution and AIDS education making condoms virtually impossible to find. As always, more work lies ahead.

No Fear

The battle over sex education is being waged all over the country. Realistic sexual education is vital for the future of America, and it is a vital women's issue as well. More than one million teens get pregnant every year, and 81 percent of those pregnancies are unintended. Female teenagers are the largest group in America to use no form of contraceptives. Two-thirds of all sexually transmitted diseases diagnosed in America are found in women under the age of twenty-five. Women between the ages of eighteen and twenty-five are the fastest-growing group contracting HIV. These staggering numbers reflect not only an astounding lack of sex education but also the negative attitude perpetuated in this country to discourage sex: the use of fear, shame, and guilt.

One way to organize in your community would be to see what local schools are doing about sex education. If nothing is being taught or the information is being presented in a biased fashion, it could be a great place to start.

SUCCESS STORY
Guerilla Theatre

On a cold winter day in 1989, a man named Marc Lepine walked into a high school in Montreal and shot fourteen women and then himself. Because of a note he left behind that raged against "feminists," his action was seen as a horrifying representation of violence against women. Dubbed the Montreal Massacre, the killing's anniversary has become a National Day of Remembrance and Action against violence against women in Canada.

At the Queen Elizabeth CVI High School in Kingston, Ontario, "there were a lot of activities to commemorate the massacre, but some of us thought an emotional aspect was lacking," according to student Mary Beth Deline. Working with male and female members of her drama class, Mary Beth developed a program of "guerilla theatre," presenting short skits about domestic violence around the school on the Day of Remembrance.

The group received support from the school's principal by convincing him that they had support from faculty and students. They presented a comprehensive plan on where to perform the skits, crowd control, and details of how the group would deal with challenges or unrest. The student committee coordinated the program with the day's other events, and many "guerilla theatre" members also took part in the guidance department's educational and counseling programs.

The three skits, which rotated through three locations in the school during lunch hour, presented contrasting scenes of domestic violence and harmony.

"Witnessing reality through drama got people beyond the nervous laughter, really talking about the issue," said Deline. "One person shouted to the actor that 'hit' me, 'Hey, man, you can't hit a woman.' Someone else in the crowd responded, 'Sure you can, man.' You can imagine the discussion that ensued."

As a sad backlash to explicit AIDS education, many school boards are adopting "fear-based" sexual education curricula. Such curricula stress abstinence and distribute medical information that is inaccurate or just plain false. This creates dangerous situations for all young people, so keep your eyes and ears open. Know the real facts—you can get them from organizations like Planned Parenthood, listed in the Resource Directory—and be ready to share them.

Look at the sexual education curriculum in your school. Your activism for the women's rights movement could start in your own classroom. The Sexuality Education and Information Council of the U.S. (SEICUS) has excellent resources for sexual education, and so should your public library. Don't be afraid to speak out on behalf of yourself and your fellow students, whether about changing your school's sex education policy or about instituting an informational campaign directed at your classmates. Balance the "shock value" of your information with a demonstrated willingness to work with school officials if they will acknowledge their responsibility to inform students thoroughly and accurately about these issues. Seek support from parents' organizations and local health care providers.

Women and Bias: Making the Connection

In 1992 the Supreme Court's decision, *Planned Parenthood of Southeastern Pennsylvania v. Casey*, was handed down, dealing the final blow to *Roe v. Wade*, the 1973 decision that guaranteed a woman's right to obtain an abortion. The restrictions supported by the *Casey* decision included a twenty-four-hour waiting period, two-parent written consent, and other items that made obtaining an abortion much more difficult for all women, and especially for young women. The Casey decision led to a surge of pro-choice activism by highlighting the risks still facing women's reproductive freedom. One of the groups that worked on this issue was the Women's Health Action Mobilization (WHAM!). A direct action group that grew out of the New York City Pro-Choice Coalition, WHAM!'s mission was to demand, secure, and defend a woman's right to absolute reproductive freedom, and quality health care for all women.

Through WHAM! many in the reproductive rights movement began to confront the issues that are less obviously linked to women's concerns. We were all pro-choice, but more than that we shared a feeling that the agenda of "choice" should be redefined—pushed beyond just abortion. Our group was concerned about other aspects of women's health, such as contraception, prenatal care, child care, and low-cost health insurance.

Looking more closely at how these issues affect women of different ethnic and class backgrounds and sexual orientations was another lesson in mapping the "web" that is the women's movement. Think about fear-based sex education again: The problem with explicit information about AIDS is that it makes schools deal with gay and lesbian issues. While our generation more or less recognizes the existence of the gay community and the right to choose one's sexual partners, this is often not true of our parents' and teachers' generation. Fear-based sex education isn't just about restricting young people's access to accurate information about sex, it's about sweeping the existence of these issues under the rug rather than dealing honestly with them.

Within WHAM! we had to deal with issues of race and class on a very concrete level: We had to reexamine our own tactics. Many of our actions could result in our arrest, and they usually took place during business hours, necessitating time off from work. Ask yourself the questions that we asked ourselves: Are women of color treated the same way by the police as white women? Are women of color afforded the same opportunities as white women at jobs? The answer in both cases is no. We struggled for several years to reconcile our concerns about these societal issues with our desire to engage in smart, media-savvy, direct action.

These discussions, although heated and sometimes bruising, were very important and necessary. They enabled WHAM! to find its focus for action and brought up issues vital to the feminist movement.

Of course, you may not find this to be the case when you organize, particularly at the outset. Don't worry, there's no shame in starting with a more limited scope. Whether or not you seek to address the whole web of issues at once is up to you. A good look at these issues will make you aware of how their interplay affects our daily lives. Look for ways that you can use one issue as a vehicle to get involved in broader issues of social justice, and how—even if you can't work directly on all issues (and you can't)—you can support another activist who is working on those issues.

Bringing in the Big Guns

Other opportunities for women's activism lie in connections with the many organizations that have been created to support women's rights. The National Organization for Women (NOW) has chapters in hundreds of cities and towns throughout the United States. Their activities range from one-day projects, such as walk-a-thons, to extended involvement in all sorts of arenas. Most states also have a chapter of NARAL, the oldest organization dealing with reproductive rights.

Especially with an issue that strikes as many deep emotional chords as reproductive choice, involvement in established organizations has many advantages. The programs are often well established and have name recognition. Often, this will make your community more readily accepting of your action than if you strike out on your own.

Forge Ahead

The exciting thing about direct action is that there is very little territory mapped out for young activists. The underlying commitment is to educate and empower people, and to provide a vehicle for change that is action oriented. Creativity and brainstorming lend to successful projects. The only limits on your projects come from within.

The possibilities are endless. If you are interested in the arts, start a women's awareness theater troupe. To get involved in direct service, volunteer at a battered women's shelter or work on a crisis hotline. Start a youth project through an established service organization or begin a political organization or rap group at your school. Write a media-busting feminist newsletter and distribute it in your community. These are just a few ideas to spark your imagination.

Swimming Against the Current

None of this will be easy, however. All activism is a struggle, and the joining together of personal feelings and political activism can be an emotional challenge. It takes a lot of determination to see a project through to the end, and it can be hard as hell to stay empowered when you run up against the kind of apathy and resistance you're likely to face. You may find that an important first step will be just to create a space where you and your fellow activists can talk through the issues that concern you. Overcome the discomfort, find common ground, and then get active when you know you're coming from a base of mutual support.

There will be much resistance along the way. Not all people will recognize or accept the need for women's activism. School administrators, parents, and friends will have to be convinced about the value of your project. In all likelihood you'll hear many of the same things I heard when I started out in this field: "These are special interests." "No one will take you seriously if you just discuss women's issues." "You're overreacting; it's not really that bad."

Don't let these people get you down. Know the facts and be prepared to express yourself firmly and passionately without getting hysterical. Your job as a consciousness-raiser is to change minds, but realize that there are some people who will believe what they choose in spite of the facts. The majority of people out there, however, will be willing at least to listen and often to support you as well. In the end, if you change the way women are seen or treated in your community or even if you just get people to think hard about the sexual attitudes we're taught by society, the pride and value your project will bring to you and to those around you will be worth it.

18

Dealing with Power Issues in Activism

MARK FRAIOLI

Mark Fraioli, twenty-four, is the former director of the Sierra Student Coalition.

Whenever we try to change the world, we are forced to confront a human trait that makes us all squirm: power. To people who are trying to make a difference, power represents a contradiction. On the one hand, we change the world by calling into question those who are in power—influential officials, entrenched programs, well-established institutions. On the other hand, in order to change this status quo, we have to tap into alternative sources of the same trait: power.

For instance, if you would like to start a tree-planting program at your school, you have to send the principal a tricky pair of messages. You first have to tell this person that the ecological landscaping of the school is terrible and that many students would support you in your opinion. At the same time you have to seek this person's approval for your improvement idea.

Making real changes in the world means navigating a sometimes tricky course between these two contradictory needs. Many activists fail by ignoring the delicacy of this task. Some mix a pound of criticism with only an ounce of cooperation, pushing their shrill cries for change out to the political margins. I remember in particular a group of activists who energetically promoted an unprecedented, radical wilderness bill. While many environmentalists, myself included, would have liked to see it succeed, the bill simply had zero acceptance from Washington lawmakers. The more its promoters pushed, the more the public were alienated by their efforts.

Other activists have failed by going too far in the opposite direction, pulling their voices into political acceptance while reducing their cries to whimpers. I remember in particular the leaders of my school's student government, who always agreed to work with and never against the school administration. As a result, student leaders found that they had no say on issues they cared about, such as the overprominence of football in the sports program. Instead, their influence was restricted to silly issues, such as what is included in the salad bar at lunch. By being too gentle, these student leaders allowed school higher-ups ample opportunity to shove aside their feeble requests for change.

How do people like you and me chart a middle ground between being too strident and too gentle? I don't pretend to have any magic answers to this question; however, eight years of in-school activism have taught me a few moves that I'd like to share with you here. Given below are the five most common power dynamics, sticky issues that confront all students no matter their gender or race. They are in no particular order because you will face a different combination of these issues in every situation and will have to sort out how to deal most effectively with the problem.

Since you and I are in the business of fighting the status quo, I will phrase each dynamic in terms of what the powers that be are trying to preserve—the images and influence they're trying to maintain. You're out to acquire some of this power and do so in a way that you neither alienate nor find yourself co-opted by the people whose support you need to do your best work. As part of preparing your action agenda, it's your job to understand how these dynamics are seen by influential individuals, and then turn them on their head to work in favor of your cause.

Preserving Unity

Imagine walking into the principal's office and informing her that you'd like to organize a club concerning environmental issues. You get a lukewarm reception. "Are you going to incite political rallies in the school?" she asks. "Are you going to cooperate with partisan groups?" Many authority figures fear that the existence of debate and dissent in their jurisdiction will reflect poorly upon their ability to lead. In my old middle school, for example, a vice principal told me flat out that working for change was simply not allowed in "his school."

Given our high expectations of those in power, a fear of dissent on their part is somewhat understandable. Dissent brings potentially volatile disagreements into otherwise placid communities and thus makes an administrator's job even more complicated and challenging than it already is. But to stick up for common sense, a fear of dissent is totally undemocratic. Free societies are built on dissent. Fear of dissent runs not only against the flag on the wall but also against the assignment on the board. American students should learn the importance of democracy in their school itself.

The best way to respond to those who are trying to preserve unity, therefore, is to remind them that you are trying to apply the democracy you learned inside the classroom to school life outside the classroom. Talk about how hard you are striving to become an active citizen. Be a little cheesy if you have to. Your work as an activist is sacred because it preserves our country's greatest dream: government by the people. Let them know that.

Also, make them feel "safe" by demonstrating an interest in their precious unity. Show that you feel a sense of connection to the school and tell them that what you're trying to do is meant in the best interest of the community. There's nothing wrong with conveying a little ownership to the administration. Just don't put yourself in a position where you're always needing permission and consultation on every little thing. You should be shooting for autonomy that allows you to stretch the limits of school unity in a constructive manner.

Preserving Authority

Now imagine sitting down with your school principal to discuss some changes in the school's handling of toxic materials. You would like to change the paints used in the art department. You have already gained the support of affected teachers and the maintenance staff. You have even checked with suppliers and found prices for nontoxic paints that are cheaper than the current paints. If it's okay with the principal, you'd like to start ordering the new paints immediately. It turns out it's not okay with her. She begins to nitpick, asking, "Why didn't I hear about this earlier?" She also says, "The budget is already written for this year" and "What if we have an exclusive contract with an art supply distributor?"

True, you should have found the answers to these questions during your research, but there's more to it than that: People in authority are held responsible for everything under their command. They are often understandably concerned about maintaining control of their situation—as concerned about control as you are about toxics. Most authority figures exercise this control by getting in on plans before they come to fruition. That's why even the simplest request for permission, when it comes late in the process, can lead to a drawn-out cross-examination. When people are taking pains to preserve their authority, respond with these two gestures: inform and include. Make sure that all those in power know what you want to do, why, and how, *before* rather than *after* you do it.

Casual updates in the hallways work well, as well as informal newsletters for slightly bigger operations. Also make sure to ask those in power for their input, opinions, advice, and criticism early on. By informing and including, you reassure them that you appreciate their need for control of the situation. In other words, by putting in that extra effort with people at the outset, you have a better chance of making progress later in the game.

SUCCESS STORY

An Experiment in Clean Living

Ten years ago a group of students at Brown University started a project that ever since has combined education and environmental living. In the fall of 1985 an environmental studies class of about twenty students examined the use of resources at Brown. As they considered their own use of water and electricity in university dormitories, students expressed dissatisfaction with their inability to control basic functions like room temperature—which often meant engaging in such wasteful options as opening windows in midwinter because radiators were preset to very high temperatures—and the types of food they were able to consume through the university's food services. These concerns led to the suggestion that a group of environmentally minded students band together in a house where they had more control over their consumption.

The group studied non-dormitory housing owned by the university, and, as part of their final report, issued a proposal to the Office of Residential Life to obtain "special-interest house" status for a wood-frame home on campus. West House, as the building was called, was well suited to the project because of its size and solar exposure, and because it was being used at that time as transient housing for commuting students. Students and faculty of the Center for Environmental Studies met several times with members of the Residential Council during the following spring semester. By maintaining their focus on the West House project rather than addressing the broader issues that made food services and building operations personnel feel threatened, they eventually obtained agreement on special-interest status, and West House reopened as "the environmental dorm."

Fourteen students live in the house each year, with up to a dozen more nonresidents eating their meals in the house. Meals are vegetarian—often vegan—and the house keeps its thermostat set at sixty-five degrees in winter. The house is equipped with water-saving fixtures, and all recyclable material ends up in the right place. Some years the West House residents have purchased their food in bulk through a local environmental co-op and maintained a compost heap in the backyard.

The fourteen also participate in an environmental studies practicum class that involves monitoring and attempting to improve their own environmental living habits. Since the house's creation a decade ago, the class has turned its focus on the rest of the university. Through an organization called Brown Is Green, they and others have worked with residential, custodial, and food services officials to improve the environmental impact of the entire university.

Preserving Seniority

You've done some background research on fundraising and are sitting in the waiting room of a local company, seeking a donation for your cause. You are given an appointment with the Director of Community Relations, who seems surprised to see someone so young walk through the door. You describe your ambitious plans for bringing change to your community. He seems positive but complacent, as if to say that your ideas are good, but perhaps your experience is not up for the job.

We've all encountered age discrimination, but we have never gotten used to it. Why is it that adults often distrust the ability of young people? Much of it has to do with the bare facts of their experience versus yours: They have had more time to make mistakes and learn from them than you have had. Sometimes that's a good thing, and sometimes it's not. There's something wonderful about a lack of experience. Your relative newness gives you a fresh perspective: You are willing to experiment with ideas that those who came before you may have ignored or abandoned. Make this argument and supplement it with a clear well-thought-out action plan. Prove to them that, wherever they got their attitude toward young people, they're wrong to apply that prejudice to you.

This can be a touchy diplomatic act. You need to express your own youth and vibrancy without saying or implying, "You, sir, are an out-of-touch old coot." A little irreverence does everyone some good, but pour it on too thick, and you could end up shooting yourself in the foot. Appeal to the official's idea that he, too, can be hip and in touch with new ideas. Look for and draw out his youth in the process of conveying your own.

Preserving Impressions

This time you're walking into the offices of your local newspaper. You have arrived hoping to persuade them to write an article on an Earth Day event you've been planning. After telling your story to a reporter, you get asked a bunch of questions that all seem pointed in the same disturbing direction. The reporter asks, "Do the students in your school really care about the environment? Wouldn't most students rather buy a CD than give five bucks to sponsor an event like this? Isn't this event just another outlet for young people's frustration with the world?" All of these questions seem to hide the real question, which is actually a prejudgment: "Aren't you from Generation X?"

Yes, we are Generation X. We didn't come up with that name, and we did not come up with the stereotypes that apply to it. In fact, the only generation powerful enough to make that kind of broad prejudgment is the Baby Boomers. Stereotypes must be nipped in the bud because they are often wrong and, more important, because they are stereotypes. This is not a time for preserving impressions but for eliminating them. Wherever they obtained their impressions of Generation X, they can discard them now because with you in town, those impressions are wrong. Our democratic society is built on a profound belief in the ability of the individual. When we are prejudged, we are not free. Appeal to the very simple concept that you should be judged on your merits and actions, and not on your age or anything else that falls under the rubric of "first impressions."

Don't pretend to represent your whole generation. No one can do that. Represent your own ideas and convey the fact that *you* are not the apathetic ones—and you're about to prove it. If that's not "news" to your cynical reporter friend, he should turn in his press pass.

Preserving Accomplishments

Imagine walking into a municipal supervisor's office with a request that curbside recycling be implemented across town. When you make your suggestions, the supervisor begins to get testy. "We are already doing enough," he says. "Why can't you appreciate the way things are rather than focus on being critical?"

When this happens, it's important to ask yourself whether the official is lashing out at your ideas or your approach. Often "the way things are" is the result of many years of hard work on the part of the person you're sitting across from. In other words, perhaps the recycling situation was much worse when this person first arrived at his post, and perhaps he was only able to improve it to a limited degree. I've seen many activists seriously disempower themselves by walking all over someone else's pride.

When you run into a person who acts like this, you just found a new friend. This person cares about the same things you do and is probably just as frustrated as you are at the amount of progress they were able to make on their own. Respond to this situation by saying how much you appreciate the work your new friend has done. Ask how you can help. In order to avoid further frustration, present suggestions that describe tangible goals that can be realistically met soon. Taking a step back from the confrontation and recognizing that you and the supervisor are after the same goals, and that each of you can help the other achieve them, is a vital first step. At the very least, it's good to know that there are others who care—sometimes as vehemently as we do.

Mix and Match

These five tools can be used in any number of situations. Think about how you might approach a teacher about becoming an advisor to your school club. Think about how you would talk to a friend's parents about donating some money to your cause. Think about how you would talk to a magazine about running a story on your accomplishments.

Think about how you would talk to your senator. This last situation is more complicated than the others and therefore merits a little more attention. Unlike many of the other people you often deal with, elected officials always need to accumulate accomplishments rapidly that are very tangible. If the voters are not satisfied with an official's record of accomplishments, they will make their voices heard in the next election. When you go before your elected representative, therefore, you have two jobs: First, you must make your concern clear in at least broad terms—saying, for instance, "I care about abortion rights." Second, you must let the elected representative know that you vote or, even better, that you know many people who vote in that person's home district.

If you appear before your elected official as a representative of a public interest organization that lobbies on specific bills (see the Resource Directory and Chapter 5 on lobbying), you will be given a much more specific list of points to make. In all situations the basic principle remains the same: Let people know what you care about and let them know that you are connected to their electorate. When democracies work, they don't do what's right, they do what the people want. Let your elected officials know what the people want.

As you may have noticed, most power dynamics have nothing to do with the real issue at hand and everything to do with how other people relate to you. In the end it is other people's responsibility, not yours, to create a world where it is easy for people like you to work for positive change. Unfortunately, some folks fail at that responsibility. But never fear: When that is the case, just pull out this little bag of five tricks, run through them in your head, walk back into the room, and win.

19

Act First, Apologize Later

ADAM WERBACH

Adam Werbach, twenty-three, is the founder of the Sierra Student Coalition (SSC) and in May 1996 was elected as the youngest president ever of the Sierra Club, America's oldest environmental organization. Both of these organizations—as well as the Sierra Club conservation staff and board of directors—contributed information to this chapter.

> Attention Kmart shoppers: There's a blue light special on lands preservation right now. Proceed to congressional lobbying immediately.

I envy Kmart shoppers. I wish I was propelled toward the best bargain of activism at any given moment, just as Kmart shoppers are sent scurrying to buy the world's best soap-on-a-rope. No such luck. We are left as individual activists to forage for ourselves. Deciding to get involved is just the first step. Wisely investing in your work to promote the greatest good is the tricky part.

Let's put it another way. You decide you want to travel from Maine to Florida. You're not going to slap on your Air Muirs (John Muir founded the Sierra Club in 1892, and Yosemite is a national park because of his activism. Once, to better understand the American landscape, he walked from Maine to Florida and then wrote a book about his adventures.) and hoof it down there to chill with your grandparents. You'll consider how much money you have, whether or not you can scam a car, where you have friends to hang with, and how much time you can stand to be away from your favorite kitchen appliance. Armed with this data and using it to make the best decision, you'll have a better chance of getting to the beach and sipping frozen cocktails.

Activism works the same way. Without a road map, a compass, and a good set of shades your good intentions will take you only so far. Now more than ever it is crucial for you to hone your skills and become a superactivist. The bad guys are getting organized, too.

Astro Turf

Here's a secret that corporate America doesn't want you to know: People like you are their worst nightmare. They want you to buy their shaving cream, deodorant, and aluminum siding, then go home and watch TV so they can advertise more useless junk. But you're not like that. By reading this book you're demonstrating that you've broken out of their mold and decided to live your life consciously.

Corporate America can't fake people like us. When we call up our congressional representatives to tell them we won't stand for Dow Chemical polluting our New Jersey neighborhood, someone at Dow corporate headquarters is grabbing for his bottle of Advil. When we get our friends together and hold a rally in Oregon to protest the clear-cutting of our cathedral forests, some rich timber barons are looking for a rock to crawl under.

No matter how much polluters spend, they can't buy our integrity, sincerity, and virtue. We are the grassroots. Diverse, broad, and hearty, we are the foundation of the American political system.

But that doesn't mean they don't try. Big oil companies like ARCO, Chevron, Shell, and British Petroleum, for example, go to great lengths to create the illusion of grassroots support for their anti-environmental ways. And they have bucks!

In one campaign I worked on, we, the good guys, spent almost $4 million—by any estimation a staggering amount. (I could buy a ton of CDs for that!) I remember a little girl named Sarah sending us $75 worth of pennies and nickels she had been saving for a new bike. Yet even all of Sarah's pennies couldn't help us match the $12 million—that's six zeroes there—that the bad guy spent. Even though we worked hard, we lost. But from the ashes of that defeat, a powerful new student organization, the Sierra Student Coalition, came to be.

Where did their $12 million go? To a new brand of genetic Terminator. Fake grassroots. What we like to call Astro Turf. Astro Turf groups try hard to look like you and me but usually fail. (Because, by golly, we're not that stupid!) They pay people to go to public hearings and pretend to care about "their" issue. They create front groups that only appear to be run by citizens. In the environmental movement the Astro Turf often calls itself the "wise-use" movement. Now I'm all for the wise use of our natural resources, but their version of wise-use means tear the stuff down and sell it cheap!

You need to direct your energies properly, know that you are working with accurate information, and make sure that others don't get conned. Being able to spot Astro Turf groups and publicity, and avoid them, is an important part of this skill.

Media Abuse

If the anti-environmental movement is bogus, why has it gained so much media attention? Environmentalists have dominated the editorial pages of the American news media for more than twenty years. Thanks to a coordinated media effort and the overwhelming support of the American people, the news media have reflected our "natural" priorities. We all believe that it's important to protect America's environment for our families and for our future, right?

Recently, however, the anti-environmentalists have caused their own stir in the media. Papers are sold when there's conflict, and the wise-use "movement" is nothing if it's not conflict. Even though the wise-use movement is not a movement at all, the media overplay their significance in the interest of "a good story."

This is the nature of media. Conflicts are reported as having two sides, each more or less equal. A story reporting that "rich industry front groups have little public support" is boring to the people out there. Americans would rather read "Environmentalists battle the rising tide of anti-environmental sentiment," even though the tide isn't rising. So the wise-use crowd benefits from the media's needs.

The wise-use movement includes bad guys that we already know, like the National Rifle Association, which continually lobbies Congress to allow hunting in all our natural parks. But it also includes harder-to-spot groups whose names make them sound like our friends but that are actually funded through big corporate money and private land developers. How do they work? A wise-use group such as the Environmental Conservation Organization sends out press releases and pamphlets that begin by describing their environmental goals. To the untrained eye they seem to be genuinely concerned about the environment; in truth they support compromises that benefit corporations at a cost to citizens.

Some anti-environmental groups fight to remove restrictions on developing wetlands in order to build more strip malls. Scientists say that our few remaining wetland areas are crucial for the purification of our water and the protection of wildlife. In states like Ohio and New York, over 70 percent of the native wetlands have already been destroyed. The groups claim to be conservationists because they "protect" the tiny sliver of the wetlands that they're building on.

Here's another example: The Sierra Club has been working with a large coalition of environmental groups to pass national legislation that would protect the most important pieces of Utah wilderness from imminent destruction by miners, developers, and cattle grazers. America's Red Rock Wilderness Act would protect 5.7 million acres of some of the most stunning and unique wilderness in North America. Knowing that there was wide public support for the creation of these wilderness areas, Utah's congressional delegation, at the request of the mining companies—large campaign contributors—introduced a "compromise" bill that they claimed would save 1.8 million acres. Suddenly environmentalists had to justify why they needed so much wilderness.

That's often the wise-use "catch" for environmentalists: Their compromises seem reasonable until you read the fine print. With

WOLVES IN SHEEPS' CLOTHING: WISE-USE FRONT GROUPS

The following groups have names that sound worthy of your support, but, in fact, they are bought and paid for by polluters:

Alliance for America
American Freedom Coalition
Center for Defense of Free Enterprise
Environmental Conservation Organization
League of Private Property Owners
National Wetlands Coalition
People for the West!
Wilderness Impact Research Foundation

---

less than 2 percent of the original wilderness areas of the United States remaining, "so much" is a misused term. Reading the compromise bill more closely, environmentalists also found that it contained "release language." Release language allows all the land that is not specifically saved by the bill to be released to developers. What was presented as a compromise was actually a trick. If environmentalists had supported the bill while planning to fight for the rest later, they would have lost big. And in battles like these, losing means depriving our grandchildren of a natural treasure that was around long before any white man walked here.

We're all still working on saving Utah's last remaining wilderness. And we always read the fine print.

Wise-use Tactics

Here's the second wise-use trick: The anti-environmental movement's organizing techniques are our organizing techniques. You will recognize their strategies because they're copies of our strategies. The wise-users have discovered the progressive movement's organizing guides and have done their homework. They know how we get people to a rally. They know how we run phonebanks. They know how we help bring focus to the public's rage. We're fighting the very techniques we pioneered. There's a simple solution: Create new techniques. Young people need to lead the progressive movement toward greener organizing pastures.

We've grown up with computers; we need to use the Internet more effectively to organize networks for action. We've grown up in a generation that watches MTV; we need to tailor our messages to those with a short attention span. (Perhaps this is our turn to take our cue from corporate strategy, but with a twist of honesty and forthrightness that the big ad firms would never understand.) Think about what motivates you to act. Think about what you need to harness that energy and go for it. Use the selling techniques that have been used on you. Sell your issue the same way that the Gap sells its clothes. We have already begun to change the movement; it's our responsibility to use our creativity to give us the edge. There's no idea that we can't make better.

Wise-use Legislative Tactics

Standing on the wise-use Astro Turf is an army of slick lobbyists who are nothing more than glorified used-car salesmen. The corridors of the U.S. Congress are called "Gucci Gulch" because of the pricey threads they wear. These lobbyists focus the Astro Turf's efforts on obscurely named bills that sound unrelated to the environment. Budget reconciliation bills, funding riders, and appropriations bills have all held hidden evil environmental provisions put there by industry lobbyists. Here are some examples.

Takings and other wise-use strategies. The American public supports the protection of their environment. Knowing this, the wise-users have devised confusing and complicated campaigns to draw support for their agenda. The wise-use movement has found ways to amend routine bills with destructive substance. Recently, Congress put a halt to protecting wildlife by attaching a bill to the Defense Department's budget that stopped listing species with the Endangered Species Act. That doesn't sound like defense to me.

Here's a new word to add to your list of "words that I don't know but other people use to sound cool": *takings.* It's a legal term that's derived from the U.S. Constitution. According to the Fifth Amendment, the U.S. government is constitutionally forbidden to "take" the property of U.S. citizens. It says in part, "nor shall government take private property for public use without just compensation." The wise-users say this means that the government has to pay them if they can't do any environmentally hazardous activity on their property. Proclaiming themselves advocates of "private property rights," the wise-use movement has introduced "takings" legislation in over thirty states to sharply limit the controls on environmental laws such as the Clean Water Act. They contend that environmental laws like wetlands-protection statutes is a "taking" of property without payment because they have to spend money abiding by somebody else's rules. This, they say, is prohibited by the Fifth Amendment.

Here's my perspective. If the government wants to knock down your house to build a highway, you should be compensated. But when you're asked by the government to do your part to protect the fragile ecosystems of the Earth, it should not be their responsibility to pay you. If I was your neighbor and decided that I wanted to build a bomb-testing range in my backyard, you probably would call up your county zoning board and ask them to stop me. By the logic of takings legislation, if I was stopped, the government would be responsible for paying me the amount of money I would have made if the bomb-testing site was built.

The word "takings" is confusing to the American public, which is exactly what the wise-users want. Most Americans support private property rights, but not at the cost of clean drinking water. If takings legislation hasn't hit your state yet, it will soon. You can call your local Sierra Club field office if you want more information on how to fight it.

Greenwashing. Walking around my local supermarket I'm amazed at the number of products that claim to be "environmental." With the advent of corporate greenwashing—making a product appear beneficial to the environment—everyone seems to be claiming that products are good for the Earth. Marketing geniuses have slapped pictures of trees and birds all over rock salt and pes-

TWO WISE-USE BUZZWORDS

Unfunded mandates: Every time the federal government passes a law that says states or localities must do something but doesn't provide funding for it, they have given an unfunded mandate. Anti-environmental forces propose that we abolish unfunded mandates, which are the basis of U.S. social policy. What would this do? Well, for starters, you could forget clean air standards. Forget child labor laws. Forget the basic protections that the federal government ensures for you.

States' rights: Another buzzword for reducing all federal social assistance, such as the Environmental Protection Agency and Head Start. Federal environmental laws are typically more stringent than state laws. By giving states more power to "enforce" environmental laws, politicians hope to get around legal protections for the environment.

ticide containers, and McDonald's puts a "recycled" logo on their napkins while still supporting the destruction of the Latin American rain forest to grow their beef. Meanwhile, oil companies sponsor environmental awards in a sad attempt to distract us from the destruction they wreak.

Don't be fooled. Here are some simple things to look for:

1. Do you need it? Less is more when it comes to environmentalism. Americans consume too much of everything. Before you buy your next "energy-efficient" electric can opener or plug-in air freshener, ask yourself if it's really necessary. Make a personal commitment to find old-fashioned alternatives when you can.

2. How much post-consumer recycled content does it have? Unless it says post-consumer, "recycled" can mean that all they did was pick up floor scraps and put them into the mix. Post-consumer means that the source of the paper is community recycling. Aim for *at least* 10 percent post-consumer recycled content. Also watch out for the new beast, the "recyclable" container. It's recyclable all right, but it's not recycled. Just because you see that familiar recycling logo on the box doesn't mean it's not virgin material. Again, read the fine print!

3. Question "biodegradability." Many products claim to be biodegradable—that is, able to break down once they're thrown away. Don't believe it. Most products require sunlight to break down, and there isn't much sunlight deep in a landfill. Again, less is best: Bring a bag when you go shopping.

4. Can you understand the ingredients? A large toxic spill recently occurred at a manufacturing plant that brews the chemical that makes the sugar stick to Kellogg's Frosted Mini-Wheats. The lesson: Just because it ends up in food doesn't mean it's not harmful at some point. Strive to buy products that contain organic ingredients that you recognize.

5. Is it reusable? If you can refill it, you're saving one more piece of plastic from your local landfill.

6. Is it local? Support products that come from as close to your backyard as possible. Buy the local diner's famous apple pie instead of a tasteless apple pie stuffed with preservatives by Hostess. This cuts down on the environmental impact of your purchases because what you buy hasn't had to be shipped so far (on polluting tractor trailers, barges, and so on) and has the additional advantage of keeping the money in your own community—something people of all political stripes can support!

Fascists or Friends?

There is a running argument in the environmental movement over whether to "love thine enemy" or make them pay for their digressions. I say, make them pay. As Dave Brower, my personal hero and the founder of the modern environmental movement, likes to say, "You say what you want. Let the politicians make the compromises!"

They expect us as young people to be a little wild and crazy; let's take advantage of our youthful exuberance and push the spectrum even further. I'm sick of hearing mediocre proposals for saving our last few stands of ancient forests. I'm sick of hearing that there's not enough money to clean up deadly hazardous waste sites near schools. There was enough money to put them there! Remember, knowing who your enemies are is just as important as standing firm against them. I will never say not to work compassionately with those who oppose you. Hunters, for example, can be powerful allies of environmentalists. Both groups share the goal of preserving our natural resources for the future. I will say, however, that there comes a point when you know who your friends are and don't owe anything to anyone else.

Finally, a story. There once was a man who lived next to a river. During a wicked storm, the river began to rise. The farmer stood next to the river and watched it rise till it reached his ankles. His friends came by to help him evacuate. The man refused to go, saying only, "I'm going to wait for God to save me."

The rain kept falling. Two hours later the water had reached the man's waist. More friends came, this time in a raft, to rescue their friend. The man refused to go, saying only, "I'm going to wait for God to save me."

The rain kept falling. Four hours later the water reached the man's neck. This time the National Guard came in a helicopter. "C'mon!" they yelled. "This is your last chance!" The man shook his head and shouted a garbled response as the water came over his head: "I'm going to wait for God to save me."

Sure enough, the water kept rising and the man drowned. A short while later he found himself in God's waiting room. "Boy, am I going to give God a piece of my mind," the man thought. When it came time for the man to see God, the man, not waiting for God to speak, said, "God, I haven't sinned that much. Why didn't you save me?" God chuckled. "What do you mean? First I sent you your friends, then I sent you a boat, then I sent you a helicopter."

The moral: The world needs your help now. Write that letter. Call your representative. Run for office. We have the chance to save the world if we get to work. It won't be easy. As the activists who will carry the world past the year 2000, we have a lot to accomplish. It's our future. Act first, apologize later. The world is in too much danger for us to wait.

20

The Ins and Outs of Local Government

HUNTER SCHOFIELD

Hunter Schofield, twenty-five, is an environmental activist and a member of the town council of Boone, North Carolina.

Look around you. Look out your window. Think about who's in charge of maintaining your community, providing basic services, and running your school system. As activists we often think about national legislation because that's where "big change" can occur. But big change only comes as the sum of many smaller changes. As student activists the best place for us to be involved is the place we can access most easily and in which we have the most stake: our own communities. In this chapter I will try to give you a brief road map of local government—explaining how it works and where to go for help—and talk about the ways you can affect it most successfully, including running for office.

This overview is by nature limited. Local governments vary from place to place in how they're structured and in the more subtle question of how their "culture" will affect your ability to work for change. I can't include all types of government bodies, but I can try to give you some ideas that will help you find your way around your own municipal system. To be an effective activist and focus your campaigns in the right direction, you must know which individuals are in control of certain aspects of community life and where they get their power and resources.

The State of Things

Whether it's Chicago, Illinois, or Boone, North Carolina, all the powers that a local government ("locality" or "municipality") has are granted to it by the state. The powers and rights granted to a locality are outlined in state statutes; some states provide more flexibility for local decision-makers than others. This flexibility, called Home Rule, often focuses on the ability of a locality to generate income by taxing residents without permission from the state legislature. For example, in Colorado—a Home Rule state—the city of Boulder put a referendum on the ballot that would raise the local sales tax by half a cent to pay for the protection of natural areas around the city and construction of more sidewalks and bike paths. The referendum succeeded, and today—almost thirty years later—Boulder has been able to purchase and preserve more than thirty thousand acres of surrounding mountains and has built one of the most extensive bikeway-walkway systems in the United States.

In North Carolina, on the other hand, only the state has the authority to raise sales taxes. Municipalities like Boone have to raise their money in other ways, such as through increased property taxes, the principal source of income for towns and cities. The state has made a uniform sales tax a higher priority than the ability of local government to raise funds for their own work. Your state representative or a municipal official can tell you how certain powers are divided between the state and the locality. This is an important part of knowing where to go to make your case, particularly when what you're asking for is going to have an effect on the public coffers.

Governing Bodies

Every locality is governed by a group of elected citizens usually called a town council or city council (depending on the size of your municipality; over fifty thousand is usually a city, less than that is a town). At its most basic level, local government is simply a service organization: It is elected to decide what services to provide with residents' tax money. This includes the obvious services—trash removal, water and sewer, police and fire protection—as well as some less obvious ones like recycling, parks and playgrounds, and services for the poor and homeless. Sometimes the work is conducted directly by agencies of the government and sometimes by local businesses or service organizations with government support.

The council also passes and enforces ordinances (laws) and can revoke them as well if they no longer agree with them. Examples of ordinances would be regulations against burning leaves and debris without a permit or against placing a billboard in a residential neighborhood. Less common ordinances might include regulations requiring developers to preserve trees of a certain size when developing a piece of property or requiring schools and businesses to participate in municipal recycling programs.

How "Policy" Is Made

The decisions of a good governing body should be based on a comprehensive vision or plan for the kind of community to be created or preserved—what politicians call "policy." A policy is not a law but a written statement or traditional practice that expresses goals and helps provide direction for future decision-making. Many communities have gathered their policies together in a Comprehensive Plan. Such a plan is developed by a group of prominent citizens, hopefully representing diverse groups within the community. The idea is that these citizens will draft understood community goals into a plan that local officials should consult when making decisions that affect the community. Written policies on economic development, community appearance, environmental quality, and public safety are usually included in a Comprehensive Plan; it is usually updated every seven to ten years.

It's important to remember that even a Comprehensive Plan—much less a community's unwritten tradition—is not law, and the governing body does not have to follow it. For example, if a large manufacturer wants to put a "smokestack" industry in the com-

BUZZWORDS FOR BUREAUCRATS

Home Rule: state policy that gives localities more control over their own affairs, particularly vis-à-vis tax policy. North Carolina, for example, is not a Home Rule state; localities here can't raise their sales tax without state approval.

Locality/municipality: a town or city, in administrative terms. Your locality may be headed by a mayor or a town/city council. It is responsible for providing some services and gathering some taxes. (The county and state are responsible for others.)

Ordinances: laws passed by the local governing body (locality) that regulate certain actions within the community, usually forbidding or mandating certain actions or behavior by citizens.

Referendum: a question posed as part of an election ballot, usually asking voters for a yes or no response to a question about policy (such as, "Should Boulder charge an additional 0.5 percent sales tax, with the proceeds to go to purchase undeveloped lands for the purpose of maintaining nature?").

Statute: the written laws that guide state policy; for example, a certain state may have a statute that mandates (or forbids) Home Rule.

munity, the governing body has to make a decision: The factory will create jobs but will also be loud and unsightly, and will discharge pollution into the community. Two community goals—economic development and quality of life—are at odds in this situation. The council's actions will speak louder than the words of their Comprehensive Plan. In the final equation, a governing body's "policy" is the sum of its decisions. Hence you can see radical changes in policy based on the changing political makeup of the governing body. You should still get hold of a copy of your town's Comprehensive Plan, however, because it may often support your position on an issue.

New Puzzle Piece: Counties

How local and regional governments impact your daily life will depend on whose jurisdiction you fall under. We've already talked about municipalities, but there's one more piece of the puzzle of government within each state. Whether or not you live in a city or town, you do live in a county. Every state is divided up into counties like a jigsaw puzzle. Wherever you are, you live in a county. Counties are the administrative framework on which states are built, and they are the bodies that affect how state law is applied and how municipal law can be made and carried out. Like municipalities, each county has a governing body, usually called county commissioners or county board.

If you live in a town or city, you are a citizen of both the town and the county that contains your town. The important difference is that as a citizen of the town or city you are entitled to a different set of services—the services provided by your municipality in addition to county services. The catch is that you also pay municipal taxes on top of county, state, and federal taxes. As a local activist, knowing whether the problem is in the jurisdiction of your town or the surrounding county is essential in identifying the people who are responsible for correcting it.

Board Yet?

Boards and authorities are committees that control one specific aspect of community life. The school board, water authority, and municipal planning board are three examples. Members of these entities are either elected to their position or appointed by another governing body. They may be independent of the other governing body or serve it directly. Likewise, some depend on the municipality or county for their funding, and some—such as the water authority, whose income comes from everyone's water bills—are financially independent of the government. Understanding both the political and financial accountability of the board you're working with is important. Where I live, in Watauga County, North Carolina, for example, the school board is elected directly by county citizens; it is politically independent of the county commissioners and therefore free to make decisions without fear of retribution from the commissioners. But it does depend on the county for a quarter of its funding and commissioners could use this fact to pressure the school board into certain decisions. So if you're trying to get the school board to change its policy, you will have to be aware of the school board's potential manipulation by the county commissioners, and if you're looking for increased funding for some special project within the school system, you may need to go directly to the county commission or the state for the financial support.

A planning board is something very different. Planning boards are established by towns, cities, and counties to decide whether a certain proposed activity—putting up a billboard, subdividing property, allowing "adult entertainment" to operate—is within the legal limits of government ordinances, which are often vague. The board then makes its case before the governing body, which votes accordingly. Needless to say, with the serious decisions found on the planning board's agenda, appointment of its members by the larger governing body can be very political.

Finally, there are often dozens of other committees, made up of local citizens, that serve an advisory role to the governing body. They bring in proposals to expand services, offer policy recommendations, urge approval or denial of construction projects, and serve a host of other needs for local government. Join up. Volunteer boards are a good starting point for affecting local policy making. How to use them to your advantage will be discussed in greater detail later in this chapter.

Implementation

Once decisions are made by the government, they have to be put into action. This is the role of departments, often called "agencies," at the state or federal level. Responsibility for every aspect of local government is delegated to at least one department, and responsibilities are often divided among several departments. A list of your local government departments can frequently be found in the phone book under the name of the municipality or county. Some examples that might be relevant to your work include Environment, Housing, Human Services, Landmarks Commission, Parks and Recreation, Planning and Inspections, and Zoning.

Again, find out who is in charge of your problem as you plan your effort. Within the limits of the money allocated to them by the county and city, department heads often have a great deal of flexibility in how they use their personnel and resources. Make an ally, and you can use this to your advantage.

Three Scenarios

Now that you have an idea of how local government is structured, let's consider several scenarios in which you as an activist would have to deal with it. Unless you live in a large, bureaucratic city, information should be fairly easy to come by. What's not so easy is accepting that information as right and just, or working to change policy for the better.

Scenario Number One: Your community does not have an effective recycling program, and you want to see the service expanded. Recycling is a very expensive service for local government to supply. Unfortunately, the marketplace is still geared toward the production of products from virgin materials instead of recycled ones. But this will change, and you know that for recycling to become part of our lives it needs to be more accessible and convenient. Your first step is to find out what your local government is doing about recycling and which department handles it. Give the department a call and set up a meeting with the department head or recycling coordinator. Get all the information you can at the meeting, including an itemized list of the government's expenditures for recycling. Tell the department head what you'd like to see done and ask for suggestions on how to make it happen. Sympathetic municipal employees can be especially helpful with strategy and can direct you to the elected officials who may support you.

Ultimately you will have to make a thorough and reasonable request to the governing body to expand recycling services. Do your homework and get everything moving through the official channels (your elected official can explain the exact procedure). Get relevant volunteer boards on your side. Send your request to individual members of the governing body in advance of the meeting where it will be considered. Follow up with a phone call and make it clear that you're representing a sizable constituency that wants this change made. (Survey results, letters of support, or a petition are good ways to show the strength of your numbers.) Don't assume that these people know the status of their own recycling program; they probably don't. By becoming their source of information, you will have a central role in shaping public debate. Appear at the meeting where your proposed measure is considered, and speak on its behalf. Try to bring out as many people as you can to support your position. If your measure doesn't pass, talk to board members and find out why. Use this information, and further meetings with those who supported you, to tailor a different request for next time.

Scenario Number Two: You're concerned about domestic violence and think your local government should be doing more to address the problem. Find out what your government is doing. You'll probably find this issue—like other issues of health, family, and aging—handled by the county social services department. Also familiarize yourself with what private agencies and service organizations might be doing about the problem; do not, in your haste, duplicate another program when you could do more by supporting it. Find out if public money is going to these private services. (This is often how local governments handle such issues.)

What you're probably after is increased government spending on the issue, whether through greater outlays to private shelters or improvement of existing government programs. Make sure your request is feasible and well timed. A well-timed request will be one submitted when the governing body is drafting the budget for next year. This usually means May or June, but confirm the exact time with a sympathetic staffer or representative. See if you can get the city to contribute some money if the county does the same; no bureaucracy wants to feel it's the only one footing the bill. Or how about a private fund-raiser and a local government pledge to match the proceeds with public money?

Scenario Number Three: A lot of development is taking place in your otherwise attractive community, and you want stronger building restrictions. In this situation you're looking to change the building regulations—ordinances—of your local government. Getting the government to rewrite its ordinance on development will take some convincing. Make an appointment with the director of the planning and inspections department or planning committee and share your concern. Learn the existing ordinances and how they work. Look beyond your community to find out what towns with similar problems are doing about it. Show your government that this is something a lot of people care about. Build a grassroots network to support your initiative.

The first step may be to ask the government to study the question; see if you and other sympathetic individuals can get onto the volunteer committee. A committee's recommendation will carry a lot more weight. Approach the problem from all sides and look at possible ramifications of your policy change. Don't be like the U.S. Environmental Protection Agency, which at times has passed laws that were intended to help but ended up doing more harm than good by creating unforeseen new problems.

A few years ago we had the chance to restrict hillside and ridgetop development in Boone, but because we moved too quickly and went for too much change—including changes (such as restrictions on what color you could paint your house) that became publicly heated but were not really essential parts of our legislation—the effort was a disaster. We didn't take the time to convey to the public what we were trying to achieve, and we allowed our opponents to play on public sentiment to make us look bad. Controversy and misunderstanding so clouded the issue that even our supporters had trouble reaching consensus on what we were after. Take your time and be clear about what you want to do.

Involving Young Voices

How can someone who is not old enough to vote or a college student who isn't from the area be effective in local politics? The most direct way is to identify a local office candidate who best represents your concern and volunteer for his or her campaign. Whether you're stuffing envelopes, canvassing, or "getting out the vote" on election day, you are making your mark on the campaign and earning the indebtedness of the candidate. When the candidate wins, you win, because now you have a friend and a voice in local government. The more you do for a candidate, the greater your ability to influence that person in office—another reason that groups are a strength! Be up front with the candidate about what your agenda is and be sure that the candidate is willing to go to bat for your issue when the time comes.

Another inroad is by establishing a dialogue with your elected officials. Write and introduce yourself. Share your concern and ask politely for their response. Build a real relationship—stop by and see them sometime. Maybe you can talk them into introducing legislation on your issue. Except in big cities, local government is relatively free of the corruption of big-time public office. Most local officials are "regular folks"—people you'll run into at the grocery store or high school football game. Some of them have a mind for community service, others have ambition to be in a position of authority. Either way, they can be reached through personal dialogue.

Sometimes they can help you get appointed to a volunteer board on your issue. There is usually no minimum age for serving on a volunteer board. This was how I got my start in politics: I called up a council member whose campaign I'd worked on and said, "I noticed that you didn't appoint any college students to the Comprehensive Plan committee. I think students should be represented, and I would like to serve." One week later I was on the committee, where I fought for language about bike lanes, environmental quality, protection of ridges and hillsides. Now as a town council member I can refer to the Comprehensive Plan I helped write for justification of my work on environmental policy.

Referenda

Another useful activist tool is the referendum or "ballot initiative." Combined with an effective community education campaign, this is the formal way to prove that you have majority support and force action by the government. Referenda are serious matters and should not be taken lightly. A referendum—even when it's allowable by local or state law—often must be approved by a majority of the governing body before it makes it onto the ballot. In some states you can force a referendum over government resistance by collecting a certain number of signatures. Referenda are most often used to see if the public is willing to pay for a certain service—such as school renovations or wilderness protection—through increased taxes. Some explode into divisive arguments over policy, like California's 1994 "Proposition 187" to ban social services for illegal immigrants or Colorado's referendum number nine in 1992 to forbid civil rights protection for gays and lesbians.

Run for It!

Once you know your way around the system and have reached the minimum age—usually eighteen or twenty-one for local offices—you may want to make a bid for public office. Start by "reading the numbers," looking at the voting totals from the last several elections to see if progressive or conservative candidates received the most support. In what voting precincts did candidates with beliefs like yours find support? This will enable you to focus your efforts in the areas where you have the most natural support.

Here's an important question to ask: Is there a significant population of people who share your views but are not voting? For example, are there students at the local college who would vote for you if only they were registered? What about women, minorities, or members of poor communities who might not be registered? During my campaign for town council, we registered five hundred students to vote. Since they were recently registered, we had their current phone numbers. The night before and throughout the

SUCCESS STORY

Two Birds with One Stone:
Helping Ecology and Economy in Kansas City

In 1994 the environmental club of the East Magnet High School in Kansas City, Missouri, a high school that focuses on environmental science and agribusiness, hosted an Alternative Energy Vehicles Expo. This exposition brought cars that were powered by alternative fuel (hydrogen, gasahol, solar, and so forth) to the school's front lawn along with a host of informational booths from local environmental firms and government programs. The Expo generated a great deal of local attention for innovations designed to reduce non-point-source pollution and energy waste, and laid the environmental club's next project idea at its feet.

Through the Expo, the students met with staff from the Metropolitan Energy Center, a city agency charged with assisting low-income residents meet their fuel needs, and learned about the colossal waste of energy that occurs each winter because of poorly insulated buildings. The students approached the center with a proposal to "weatherize" homes in the inner city.

With materials provided by the Center, thirty-five students and a handful of teachers installed insulation, weatherstripping, plastic storm windows, and caulking around windows and doors in six inner-city homes. The group spent one day at each house, receiving enthusiastic support from residents.

"Everyone involved was educated about how to save money on energy and reduce air pollution," says environmental club advisor Bob Hubert. "We really killed two birds with one stone: We were helping people with a limited income to save money on their heating bills, and we were helping the environment by cutting down on energy use and release of greenhouse gases."

The students, many of whom come from the same inner-city neighborhood where the school and weatherized homes are located, also learned simple strategies to conserve energy in their own homes. The Alternative Energy Vehicles Expo has become an annual event, and Hubert received an "Excellence in Teaching" award from the *Kansas City Star* for the weatherizing project. The award included a $1,000 grant, which the club used to weatherize twenty-four more homes in the fall of 1995.

---

day of the election, we called them all and reminded them to vote. I won the election by four votes.

Getting out the vote is crucial, and the ability to do that, whether for your own campaign or for somebody else's, will determine your ability to affect policy from the inside. Remember, President John F. Kennedy won by less than one vote per precinct when the whole country's ballots were added together. Make every vote count.

My philosophy toward politics has always been "one foot in the system and one foot out." This means that I affect what happens in the system via my political position, but at the same time I continue to organize and work outside the system in the grassroots. Most politicians do not have an activist background and so are not knowledgeable about how to influence issues by organizing people. These politicians, who have both feet in the system, often find themselves in the position of bargaining for political support. Instead of standing firm on their convictions, they have to "wheel and deal" to get the support they need.

I started on the outside, working as a citizen-activist on environmental and social justice issues. Eventually I realized I would be more effective if I could influence decisions from both sides. That way I could prevent bad decisions before they occurred, represent the interest of citizens in my community, and provide greater recognition for the grassroots issues my compatriots and I were working on. Because I entered local government this way, I often don't have to play politics to get things done. By continuing to organize outside the system, we still have the "people power" needed when the system becomes too bureaucratic or political and stops serving the people's needs.

Make no mistake—being a public servant is no bed of roses. Although I value the chance to affect decisions from the inside and know my way around the system, people are very critical of elected officials. When a good-hearted public official makes a decision that is in the long-term interest of the community but has short-term negative consequences, citizens get upset. In addition, individuals with their own political agendas who feel threatened by your success may attempt to discredit you. Politics is not for the "thin-skinned." You're attempting to bring honesty to a dishonest profession; stay humble and remember where you came from.

Having one foot in the system, with all the protocols and standards you then have to conform to, can interfere with your activism. Because you are responsible for representing all of your constituents and not just the ones you agree with, you need to be more balanced and accountable. This doesn't mean that you can't be as active in the grassroots as you were prior to being elected. It simply means that from a practical standpoint you must be more selective in the battles you fight and the ways you fight them. Remember that politics is "the art of compromise." You can't win them all, so be prepared to make some concessions. While you will be disappointed at times, ultimately you will gain the knowledge necessary to become a strong and effective political leader.

I hope this road map of local government has been helpful. There's a lot to learn and you will make mistakes, but remember that knowing your way around is half the battle—sometimes more—and will make you a more effective activist in the long run. You must engage the system if you wish to change it. Persistence, combined with knowledge and an ability to work through the age barrier, is the key to success as a young citizen-activist. Educate yourself, organize others, and activate us all. Good luck and Godspeed.

21

Creating a School-based Peer Counseling Program

DANIEL L. SHAPIRO

Daniel L. Shapiro, twenty-four, has directed peer counseling and conflict management training in the United States and Eastern Europe. He is a doctoral student in clinical psychology at the University of Massachusetts.

Jay lies curled up in his bed, alone and crying. Earlier in the day he and his girlfriend got into a terrible argument, and now he really feels like talking to someone. But who? His best friend is out of town, he feels uncomfortable talking about personal issues with his parents, and the matter doesn't seem serious enough to seek psychiatric help.

Jay could meet with a peer counselor.

Peer counseling may sound like a scary concept to some people. Are students skilled and knowledgeable enough to counsel? The answer to that question, provided by both scientific research and anecdotes, is an emphatic yes. Peer counseling is a unique form of dialogue that enables young people to help other young people who just need to "talk something through." Instead of giving advice or offering psychological diagnoses, peer counselors act as open, nonjudgmental listeners who help friends explore and clarify problems and think through the consequences of certain decisions. Because all students encounter minor life obstacles—a bad breakup, poor grades, periods of sadness or stress—peer counseling can be an important part of the school learning experience for everyone involved.

"Peer counseling is a gift to both the counselors and those being counseled," explains Clare King, a professional consultant with Johns Hopkins University's peer counseling center. "Valuable life skills are learned, and people become more motivated to take responsibility for their actions, whether the consequences are positive or negative." In other words, peer counseling benefits the counselees—a broadly defined term for anyone who speaks with a peer counselor—as well as the counselors. Through training and experience, counselors develop a deeper understanding of their own values and capabilities. Counselees have a reliable source of support to cope with minor problems in life. Peer counseling can help them open up and understand themselves, their needs, and their responsibilities better; and they then can make wiser, more informed life decisions.

This gift of peer counseling has been implemented in different ways around the world. Many junior high schools, high schools, and universities have peer counseling centers and training courses. Some schools have a peer counseling room where students with day-to-day problems can walk in and talk to trained peer counselors. Other schools have peer counseling support groups or phone lines. Peer counseling skills have also served as a backbone for developing a variety of student-run help groups on issues such as drug and alcohol abuse, sexual assault, and suicide prevention.

What It Is and What It's Not

Peer counseling is a process of active listening. First, as an effective peer counselor you are using body language to demonstrate your interest in what the counselee is saying; leaning forward in your seat and making eye contact with the speaker are examples of good "posture" for a counselor. Second, you are using questions to lead the counselee through an intellectual and emotional process. With a good counselor, counselees will have the chance to examine problems from all sides, to clarify what they are really feeling and what outcome they are hoping for, and to consider possible solutions. You are nonjudgmental and nonbiased in your approach to the counselees and their problems.

Finally, you are giving students a friendly, accessible link to other services. You've researched the available support services for people with certain types of problems and can point counselees toward treatment programs, professional counseling, and other resources they may need. This is one of the reasons I recommend that peer counseling programs have a space of their own. In a counseling room you can keep binders of contact information and important resources such as phone numbers for an AIDS hotline, sexual assault hotline, and suicide hotline, and for professional psychologists with expertise in specific areas, including eating disorders and anxiety problems. Lists like these are often compiled by hospitals, social workers, mental health professionals, and women's organizations; your school may even have this information available. Seek it out and make knowing about it part of your training program. Also let school officials know that you have established firm contacts with such professionals, to allay their fears that the peer counseling program could find itself over its head.

The core of peer counseling theory is *not* to give advice. While that may not seem logical at first, think about it. Your role as a peer counselor should not be telling other people what to do, even when you're sure you're right. Advice-giving can cause the counselee to depend on you for every decision encountered and can also lead to resentment when your advice is carried out and doesn't result in the desired effect. Fundamentally, giving advice runs contrary to what peer counseling is all about: When students follow a peer counselor's advice, they take no responsibility for their own actions.

No peer counseling program is complete without a consultant, a trained adult who can support you and point you to resources for students whose problems are out of your league. Your peer counseling corps should meet with this person on a regular basis to discuss possible problem cases, get advice, and feel supported. If you're in middle school or high school, the first people you should approach with the idea of a peer counseling group are probably your guidance counselor and school psychologist; in college you could contact a member of the administration concerned with student life issues. Bring these people on board early in the

SUCCESS STORY

Getting Help for That Old "Teen Fever"

Iasi, Romania, is not the first place you'd expect to find a well-developed peer counseling program, but this small city on the Moldovan border is the epicenter of a peer counseling movement that is gaining national attention and respect from educational officials across Romania. In 1993, Andreea Sava was one of eighteen students to attend a seminar on peer counseling sponsored by the Soros Foundation, which sponsors educational programs promoting democracy, health, and economic development in the former Soviet bloc. Eight of these students hailed from Iasi, and on returning home they contacted the Health Education Program—also a Soros project—for funding and logistical support to develop their own peer counseling program.

The group wrote short proposals and took them to area high schools to promote the project. At the same time they rallied media support and succeeded in getting an article about peer counseling and their program in the popular Romanian magazine *Teen Fever*. By the time they had made arrangements for their first peer counseling office, open from 10:00 A.M. to 2:00 P.M. every Saturday at Eminescu High School and backed by a consulting team of mental health professionals and teachers, letters from teens across the country were pouring in. Most asked for advice on setting up their own program. The Iasi program expanded to several more schools in 1994, and the students also set up a peer counseling hotline staffed by high school students for eight hours every Saturday and Sunday. Members also had a program for teenagers broadcast each week on a local radio station.

Bringing back the American lecturer who introduced them to peer counseling, the Iasi group has organized two more seminars for high school students in the Iasi region. "School pupil's problem" boxes appeared in a number of local schools, with feedback from the counselors published in *Teen Fever*, where Andreea Sava now sits on the editorial board. With the help of further seminars, including chances for peer counselors to travel abroad for Soros Foundation events, the program continues to develop and expand its base of volunteers throughout the Iasi region and beyond.

---

process and try to build a small network of supportive professionals. Such individuals also add important legitimacy to your group when it comes time to confront administrators' concerns about your program.

Training

Peer counseling is not something you just start doing. Because you're helping people deal with problems that are very real and emotional for them, quality training is an essential ingredient. Just as pianists learn and practice scales to improve their performance, peer counselors must learn and practice communication skills to improve their listening and helping abilities. If you're starting a program from scratch, work with your school guidance counselor to find out if there are neighboring schools or colleges with similar programs. If so, ask those trained peer counselors either to act as trainers in your school or to put you in touch with the people who trained them. If no such program exists, call local psychologists to see if any of them can train your group or can refer you to someone who can.

In addition to seeking out training—or as a substitute if absolutely necessary—check out the following excellent books: *Peer Helping: A Practical Guide* by Robert D. Myrick and Don L. Sorenson; *Peervention* by Betsy E. Folk and Robert D. Myrick; and the *Peer Counseling Starter Kit* by Rey A. Carr and Gregory Saunders. Also contact the organization called Peer Resources in British Columbia; they're full of great ideas and have a library of reference materials.

Peer counseling training is a fun, exciting process of getting to know your fellow counselors and practicing your listening and guidance skills. It's also a serious introduction to respecting confidentiality, dealing with stressful and sometimes scary situations, and learning about the professionals you can "fall back on" when necessary. Although different peer counseling programs meet varying student needs, all training programs should cover the following five fundamental areas of counseling:

1. *Trust and confidentiality.* In order for peer counseling to be effective, counselors must be viewed as "safe" people with whom to talk. Specifically, counselees must feel confident that the information they reveal will be kept confidential. Within a safe environment, counselees are more likely to explain their problems truthfully. Peer counselors must be trained in the aspects and limits of confidentiality, and counselees must be informed of them.

The things that you talk about with counselees must never be fodder for gossip; even sharing them with caring friends outside the program should be avoided. Typically, counselees' problems are discussed only with a faculty consultant and a small team of supporting counselors. When counselors meet on a regular basis, issues discussed remain confidential within the small group. Even within the group, I encourage you to discuss problems and cases in general terms. If there's no need to name your counselee, don't. Asking for fellow counselors' advice on how to deal with "a counselee who's having trouble with her parents" is completely adequate; telling them that it's Jane Smith is unnecessary.

Generally speaking, confidentiality must be violated when students' actions or potential actions could harm them or others, or in situations where crimes of abuse are being or may be perpetrated against a minor. Examples include students who are considering suicide or college students who talk about sexual abuse by a parent who still has custody of a person under the age of eighteen.

When you have to violate confidentiality, be up front with the counselee about your need to do so and explain the reasons; often you are bound by law and truly have no choice in the matter (but don't say that if it's not true). Talk with the counselee about how the situation can be turned into a productive one. If a student is considering suicide, for example, you could offer to walk with

PRACTICE MAKES PERFECT

Two methods that peer counseling training uses to teach communication skills are *role plays* and *games*.

In role plays, students act out real-life situations as a way to practice communications skills in circumstances they may confront as counselors. Role plays are often done in pairs, with one person playing the counselor and the other the counselee. The counselee arrives with a problem, and the pair discusses it as if they were in a real counseling situation. After a few minutes they stop and share ideas about what worked and what could be improved. Sometimes a third person participates as an observer to offer feedback to the counselor-in-training. Ideas of good role-play situations are fights with friends or significant others, not doing well on a test, friends spreading rumors, "a certain person (or teacher) doesn't like me," "I feel lonely," or "I am attracted to the same person my friend is." Use each role play to focus on a specific strategy area, such as observing nonverbal cues or asking open questions.

Games keep students' interest and allow the whole group to be part of an enjoyable interaction. One example of a good game for teaching about body language is to have the group brainstorm a list of emotions or "feeling words." One by one, participants act out words on the list *without speaking or making any noise*. The group has to guess which emotion is being expressed. Sounds a little like charades, doesn't it? Give it a try and see where it can take you.

---

her to the guidance counselor's office and wait with her there. If a counselee is reporting parental abuse and is afraid to go home, you can work with him and school officials to find an alternative.

Situations like these are some of the most serious you will come across, so you should be sure to cover them in your role plays during training. Practice explaining confidentiality to other counselors-in-training and have some tough role plays in which you need to explain the breach of confidentiality to your counselee.

2. *Nonverbal communication skills.* Peer counselors must be trained in modeling and interpreting nonverbal communication. Many people assume that talking is our most expressive form of communication. By paying attention to body language, however, you can better understand what people are really feeling. For example, a student may claim that she is no longer angry at her boyfriend, but nonverbal cues—clenched fists or "wandering eyes"—may tell you otherwise. Armed with that understanding, you can ask questions that lead her to understand she's still pretty upset.

Peer counselors should also learn how to use body language to convey their concern. Leaning forward in your chair is an obvious example. Nodding your head occasionally to communicate that you hear what someone is saying is another. But how about some less obvious ones, like not crossing your arms because this is a closed and "judgmental" posture, or making sure that your facial expressions are similar to those of the counselee (smiling during a sad personal story, for example, is a bad idea).

3. *Verbal communication skills.* There are a number of communication techniques that encourage conversation and give counselees the chance to express themselves more fully. Try to use "open" questions instead of "closed" ones. Open questions encourage people to talk; closed questions demand a succinct answer—usually just "yes" or "no"—and lead to halting conversation that probably won't get anywhere. Think about this example: "How are you feeling?" is an open question, because the counselee can respond with adjectives and explanations. "Are you feeling okay?" is a closed question; the counselee will answer either yes or no, and the counselor will be left fumbling for a way to restart the conversation.

Open questions are especially helpful with reticent or quiet students. To get them to talk, you could open the conversation with questions like "So tell me what brought you here" or "What are you thinking right now?"

Closed questions become more useful as you and your counselee begin to focus on the problem at hand. They allow you to "rule out" certain options. But be careful: They also give a nervous counselee an escape.

Try to avoid questions that begin with "why" because they can put respondents on the defensive. They can sound scolding and cold, as when someone asks you, "Why did you do that?" Instead, use questions that begin with phrases such as "What are the reasons that . . ."

One of the most useful strategies for counselors is reflective listening: repeating back to counselees part of what they said. If a counselee says, "I feel sad today because of the weather," the counselor can respond simply, "You feel sad." By reflecting the feeling word, the counselor enables the counselee to really hear how he or she is feeling. Recognition of feelings is often surprising and eye-opening, and very useful for building understanding of what one is truly thinking. A similar strategy is paraphrasing—summarizing, for example, a counselee's fifteen-minute speech about her mother into a more manageable list of the problems mentioned. Paraphrasing reassures the counselee that she has been heard and is useful in isolating certain issues to discuss in greater detail.

And once again, don't give advice.

4. *Emergency situations.* Part of your training should be learning how to recognize and react to emergency situations or "crises." Clear guidelines should be presented outlining the organization's procedures for dealing with emergencies and connecting them to the policies of the school or county. Brainstorm other emergency situations and have the group discuss possible reactions with a mental health professional. Examples of emergencies might include a classmate's problem suddenly becoming a lot worse, a major change in academic performance, tragedy striking a counselee's family, or an act of violence. Formulate an "if . . . then" policy so counselors aren't left out on a limb when something happens.

If a suicide or other kind of violence involving a counselee does occur, counselors who had worked with that individual should seek psychological assistance. Stress to them that what happened was not their fault and that they should not blame themselves or second-guess their counseling abilities and actions.

5. *Limitations, referrals, and supervision.* Finally, be aware of the limitations of peer counseling. You are not a professional. You cannot and should not deal with someone who is exhibiting signs of mental illness. All serious problems or situations where there is

CRISES AND CONFIDENTIALITY

Crises

For counselors, a crisis exists when one or more of the following conditions holds:

1. A student's behavior (actions or speech) indicates that he is or may be in danger of hurting himself or another person or has already done so or tried to do so.
2. A student's behavior is disruptive enough that she is unable to carry out the usual functions of a student, including but not limited to academic work.
3. A student's behavior is disruptive enough that one or more friends or neighbors express serious concerns, or the student is otherwise unable to carry out the usual functions of a student, including but not limited to academic work (the situation makes the student unable to study or work).

A crisis may exist when a not-so-dramatic situation becomes more so by its duration, frequency, or intensity. For example, missing a meal is not dramatic; missing many consecutive meals may be a crisis needing attention. Crises definitely point to a need to discuss the matter further with your advisor or another professional, and may indicate the need to violate confidentiality.

Confidentiality

Counselors are expected to keep to themselves the concerns shared by counselees, with the following exceptions:

1. A student's behavior (actions or speech) poses a threat to self or others, such as a student talking about feeling very down and believing that his family would be better off without him.
2. A student makes reference to having a weapon.
3. A student describes a situation in which the physical, emotional, or sexual abuse of a minor is or might be occurring

(that is, the student talks about having been abused by a parent who continues to be caring for a minor child).

These exceptions may have been stated by the counselor at the outset of a conversation; but if they were not, the counselor is still bound by them and ethically should inform the counselee that the counselor will not be able to keep the secret which has been shared.

If you have any doubts about a crisis situation or feel that you may need to violate confidentiality, consult your advisor or peer counseling program leader immediately. Do not hesitate to ask for help in sorting out these critical issues.

(The above guidelines are courtesy of the Brown University Counseling Program.)

---

some question about the severity of the problem should be referred to a mental health professional. Develop a relationship with mental health professionals during the planning stages of your program. Be sure you know who is "on call" and when, and don't be afraid to consult directly with that individual as part of the referral process. Your experience and thoughts about a particular case can be helpful to the professional who subsequently takes it on.

The potential for coming across a problem that's out of your league again points to the need for a competent, knowledgeable supervisor within the school administration. Guidance counselors and school psychologists are usually the best choice, but even a supportive teacher who is familiar with your project and with the backup resources you have amassed can play this crucial role.

Getting Administrative Support

The idea of setting up a peer counseling program can sometimes be tough for school administrators to swallow. They are understandably nervous both about your ability to provide "psychological services" to students and about the legal ramifications of supporting a peer counseling program if something bad should happen to a counselee. Describe in detail your plans for the program and demonstrate that you have thoroughly researched and spoken with mental health professionals who are willing to serve as a backup network for the program. (They can be found in the yellow pages and through local professional organizations, and by enlisting the help of school guidance counselors and your parents to contact professionals they know personally.) Rally faculty support, particularly from guidance counselors.

Explain to administrators that, with proper training, peer counselors are often the most capable resources for helping friends and classmates. They understand the social environment, and their friends trust them. Just about every student will approach another student with a problem before he or she will go to a teacher, parent, religious leader, or sibling. Peer counseling gives friends the skills to help one another.

Some administrators may question whether students have enough training to "counsel" other students. Explain that peer counselors do not actually "counsel," that is, give advice. They listen and facilitate understanding. To illuminate, you could use the following metaphor: A teacher can sit beside a pianist and help her prepare for a recital, but only the pianist can perform during the actual recital. Similarly, a peer counselor can help classmates explore and clarify their thoughts and feelings about a problem, but only the classmates can live their own lives and take responsibility for their actions.

Also, think about giving your program a name that doesn't include the word counseling. In Romania, for example, peer counseling is known as "communication skills training," and trained peer counselors are recognized as members of the "Trust Network."

Remind administrators that peer counseling offers a sense of caring and community to the school. Fundamentally, peer counseling consists of basic communication skills, useful in all situations. People appreciate when you listen to them; they enjoy the attention and respect shown when you are an effective listener. This sense of caring within your school and home unites people in a greater feeling of community. For instance, at Johns Hopkins University in 1994, a bright, pretty, young first-year student committed suicide. The entire student population—even students not acquainted with her—was upset. Meanwhile, the student administration was fearful that another student might soon commit a "copycat" suicide. JHU's peer counselors, trained in how to recognize and refer suicidal students and how to comfort those who were upset, immediately met and offered their services. They set up impromptu rooms in the first-year dorms and made themselves available around the clock in person and by telephone. No imitation suicide took place.

Selecting Students to Be Trained

Think carefully about how to select students for training in peer counseling. While most selection processes—applications, interviews, nominations, and so on—are useful, they have a downfall: Only accepted students get to learn these listening and life skills, and therefore the peer counselors may be viewed as an elite clique. Instead of selecting certain classmates, you may instead wish to develop ways to train all students interested in peer counseling. A core staff of counselors can offer training programs through which new core members can be selected but in which anyone can participate. Work with the administration to make it part of the school curriculum if you have enough interested students involved.

One thing you should strive for is a counseling group that "looks like" the student body. People are often more willing to discuss things with someone like themselves; for example, women are often more comfortable discussing certain issues with other women. At Brown University there are three types of counselors: In addition to the basic Resident Counselor program, the university has Minority Peer Counselors and Women's Peer Counselors. Although any counselee can go to any counselor to discuss any issue, the MPCs and WPCs have received additional training in certain areas that make them more appealing—and perhaps more useful—to certain counselees.

If you decide to select a group of students to be trained as peer counselors, important factors to consider are these:

1. *Time commitments.* Will the students have enough time to dedicate themselves to learning the skills of peer counseling?
2. *Enthusiasm and grades.* Do the students seem academically motivated enough to learn the skills? Or do they have other motivations (such as the desire to help others or a demonstrated talent for rapport with fellow students) that compensate for low school grades?
3. *Conduct.* Will the students be able to behave themselves appropriately while learning and then practicing peer counseling? Do you think they will be able to respect rules such as confidentiality?
4. *Openness to new ideas.* Will the students be open to new ideas, or will they be defensive of old ways of communicating and remain unwilling to evaluate the effectiveness of their own manners of communications?

Bringing 'em In

Your peer counseling program won't do any good unless people use it, but remember: Something like this takes a while to build public trust. Don't expect long lines on day one. Begin by advertising your program's strengths: the supportive environment, the referral system, and confidentiality. If students don't know where to go for help or are intimidated by the stigma that might be attached to seeking professional help, they can start by going to a peer counselor.

Creativity is the key. Think of colorful, unique ways to grab students' attention and convey the basics of peer counseling. Do a short, humorous skit in classrooms, such as a role play of a wolf who goes to peer counseling upset because her friends call her "the big bad wolf." Build a whole school assembly around it. Or contact local media for coverage of this "human interest" story.

Create flyers and posters advertising the program. Come up

with a catchy name: At JHU, it's "A Place to Talk." Brown has "Student-to-Student."

Perhaps most important, emphasize that peer counseling isn't just for (drum roll) *people with problems.* Send counselors into each classroom to explain that the program is just a group of people with "open ears," to chat with or discuss particular concerns. Talk about training as a chance to learn communication skills—the "anybody can do that" reaction will demystify your program, and the appeal may even encourage others to join.

If you've developed a successful program, think about ways to build on it. Maybe a peer mediation program or a peer counseling hotline for after-school hours. Expand your reach: Create a multischool peer counseling coalition in your town. This will enlarge your support network and your ability to positively affect the lives of your peers. The possibilities are as endless as your imagination and ability to develop your own resources.

Peer counseling is an asset to any school because none of us gets through our younger years without a host of little difficulties that would be made a lot easier by just talking them out with someone we can trust. By setting up peer counseling programs, students acknowledge their positive potential within society and their potential to help others. On the slow days and in moments of crisis, remember: You are helping someone who could be you.

22

Fighting Bias Where It Lives

NAHID ISLAM

Nahid Islam, twenty-one, has directed anti-racism educational programs at the high school and university level. She has written anti-bias curricula and was part of a group that received a grant from the Ontario government to produce a video about racism for police, schools, and libraries. Thanks are extended to Khyati Y. Joshi for her extensive input on drafts of this chapter.

As our communities become more and more diverse, problems with discrimination and bias are visible on a much broader scale. People of different backgrounds, cultures, and lifestyles affect our lives daily. With this new development we have come face-to-face with something that used to be easier to hide or ignore: prejudice. Even within ourselves we discover a world more based on preconceived ideas and stereotypes than we ever expected. Our generation has inherited a legacy of prejudice and discrimination; our youth and our newfound diversity give us a responsibility to confront these head-on—to educate ourselves, our peers, and our parents. Our voices and actions can serve to heal these scarred perceptions of society that still live in so many minds, young and old.

Bias and *prejudice* are easy words to throw around. Everyone knows they're part of our culture and societal fabric, and people spend as much time decrying them as they spend engaging in them. But just exactly what is it we're talking about? Many of us have biases—opinions or preferences formed without any reasonable justification—without even being consciously aware of their existence. They are reflected in our attitudes toward people of a different cultural background, religion, nationality, race, class, gender, sexual orientation, or disability. As we draw generalizations about certain ethnic or religious groups, we create stereotypes that impair our ability to evaluate particular situations and take actions objectively and accurately.

The reason I use the word *bias* instead of *prejudice* is that sometimes we're going up against "positive" preconceptions—the idea that Asians are good at math and science, for example, or the heavily European bias in how we tell our country's history. Such biases are no more "right" than negative stereotypes of African Americans or Jews. Really, they're nothing but patronizing.

Why is it important to eliminate biases? How do they affect our lives negatively? When held by the dominant group in a society, they shape societal structures and curtail the freedoms of minority groups through social, economic, cultural, political, or religious power. This leaves the smaller minority group with less control over its own affairs or over how it is seen in the "dominant culture." No one is unaffected: All groups have biased ideas about one another, about themselves, and about those who make up the dominant culture. At a more personal level, prejudice hinders our ability to interact honestly and openly with others and to learn as much as we can from personal encounters. If we are indeed a society that strives for justice and mutual respect, we must strike at the root of these problems by trying to eliminate bias.

Bias issues are sensitive ones that have special meaning to each individual. For minority young people it means trying to be accepted for who they are by a society that sometimes seems to feel that if they can't assimilate—or even if they do—they are too different to be accepted as equals. For a woman it means being respected and treated equally for the person she is. It's knowing that you, as an individual, will be treated by all people equally and with respect for your basic humanity. Compound discrimination (also called multiple discrimination) occurs when a person faces more than one form of systemic discrimination. I'm a good example. As a minority woman I face three kinds of bias: The assumptions made about me as a woman, the assumptions made about me as a

South Asian, and the assumptions made about me as a South Asian woman.

By using genuine emotional support and an experience-based learning process—such as through the workshops described below—bias can be treated and eliminated before it manifests itself as prejudice and forms the ugly face of discrimination.

Intuitively, we know where biases take root. It's not at neo-Nazi rallies or through ballot initiatives like California's "Prop 187"—those are the second step. Biases are born in the "little things" that we can ignore all too easily: crude racist and sexist jokes, the presence of words like "fag" in high school slang, the tendency of some science teachers to call on boys more often than girls. I can't even think how many times friends and I have talked about how our older relatives have made prejudiced comments without a second thought to their effect on the children listening.

Too often we let these comments slip by, forcing a smile even when we are the butt of the joke, because we're afraid to speak up. But it is especially important for us as young people to question those with whom we disagree. In silence there is no change, only acquiescence to the insidious growth of prejudice. For a long time I had the reputation of being overly sensitive because I always confronted the "little things," but I know I made my point and that I was respected for it later—sometimes years later.

The anti-bias fight starts within yourself. We all have biases, and recognizing them and trying to overcome them is imperative. Unlearning this kind of conditioning is an uphill battle, especially since we're often surrounded by those with similarly biased attitudes in school, at work, on television, and at home. If as anti-bias educators we do not begin by confessing that we, too, are biased, then we end up sounding holier-than-thou and changing no one. Only if we begin with introspection can we show others how to do the same.

The role of an anti-bias activist is to educate people on the attitudes and prejudices that may exist within their community and to help point out effective ways of treating and trying to eliminate them. Biases conjure up prejudice, which results in discrimination. As an anti-bias activist you must find effective means to recognize bias and establish a way to overcome it. You are an educator, but you cannot succeed if you tell people how to think. *The task of the anti-bias activist is to ask the questions that bring people to change their own ways of thinking.* You are encouraging an evolution, not conveying a revelation.

There are two different things that an anti-bias activist needs to know to work effectively. The first is background on the issues, an understanding of the historical and social aspects of prejudice and how that history continues to play itself out today. You also need to know how to convey your ideas effectively, which is a combination of interpersonal skills and workshop design. As a friend of mine advised me, "You need to teach them, and you need to teach them how to teach." There is much more out there that you should know. Read the work of Gandhi and of Gates (Henry Louis, not Bill), of Jonathan Kozol and Edward Said and others. Discover the history of civil and indigenous rights movements. Also, get hold of handbooks on workshops and draw on the resources of existing programs such as the National Conference's nationwide "Anytown" program.

Prepare

Learn what you're up against. In the words of the Chinese philosopher Sun-tzu, "If you know neither yourself nor your enemy, the battle is lost before it has been joined. If you know only yourself or only the enemy, for every one battle you win you will lose another. If, however, you know both yourself and your enemy, your victory will be assured."

When doing anti-bias work, you will find varying degrees of support in your community. In metropolitan areas where the populace is more diverse, it will be easier to find allies and assemble a diverse coalition to work with. In smaller cities and rural areas, you may face more resistance. Sometimes you will find people who pay only lip service to diversity; they may ignore you or actively resist you when push comes to shove. Unless there has been some kind of racial incident that brought latent prejudices to light, you can expect to be told that you're making an issue out of nothing, that there's really no problem. Don't make mountains out of molehills, but if there's a mountain, call it a mountain. Also remember that sometimes even molehills need something done about them.

Because issues of prejudice are so emotional, it can be very difficult to get the kind of support you need to start an anti-bias program. School officials may not support you because they don't want to think that "racism" is something that's happening on their turf. You may feel an undercurrent of racial tension in your high school. You may go to the cafeteria and see "color lines." But if you go to a school official to talk about prejudice or racism in the school, you need more. Try to gather a diverse group of students to present the idea. It's harder to argue with a student delegation that represents all the school's ethnic affiliations. Get faculty support if you can; the image of a "mature adult" watching over your efforts is a comforting one for administrators. Or do what a friend of mine did in her small community: She conducted a survey among students, asking specific questions about race issues and the school's efforts to deal with them. When she came back with a lot of negative responses showing that more needed to be done, she had the "ammunition" for her approach to the principal.

Beware of school officials who try to keep your organization from prospering beyond the few obligatory meetings and bake sales. Don't fall into this trap. Consult with faculty and students, develop a solid plan, bring in community support when you can, and have a plan that you can adjust—even taking it completely outside of the school system—if you face strong opposition. If your cause is true and you have a concrete plan before you encounter your challenges, you'll be one step ahead.

Tools of Change: Workshops

Workshops are where it's at in the field of anti-prejudice activism. They encourage people of diverse backgrounds to come together and discuss bias issues in a safe, confidential atmosphere under the guidance of facilitators who guide the discussion by offering questions, not answers. As an interactive process based on experience (for some people their only chance to experience real dialogue with members of different ethnic groups) it helps people work through stereotypes and consider the root of their prejudices. Conducted in a small-group setting, workshops encourage participants to build on the ideas and experiences of those around them and enable emotion to be part of reasoned discussion.

As you prepare a workshop program, be realistic about what you can expect. Know that you will not magically transform racists into multiculturalists. More often you will leave people (including yourself) thinking about and questioning the beliefs they may not even have realized they had. But this is a victory. Every time you discourage racist or sexist attitudes and encourage introspection and dialogue, you have taken our world another step in the right direction. (That's why many people call our work "prejudice reduction.") You probably have also changed for the better how those people will act when they face challenges of intercultural communication.

Designing a Workshop

Tailor the design of your workshop to your audience and your goals. Use age-appropriate examples and exercises. Know whether you are trying only to encourage dialogue during the workshop program or also build a basis for future communication—like if you're bringing a pilot anti-bias program into a school that wants to develop its own. If it's the latter, you're going to want to incorporate into your workshop a discussion about "what's next," how participants can use what they learned in a concrete, constructive manner in addition to encouraging participants to share their differences and reflect on their experiences with prejudice.

Use resource materials like short video clips ("Listening Through The Walls," "The Colours of Racism," and "Prejudice: Dividing the Dream" are three good ones) and handouts to give participants some shared information to discuss. Writing exercises, in which people respond on paper to questions about their experiences with bias and then use their responses as a basis for the discussion, can also bring out ideas that people would otherwise be unwilling to share. For children, drawing exercises can serve the same purpose: "What does racism look like?"

WORDS OF WISDOM

Shedding Prejudice and Seeking Potential

It is never too late to give up our prejudices. No way of thinking or doing, however ancient, can be trusted without proof. What every body echoes or in silence passes by as true today may turn out to be falsehood tomorrow, mere smoke of opinion. . . . What old people say you cannot do try and find that you can. . . . Age is no better, hardly so well, qualified for an instructor as youth, for it has not profited so much as it has lost. . . . Practically, the old have no very important advice to give to the young, their own experience has been so partial. . . . I have lived some thirty years on this planet, and I have yet to hear the first syllable of valuable or even earnest advice from my seniors. . . . Here is life, an experiment to a great extent untried by me; but it does not avail me that they have tried. If I have any experience which I think valuable, I am sure to reflect that this my Mentors said nothing about.

—Henry David Thoreau,
Walden

In some of the workshops I have run, we played a cultural awareness game where two or three people left the room and everyone else "invented" a culture with certain traditions and taboos. When those who left the room came back, they had to figure out what was going on to understand why everyone around them looked horrified when they crossed their legs or that touching elbows was a sign of affection. All this without verbal communication. The game was an effective way of showing how arbitrary some of our own cultural norms are, and it encouraged discussion about how it feels to be the outsider. This can lead into excellent discussions about what it's like to be an immigrant in North America. Most workshop participants will never be immigrants, but in this small way they can experience similar emotions for a moment. Empathy is a big step toward understanding and respect.

Another good idea is to keep things lively by varying the "size" of the discussion, usually by breaking the group up into pairs or small groups to discuss a certain question or by using role playing to encourage participants to adapt others' attitudes (or what they think others' attitudes are). There are dozens of great workshop games that can be adapted to all age groups and specific situations. Ask your school guidance counselor, your county or state's anti-racism office, or a local firm's diversity trainer for ideas. Also be sure to check out *The Nature of Prejudice, Open Minds to Equality,* and other texts under the subjects "multicultural education" and "conflict resolution," and the resources of the National Conference, for ideas.

Always screen your resources before you use them. Materials that convey the wrong message or are just too cheesy to take seriously can spell disaster. Focus on content: If you like what something is saying, you can deal with a little cheese. This isn't the Academy Awards. And make sure that your videos aren't too long. Shoot for something under half an hour so there's still plenty of good discussion time before people need a break. As interesting as John Singleton's feature-length films are, they don't belong at the front end of a diversity workshop.

Puzzle Pieces

One great thing about workshops is that they can stand alone or be fit into all kinds of formats—from a one-day anti-prejudice event to a week-long diversity training program. Many high schools in North America have had successful one- to three-day anti-bias conferences that combined workshops with lectures and inspirational speakers, cultural events, and social time. Have some situations where everyone is together—using keynote speakers and cultural presentations—and others where small-group dialogue is encouraged.

Start with introductory exercises and identity games. Bring together a diverse panel of local figures to talk about how these diversity issues affect your community. Always allow time for "Q and A," so that even your keynote speakers get involved in the dialogue and participants consistently feel there is a chance for their voices to be heard. Allow for emotional "down time" as well. Provide breaks and try to have some kind of physical-movement game around midday to serve as stress release and give people renewed energy for later workshops.

Be sure to have a "what's next" component to the event. If you're dealing with a racially tense community, encourage panelists to talk about what can be done to alleviate the problem. At the end of the day, start people on a simple project. Even if it's just drawing thematic posters to hang up around school, it will give the participants something concrete to outlast the event itself.

If you have several days, construct a program that encourages individual initiative and leadership. An excellent example is the Canada Youth for Social Justice Conference held annually by the Oxford Committee for Famine Relief (OXFAM) in London, Ontario. The conference focuses on different social justice issues not only by bringing together speakers and workshop programs but also by involving participants in hands-on research. In the course of the week-long conference, each participant is asked to take responsibility for a part of the week's curriculum, which he or she researches in the evening and presents side by side with conference facilitators. By week's end all have had a chance to "strut their stuff" as well as to participate in more standard programs. By leaving the participants and supporters with something tangible—resources and experience as well as ideas—the OXFAM conference encourages them to continue the work and to develop new initiatives of their own themselves.

In the workshop itself, it is important to foster an atmosphere where participants feel able to share openly. Remember, bias issues are highly emotional and can sometimes be embarrassing as well. Begin by explaining who you are, your role as facilitator, and your agenda so that participants know you will participate and coordinate the workshop. Then ask them to introduce themselves and find out what they hope to get out of the discussion. If there is time, have one person act as "secretary" to record these comments. (It's especially important when working with young people that you encourage them to "take ownership" of the agenda by taking this kind of active role.) Look at the list and think to yourself how you can order these concerns to create a good flow of dis

SUCCESS STORY

March of Justice

When she got to high school in 1993, Tracy Schramm of Yankton, South Dakota, assumed she would be able to continue to play the saxophone in the school marching band as she had in middle school. Instead Schramm, who uses a wheelchair, was told that high school band was "too competitive" and that her condition would pose a danger to other band members.

The school district argued that since band was an extracurricular activity and Schramm would be able to fulfill her fine arts credit requirement by taking classes during the school day, they did not have to allow her to participate in band. Unable to convince the school to change their policy despite having the moral support of fellow band members and others in the community, Schramm filed a complaint with the federal Office of Civil Rights.

With the help of a lawyer from South Dakota Advocacy, a public-interest law firm, Schramm convinced the OCR to find her school district in violation of the Rehabilitation Act of 1973 and the Americans with Disabilities Act of 1990. It took nine months and thousands of pages of legal maneuvering, but the school district eventually capitulated, agreeing to a settlement that not only allowed Tracy to take her place in the band but also instituted a policy stating that all future students with disabilities interested and able to participate in the marching band must be provided with an aide to push their wheelchairs and with other reasonable assistance. The case is the first of its kind in the nation and has set an important precedent for full participation by students with disabilities.

The culmination of the case was a relief for Tracy, who has since filled her time by developing a school recycling program and participating in academic teams, as well as marching in the band. All the months of legal wrangling and working with adult advocates was worth it, though.

"Now I know they can never do this to any other student down the line," says Tracy, who began marching with the band again in the fall of 1994. "That"s the most important thing."

cussion, then use the list to guide your questioning so the conversation touches on the group's areas of concern.

Find out what the group knows about bias issues. Most people today are aware of "the diversity thing," and many may have some idea of the philosophical arguments behind multiculturalism. Encourage these people to express their understanding of why this kind of dialogue is important. Remember who these people are so you can come back to them as possible peacemakers in a conflict situation. See if you can get a sense at the outset of what kind of group you're dealing with and how certain parallels might be drawn among different participants' experiences. Bringing out people's own stories of prejudice will be an important part of the workshop. The best way to do this is to offer some of your own; provide a model by sharing your experiences and feelings in the ways you hope participants will.

When arranging the seating for your workshop, make a circle without any table or other objects in the center. This helps break down two traditional settings—the teacher-student lecture setting and the confrontational debate setting—and encourages all participants to interact as equals.

Role of the Facilitator

As the facilitator—or better yet, co-facilitator with someone of a different background whom you know well—you are only a guide, not a leader. You need to keep the group "on topic," of course, and should come in with an outline of possible discussions and an arsenal of questions to keep things moving. But ultimately you guide discussion and use your questions to bring out ideas and thoughts that point people toward understanding. It's a very intuitive process, which is why it's often good to participate in workshops with experienced facilitators before trying to run your own.

What you can expect from participants depends on how participants for your workshop were selected. A "self-selecting" group—students who chose to participate—have already demonstrated interest and openness to the issues; your path will be easier. More challenging and more interesting is the experience of workshops where not everyone wants to be there. Many school-sanctioned anti-bias programs give teachers the chance to refer people to the program; this is when you're more likely to come face-to-face with heavy-duty prejudice and sometimes heavy-duty resentment about being there.

Because of the emotions that bias issues arouse, you need first and foremost to show emotional support for participants. Let them know through your words and actions that they can express themselves freely without fear of ridicule or retribution. Establish "safe space," a set of preestablished rules for personal interaction designed to create an atmosphere where people can speak freely (for more details, see the next chapter). And remind all participants that the principle of confidentiality—what's said in the room will not be repeated outside the room—is in full effect throughout the workshop. Convey to participants their responsibility for the workshop's success; confidentiality doesn't work unless it's agreed to unanimously. Also make it clear that you will be available privately after the workshop for people who are too uncomfortable to speak in the group, but try not to give people an easy out. Say you'll be available "for further discussion" or "follow-up."

It's important to show that you share the same fears, hopes, and aspirations as your participants. Throughout the course of the workshop there will be differences of opinion voiced, but make sure that all involved know that this is just that—a difference of opinion. Be sure to separate the personality from the activity. It is human nature for people to become defensive when they feel personally attacked. When a conflict seems to be brewing, encourage the group to respond rather than prolonging a dialogue between just two people.

Your authority as a facilitator comes from your knowledge of the topic and, more simply, from the fact that you are there as the facilitator. Age will often be part of that equation. I've found that an age difference of two or three years between you and the participants is ideal. You are close enough in age to be a peer to them but "older enough" to maintain respect and control with your demeanor alone. Introduce yourself to students as someone just like them in that you have experienced bias. Acknowledge your own biases as a first step to helping participants acknowledge theirs.

Find parallels among participants' stories and point these out to illustrate how thinking about one's own experiences can be part of understanding others'. When someone is describing a bias experience, listen respectfully but don't be afraid to interject questions that encourage them to think more about how the situation played itself out: "Why do you think he said that?" "How did that make you feel?" "What could you/he have done differently to prevent a conflict?" Encourage participants to "get inside the heads" of the people they have had confrontations with.

Bring your own experiences into the discussion when they're appropriate, especially when they're useful to show empathy with someone who has just told a difficult story. Be up front about where you're coming from. You cannot be afraid to share your own thoughts and feelings because if you won't, how can you expect them to? When they feel you holding back, they will start holding back. That's why facilitating is a game of both self-expression and self-control.

In situations of conflict we have a reflex to try to instantly reestablish tranquility. Resist this temptation if you feel that the thoughts and emotions that will be brought out by a higher-pitched discussion will be important or useful for the group. Never encourage conflict, of course, and don't ever let a shouting battle ensue, but when conflict begins to occur, think about how you can channel it constructively. Ask those who are speaking why they are angry and try to get them to verbalize the root of the problem. Sometimes when discussions become arguments, the people involved are not the only ones in the room who feel strongly about the issues at hand. Allowing a heated discussion to play itself out—keeping things under control with remarks like "Remember, we are here for a constructive discussion" or "Let's try to take the hostility out of this debate"—can be educational as long as the group returns to quietness and some sort of consensus by the end. In other words, it's fine as long as everyone can leave the room feeling that something was resolved and that peace was reestablished.

Whatever you do, do not attack participants even when you find their views repugnant. In one of the first workshops I ran, a woman of color in the group talked about her own experiences of bias but then said that Mexicans in her school deserved what they got. Unfortunately, I lost it. I rebuked her loudly and in no uncertain terms. By doing that I lost my legitimacy with the whole group by destroying the safety of the space and showing that I could not control my own emotions. Difficult as it is, you must keep your cool as a facilitator. When faced with very prejudiced remarks from a member of the group, respond again with questions: "Has anything like that ever happened to you? How did it make you feel?" "How do you think that person felt?" Usually, others in the group will get into the act, and you will be able to bring the person around to saying, "I guess I never looked at it that way before."

Watch out for "groupthink," where participants only express agreement because they feel they should "go along" and not question the consensus rather than being singled out for thinking differently. People who know that they are prejudiced, particularly those who don't see anything wrong with it but don't want to look like the bad guy, will often keep their mouths shut when put in a workshop situation. Encouraging these people to speak out by demonstrating a willingness to air all opinions will be an education for everyone and will give you a chance to get through to them. As always, focus on ideas and not individuals so the discussion can remain civil, and avoid vocal confrontations when it's possible to do so. (This also takes a little practice.)

Co-facilitating, running the workshop in tandem with another facilitator, can be very helpful. If you and your co-facilitator come from different backgrounds—one man and one woman, one European-American and one person of color—it will convey to the group that the leadership is not necessarily coming from a certain social or ideological position. By having a diverse pair of leaders, you will also enable more students to identify personally with you, and this will encourage them to speak out more. Co-facilitating is also a good way to train younger facilitators so they can learn by doing but not without a "safety net."

More than anything, that is the key to facilitating: getting participants to come to the right conclusions on their own by guiding the discussion with questions that bring out your point from members of the group. The great mistake of many cultural-encounter programs is that they try to force a certain ideology on participants. The only way to have a lasting effect on participants is for them to feel they came to their conclusions on their own. That's when you've changed a mind.

Other Paths

I've spent most of this chapter talking about workshops, because they're a central part of anti-bias work and represent the kind of interactive setting that I feel is best for what we're trying to do. But there are other kinds of anti-bias work you can do. Videos and speakers about anti-bias issues can stand alone and can often be a good way to introduce your school to the basic concepts. Cultural festivals can be a fun and informative adjunct to efforts to break down misunderstanding, particularly if you live in a "divided community" where people tend to associate only with members of their own ethnic or religious group.

You can also use the basic strategies of a community education campaign to bring bias issues onto the agenda. Postering, canvassing, and letters to the editor can bring the issue home to people in your community or school. These displays begin dialogue, which can help you either to develop interactive programs or simply to present your viewpoint "take it or leave it." Be creative.

In this short chapter, I've only been able to give you a cursory view of anti-prejudice workshops and other activities. I encourage you to seek resources such as the ones mentioned, to learn more about the issues that surround "bias" for people in your community and nation, and to attend organized prejudice reduction workshops before embarking on your own. You will develop your own perspective on the issues and your own style of effective leadership, and you will create anti-prejudice campaigns in your own community based on an understanding that no outsider could have. Know your limits but appreciate your capacity.

Always remember that you are, in your own way, making a difference just by getting the ball rolling. Nothing you try to accomplish is too little or too big. For every person who comes into contact with you, listens to what you have to say, and walks away from your program with new knowledge about these issues, you have created an enormous success. You cannot work miracles, but you can help change minds one at a time. And that will save our world.

23

Building Coalitions in Diverse Communities

MALIK YOBA

Malik Yoba, twenty-six, is a founding member of City Kids and star of the Fox Television series "New York Undercover."

Everyone knows that there's strength in numbers. What more and more people are starting to realize is that there's also strength in diversity, particularly for activists working for social change at the community level. Whatever you're trying to do—from stopping a local project with serious environmental consequences to increasing the peace in your school system—the more parts of your community that are represented in your campaign, the stronger you will be in political, moral, and numerical respects.

Let's start by defining the word "coalition." A coalition is a group of people representing different and diverse backgrounds, be they from different organizations or different ethnic or social groups within a certain area, who come together to address a particular issue. This focus on a goal is what gives coalitions their unique strength. Although each group represented in a coalition may have a different reason for being there, they are united by seeking the same end result. When you're organizing around a particular issue, look at how that issue will affect all the different groups around you and seek coalition with those who have an interest in the same outcome you're working toward—even if not for the same reasons. Ask these groups what the issue means to them and what they'd like to see done about it. This is the first step toward pulling together a working coalition.

Making Contact

So what if you're interested in coordinating efforts with a certain community—African-American residents of a particular neighborhood, "jocks" at your school, etc.—but don't know anyone that's part of it? Religious or social centers and cultural organizations are good places to start; approach clergy and administrators. Approaching schools in your area can be done through a student organization, parent groups, faculty, guidance counselors, or the principal. Mostly, just ask the people you know. In almost all cases you'll be able to find a personal contact, someone who knows someone in the group you're trying to reach. If you go in good faith, the right people will receive you with open arms. Trust in that, and don't give up if you don't make the right contact the first time.

Consider both official and unofficial leaders when you're looking for a broad spectrum of people. When I worked with City Kids, we would go into a school and meet with their leadership class, the "official" student leaders, and then ask who were the unofficial leaders of student opinion: the kids who were running people out the back door to cut class, the fashion kings and queens, the popular jocks. We'd bring all these students together in a classroom after school and say, "Listen, we're here to help you have a voice."

The most important part of organizing students is validating their needs and concerns. Young people aren't asked what they feel about things or to contribute. Instead, we're told what to do by older people, and then they wonder why they get no respect, why defying authority has become so appealing to young people in the 1990s. If you're reading this book and preparing to organize around a certain issue, you've already learned the value of what you have to contribute. Probably, you've had your concerns validated by caring parents or supportive teachers. Remember that everyone hasn't been so lucky, but if you bring that validation and attention to people who haven't gotten it before, you will be able to build a strong base of support that no one else even appreciated as a possibility.

I facilitated a one-day youth workshop program in Belize last year and began by asking the group, "How many of you believe the answer to Belize's problems will be found in this room?" Three of the seventy participants raised their hands. For the next five hours I took them through a process of self-discovery modeled after City Kids. We started with an introduction exercise involving physical movement: speak your name loudly and do a movement, and then everybody mimics you. This began a process of dialogue, of really looking at the issues facing Belize from the standpoint of how each individual could have an effect. We conducted an exercise designed to get people's internal creativity flowing by envisioning a magical world of their own creation and being guided through it by questions from the facilitator ("Now you're on the beach, and you see a box. What's in the box? What does it feel/smell/look like?" and so on). Then we divided the students into small groups and asked them to look at certain problems and come up with solutions that they themselves might be able to implement. By the end of the day more than sixty of those young people raised their hands when I again asked how many saw solutions for Belize's problems within that room. What an appreciation that gives of the power of team-building exercises to bring people to new ways of looking at their surroundings!

You and I need to be able to reach people where they are, socially as well as geographically. We may have these grand, utopian ideals, but unless we're willing to bring them to a level where people can understand them and where their own needs can be incorporated into the scheme, we're wasting our time. That's one of the reasons that City Kids has focused much of its effort on using the arts to educate. The City Kids repertory company goes into schools with a very hip music and dance production in order to reach kids through a medium they understand. This approach—bringing kids in through what appeals to them—makes the follow-up programs of workshops and student organizing that much more successful. We pull in more young people at the outset and give them the opportunity to proceed in the directions they decide are the most important.

Likewise, student organizers have a particular responsibility to understand how limited their own realm of experience is, and they need to learn from people they work with. You have no idea what another person's life is like until you ask them, and you may be very surprised to hear the answer. My story is a good example: As you sit and read this chapter, you know me as an author, an activist, and maybe as the star of "New York Undercover." I'm all those things, but do you know that when I leave the set and try to go home for lunch, I can't get a cab because to those who don't know me I'm just another dangerous young black man on the streets of New York?

These are not unusual experiences for young African Americans; my celebrity gives me the opportunity to talk about them. Your desire to work with me gives you the responsibility to learn. And that goes for everyone.

Eye of the Beholder

Perceptions and preconceptions are a part of life, and student organizing is no exception. We'd like to believe that our higher purpose gives us some immunity from being judged by where we come from or what we look like, but it's just not so. When building a diverse coalition, you need to anticipate the assumptions that members of various groups will make about each other and about you.

Try to understand where others are coming from and where you yourself are coming from as well. This doesn't mean making your own assumptions based on where someone lives or how she dresses. It does mean trying to see the world, yourself included, through their eyes—to "walk a mile in their moccasins," to quote the old saying. Issues of race, which I'll use as an example because they have greatly influenced my experiences, must be faced head-on.

Realize that whatever issue you're dealing with, no matter how "unracial" it seems to you, will have racial aspects for members of minority groups. If you're focused on some broad topic like the environment, seek the input of people from many backgrounds as you focus on your priorities. There's a perception among many minorities that white people will try to save the rain forest and the whales and the baby seals and just about everything but people. Right or wrong, that's the perception. If you want to bring a broad racial cross-section into your group, you need to focus on issues that matter to everyone in that group—environmental justice issues, urban environmental problems, and so on. If you're not ready to do that, think twice before trying to bring others in on your agenda. This will not only show that you're concerned about issues that are tangible to many minority groups, it will also smooth the path when you want to bring global issues like the rain forest into the picture. Remember that I'm focusing on race as an example here: Similar arguments apply to issues of gender, socioeconomic class, sexual orientation, age, and disability. Think how people with "a different demographic" from you will see you and your effort, and about how they would wish to be seen by you.

Organizing around bias issues can be a double-edged sword for minorities and whites alike. White groups going to African-American or Latino communities to develop an anti-racism program will often be met with a response like, "What do you know about it?" The answer is usually, "Not as much as you do, but I want to learn and to change things and I need your help." At the same time, minorities organizing around these issues may be accused of rocking the boat, making a mountain out of a molehill, or seeking "special privileges."

Face the Music

It's important for our generation to face racial issues head-on. America has spent too much time denying its own past, and a big part of organizing diverse communities includes acknowledging that many inequities have a basis that stretches far back in our country's history. Acknowledging these injustices—but not allowing them to limit the ways we shape the future—is step one.

The past few years have seen a real resurgence of "nationalism" in all parts of American society. The pride that people of color are now able to express in their backgrounds is an important thing.

But activists have to remember that we have no more right than anyone else to define our allies in terms of their skin color or religious affiliation. When we don't want to hear from other people anymore, we become the losers. Cool out a little bit and recognize that there are allies out there. Seek them out wherever you find them, even when they "look like" what you think you're fighting. Pride taken to the point of exclusivity serves no one; in the long run it will only hurt you and the goals you think you're striving for.

Tokens Are for the Subway

Obviously, questions of public image are a part of why you're trying to pull together a diverse coalition. The appearance of leaders from many backgrounds will strengthen your legitimacy with all the communities represented in your group. There's nothing wrong with this as long as it is a by-product and not a goal. Unless all participants are equally engaged in the planning, execution, and outcome of the work—and are not just there to "add some color" to your press photos—you're engaging in tokenism. This kind of race consciousness has no place in student activism and will eventually lead to the unpleasant dissolution of your coalition when members get tired of being nothing more than their skin color.

As an organizer, you need to be aware that people who are minorities within the group may begin to feel like tokens even if that thought never crossed your mind. Make it clear that these individuals are equals within the group by showing neither negative nor positive preferences: Don't shut them out of decision-making but also don't patronize or label them by forever seeking "the black angle" or "the Latino voice." Whether you're doing this out of ignorance or out of hypersensitivity about racial issues, it serves no one. No well-informed view is is more or less important than—or qualitatively different from—any other.

You need to be very up front about not wanting participants to see themselves as anything less than full and equal members. Be honest and build trust by saying, "What will it take for you not to feel like a token?" Listen openly to the answer and show

SUCCESS STORY

A City-wide Environmental Coalition

It began with just two students who traveled from their native Tulsa, Oklahoma, to an environmental summit in Connecticut in 1993. The pair, who came from different high schools, decided to increase their own groups' effectiveness by networking across community lines, so they founded ECCO, the Entire Community Conservation Organization, which brings together students from all over Tulsa on environmental projects of local and global importance. In its first year ECCO helped foster ecology clubs at elementary and middle schools, and engaged in a number of direct-action projects—from cleanups at local prairie conservation areas to helping local officials post signs marking protected nesting sites of least terns along the Arkansas River.

Last year ECCO organized an Earth Day benefit concert called "Earthwaves '95." In planning the event, the group came up against a number of obstacles. Because of their youth, questions about liability almost kept them from finding a site. Local businesses were reluctant to contribute to the project because the group was not a certified nonprofit entity. They also allowed themselves just three months of lead time—not nearly enough for a project of such scope. Just as the group was preparing to accept failure, one organizer was introduced to a local radio personality through a mutual friend, the city's recycling coordinator. The station, Tulsa's Z-104.5 The Edge, took ECCO under its wing and used its contacts to arrange for the concert to take place at a local amphitheater. By endorsing the project and offering technical assistance, The Edge was able to convince the ampitheater's owners to back the concert. The publicity generated for the group by the radio station encouraged other local sponsors to come forward, and soon even local bands were asking for the chance to play in the concert.

The concert raised more than $15,000, which was distributed to the Nature Conservancy (which had backed the group with a small contribution and "turned a profit" on their investment), Trees for Life, and disaster relief for victims of the Oklahoma City bombing. The disbursements were announced at a series of press conferences that further increased the group's visibility. Perhaps even more important, the concert raised local awareness of environmental issues, so much so that more than one hundred attendees stayed around after the concert to clean up the area. Plans are already under way for "Earthwaves '96."

Also important is the role ECCO has played in giving young people of all backgrounds the chance to exchange ideas and work together on ecological issues. The group meets weekly at a local coffeehouse, making it very accessible to students throughout the community. In the words of a magazine article about the group, "Membership is easy: Simply show up at Java Dave's Coffee Shop near 31st and Peoria . . . every Wednesday night at six."

---

that you respect those needs. Be prepared to be hurt or taken aback by negative views of how things are working. As part of this discussion, make it clear that you may make diplomatic mistakes within and beyond the group but that they are not meant with malice.

As an activist of color working in a diverse group, I can choose to be either an individual or a "representative." It's always just me who's talking, but because of who I am, I have the chance to speak for a large group of people—African Americans and particularly African-American men—who don't always get a voice. When I'm comfortable being a representative of people like me, it helps me feel the strength to speak up even when I am the only black man in the group. But just as often I am speaking simply as Malik, giving one person's opinion. This is a hard difference to explain, but you'll get a feel for it as time goes on.

Or take the example of a friend of mine, who is the only Hindu grad student in her school's religion department. Is she the token Hindu, or has she been given the chance to represent and educate others about her faith? At one time or another she has felt like both. It's important to make clear to all participants that they are only representatives of people beyond themselves if they want to be. Ultimately, it should be their personal contribution that the group wants to hear.

It's a reflex for someone who is feeling like a token to want to run away. Remind this person and yourself of the greater good. Make an appeal not on behalf of the group or of yourself but on behalf of the goal that you have set out to reach.

Creating Safe Spaces

An important part of opening up your group to this kind of brutally honest dialogue is establishing safe space to air these issues in a constructive manner. "Safe space" refers to a way of organizing roundtable discussions in your group based on an agreed-upon set of rules regarding conduct. I will give the basics of safe space here, but for a more thorough set of guidelines check out City Kids' forthcoming handbook. Safe space is especially useful when working with diverse groups of students, both as a program designed to foster dialogue and as a tool to aid in group dynamics.

The goal of safe space is to overcome participants' unease about how and what they can talk about, about what risks they can take and what kind of response they can expect from their peers. The first step is to establish the Laws of the Group, within which everyone will feel free to participate fully in whatever is being discussed. Use a blackboard or big pieces of paper to create two lists: "We agree to . . ." and "We will not accept . . ." The first list may include things like "not interrupt," "call people what they want to be called [names and racial categories]," and "keep what's said here confidential." The second may include "personal attacks" and "name-calling" or even "gum chewing," if you're so inclined—whatever it takes for all participants to feel they can speak freely.

Once you've established the Laws of the Group, let them be the boss. The laws are the strength from which the facilitator's authority must grow. The role of the facilitator is not to enforce but to remind the group of its own commitments. If you are the facilitator, be firm in your application of the rules but remember that your voice is more that of the group conscience than of some kind of police officer. The criteria for the facilitator to ask people to leave should also be preestablished so that no one feels unjustly excluded.

The other crucial guideline for safe space—and, it seems to me, for any kind of group meeting—is that anything said should be in the interest of uplifting the group and moving toward its goals. The word "constructive" should always fit in front of the word "criticism." Extraneous discussions also have no place in safe space.

One guideline I always urge groups to follow is to use language that personalizes statements to the speaker. Rather than making possibly unfair generalizations, begin opinion statements with "I think" or "in my opinion." When responding to someone else's remarks or actions, use the structure "I feel [emotional response] when you [other person's statement or action] because [reason]." An example: "I feel unfairly judged when you talk about suburban kids as spoiled because the reality is that we just have a different set of problems and needs." Then go on and explain what you mean.

Dealing with Conflict

Of course, all these guidelines cannot prevent conflict. People will get offended, and no amount of preemptive effort will prevent that. When conflict occurs, bring the group away from the point of conflict for a brief period. Allow people a chance to cool down by stopping for a moment of quiet reflection. Seek a way to talk through the conflict or, barring that, to agree to disagree in order to move forward. "How can we come to consensus and get back to the goals that brought us together?" Deal with the problem directly and allow people to express their positions (within the bounds of the Laws of the Group). If the discussion becomes heated, to cool things down go to the peacemakers of the group—those individuals whose voice can bring on an air of conciliation or the usually quiet people who may wish to express an opinion but are intimidated by the conflict.

If someone storms out as a result of the conflict, talk to that person later the same day. If necessary, arrange a meeting with group leaders, come up with some mediation scheme, or orchestrate a group apology—whatever it takes to bring the person back to the group as a constructive participant. Don't just ignore the problem in the hopes that it will go away. Such sores fester, and need to be treated as soon as possible.

The advantage of "safe space" strategies is that they can be used in dialogue-oriented projects—for example, bringing diverse groups of students together in a racially strained school—and also to keep regular groups on track. It becomes a tool for dealing with issues of group dynamics outside "your issue." Participants who need to discuss something can "ask for safe space" during or after a meeting, or it can be made part of weekly meetings to head off conflict before it occurs.

Bringing together diverse, sometimes antagonistic groups within your school or community is not an easy thing to do. "Coalition building" is a facile phrase for something that can be a complex process of diplomacy and power-sharing. It means taking risks: trusting the people you're working with when you're not sure if you should or when you're not sure that they trust you; showing a commitment to focus past differences when it means having the chance to achieve a shared goal; reaching out at a time when groups in your community may be pulling apart; establishing open lines of communication through a sea of social static. It is an act of moral courage as much as one of planning and coordination. Most of all, it is an active process and not a passive one—psychologically, ethically, and logistically.

The process—as with all that we try to do to make this world a better place—is neither easy nor short. But keep your eyes on the prize. It's worth it.

24

Bringing the World Inside: The Value of International Exchange

VIRGINIA ROBBINS

Virginia Robbins is the former coordinator of the ONEIS International Peace Camp and a member of the founding board of the Santa Barbara-Yalta sister cities association.

An American, a Mexican, a Japanese, and an Israeli walk into a pizzeria. Sounds like the first line of a bad joke, but for me it was the beginning of an evening I still remember fondly. The people I've met and the things I've learned through participation in several international exchange programs and the Sister Cities programs of Santa Barbara, California, are emotional treasures and educational wellsprings. What course in "modern diplomacy" can teach as much as a summer in Russia? How many documentaries on the Middle East peace process can compare to sitting down in your living room with a Palestinian and hearing what things are really like in east Jerusalem?

There are few experiences more rewarding than the chance to share your culture with someone from a different place and to learn about their cultural and geographic roots. International exchange gives us all the chance to convey America—not McDonald's or Hollywood, the crap that television sends to all corners of this otherwise beautiful planet, but the real places and experiences that characterize our lives and form our ideals—to someone from abroad and to learn about how things are done in another country. No one has more or less to learn about others, just the basic human need to revel in the sharing of oneself, of understanding and being understood.

There is so much more to know about the world than you can get from the Associated Press and CNN. As citizens of this shrinking world, we have a responsibility to learn about the humanity behind the headlines and, just as important, about the billions of people who aren't in the headlines but still have human dreams and needs and fascinating things to show us. Don't think that you have to be sitting across from Bosnians or Rwandans to learn about how the world works. In the 1980s I worked with an organization that brought together Soviet and American children through summer theater programs. One of the wisest things that organization ever did was bring in students from other countries as well, so the Soviets and Americans could learn not only about each other but also about the Poles, Dutch, and Nicaraguans whose countries were caught up voiceless in the superpower conflict.

To learn about others is to better understand ourselves as well. One program I worked with several years ago distributed with its host-family instructions an essay called "The Values Americans Live By." It was a description of Americans "from the outside," contradictions and all—the view of ourselves that we can gain by bringing the world into our living room for a look around. Through international exchange we learn not only about Greek cuisine or South African politics but also about the phenomenon of difference. We learn the strategies of intercultural communication, strategies that will be demanded of us every day of our lives.

Don't fool yourself. Inviting a handful of Israelis and Palestinians to your sleepy town or bustling metropolis will not solve the conflict in the Middle East. But it will give you and your neighbors a chance to hear firsthand the real concerns of people in the region. And if all goes well, it will probably earn you an invitation "back" to your guests' home country. There is something very comforting in the fact that after my years of working on projects like this, I have a warm welcome waiting for me in almost every country in Europe.

SUCCESS STORY

Passing on the Wisdom

With two global environmental youth summits under its belt in just a few years, a group of high school students in Loveland, Colorado, has brought together more than five hundred teens from thirty-one countries to discuss and organize around ecological issues. Nearly two years of planning went into each event—the first in 1993 and the second in 1995—with more than three dozen students organizing into committees, contacting foreign embassies and local businesses for assistance and sponsorship, and pulling together a speakers' list that included some of the world's biggest environmental leaders.

The diverse, multiage group benefited from a very supportive school, which provided a two-room outbuilding with its own communication equipment; the group also received assistance from another high school club, VERTERRA, in suburban Chicago. The connection between these two groups came through their teacher sponsors, the brothers Joe and Chris Fontana, who made sure communication was maintained between the groups and played the role of "responsible adults" when it came to issues of liability. The students raised nearly $200,000 from more than a dozen corporate sponsors and provided travel scholarships for many students from the Third World.

The 1995 summit expanded on the 1993 event by bringing together students from forty states and thirty foreign countries. The summit organizers incorporated many facets of activism into the one-week event, dividing participants' time among issue-oriented speakers, workshops with a creative or activism-oriented focus, an "Eco-Expo" with environmental products and information from around the world, Buckminster Fuller's "World Game," nature outings, and a rally at the Western Hemisphere Economic Summit in Denver.

Continuity also played an important role in the students' ability to learn from and improve on the first conference. The 1995 event was organized largely by juniors and seniors who had been peripherally involved in organizing the 1993 event. Likewise, the small army of younger Loveland students involved in 1995's summit are already developing plans for another one in 1997.

These experiences are gifts you can bring to your family, school, and community by organizing an international exchange. This kind of project is usually the work of huge organizations like the American Field Service (AFS) and Youth For Understanding (YFU), but they can be developed on a small scale by individuals like yourself. All it takes is plenty of advance planning, some creativity in developing contacts abroad, a dose of cultural sensitivity, and a willingness to wade through some red tape.

Establish a Coherent Vision

Think about the character of exchange you want to create; in other words, begin by defining why it is you're bringing someone of a certain background into your community. There's nothing wrong with international exchange for its own sake, of course, and you will learn plenty from it. But if you're going to put a lot of your time into a project like this, think about the bigger picture: Have a vision beyond just meeting and talking. Do you want to learn about what's happening in a certain global "hot spot"? Do you want to bring together students dealing with similar issues, such as human rights, fostering democracy in central Europe, or development-related ecological crises? The answers to these questions will determine not only what countries you'll be trying to bring students from but also what organizations you work through. For example, the Brazilian embassy may not be much help in reaching young people who face the dangers of government-backed violence against street children, but the Brazilian Street Children's Movement and its U.S. contact, the National Child Rights Alliance, probably would.

The "reasons" for your exchange will also point you toward certain types of events: having your guests speak to local schools, convening a panel of academics and diplomats on a certain issue, or coordinating the exchange with an environmentally oriented direct action in your own community, for example. At the same time, don't make your issue all there is to the exchange: Take your South African friend to the mall and the movies as well as involving him in anti-prejudice projects and speaking engagements in your community.

Find something that your school and community will support with enthusiasm; that will strengthen your ability to get financial backing from the government and local businesses. This could mean tailoring your project idea to current events—the reason that Soviet-American programs were so huge in the mid-1980s—or focusing on something special about your community. You might want to focus on a certain industry, bringing in people from a foreign city with the same economic base. Or, inspired by a strong local ethnic group, you could develop a project that brings young people from a certain country together with a large pool of first- and second-generation immigrant youths in your town. Or find another creative angle, like the somewhat morbid decision of some Harrisburg, Pennsylvania, residents to link up with Hiroshima and Nagasaki in the wake of the 1979 Three Mile Island nuclear accident.

Don't play the role of savior. Don't try to "save a refugee" or play cultural or religious missionary to some poor heathen. These kinds of things are the height of cultural disrespect and have no place in a progressive movement.

Essentials

International exchange programs are very resource intensive. To create a successful program you'll need to budget a lot of *time.* The challenges you can expect include finding and establishing a relationship with your would-be guests, filing visa applications, dealing with other bureaucracy and paperwork on both ends, and communicating internationally via letter, phone, or e-mail (even without a language barrier!). Unforeseen challenges could be anything from a last-minute illness, flare-up of a regional conflict, or just long delays in the standard processes. Some years back a friend of mine was working to bring a Russian student to his high school for a month. He planned nine months in advance and still didn't get all the paperwork through in time—the trip was postponed from the spring of his junior year to the fall of his senior year.

This is an extreme example, but if you want to be safe, give yourself about a year of lead time. Every country and organization is different; consult with people who know the kind of paperwork you will face and how much time you'll need to wade through the bureaucracy.

International exchange is one of those fields where you have to be sure to "dot all your i's and cross all your t's." Speak to people familiar with the country in question to find out what kind of diplomatic issues (read "delays") your guest may face. Also, give a call to the State Department in Washington, D.C., which has a desk for practically every country in the world, and ask for the full list of rules and regulations that you and your guest will have to adhere to. Believe me, there are some pretty arcane ones out there. Ask the same of the country's embassy in Washington.

Then submit all your forms—and wait. If things seem to be taking way too long (a phrase you'll have to define with the help of people who know), start pestering. Sometimes only tenacity—the kind that gnats exhibit on hot summer nights—will get the people who process visas to push your papers across the desk.

Essential number two is *money*. There are fees on this end, fees on that end. The plane fare. The thirty-buck cab ride from Kennedy Airport to Manhattan. Also remember the peripheral costs: Telephone and fax communication with your friend in Bolivia will eat away your allowance in short order. There will also be incidental expenses, for which you'll want to have a few hundred dollars as a "slush fund" to draw on as needed. Depending on where your guest is coming from, he may also need some spending money for his time in the United States. Seek help from local service clubs and ethnic associations, your school and local government, and anyone else who will benefit from the exchange. If your guest will be speaking at several high schools, ask each for a small honorarium to help defray costs. Schools that can't even cough up $100 belong at the bottom of your priority list when planning your guest's itinerary.

Try some creative projects that get a lot of students involved in the exchange—a school-wide service project to raise funds, for example. My friend who brought over a Russian student coordinated the exchange with his school system's "international education week." As part of the lead-up to the event, he received permission from the elementary school principal to send home a letter with each student asking parents to let the student do "a simple job around the house" to earn one dollar toward their Russian "friend's" plane fare. And he covered it, with a few bucks to spare.

During the big span of time between submitting all the forms and your guests' triumphant arrival, flesh out their itinerary. Go back again to more schools and organizations where they could speak. Pull more people into your coalition or get more local students signed up for the cultural weekend.

Create a diverse itinerary for your guests. No one wants just to be shuttled from speaking engagement to speaking engagement. Program plenty of down time, especially in the first few days when jet lag may give them some pretty weird hours. Sprinkle liberally with fun but make it safe fun. You have a responsibility to return your new friends unharmed to their families. Avoid the "wild life" and never involve your international guests in anything illegal, even something as apparently harmless as a beer with your high school friends. Consequences for noncitizens involved in illegal activity can be very serious. More than that, it's not right and it's not necessary.

Personal Diplomacy

This chapter is not about how to treat your guest and overcome cultural misunderstandings. These are important things to learn, however, and you should encourage individuals who will be hosting foreign guests to check out materials available from the National Council for International Visitors and other material on cross-cultural understanding—and, of course, to read up on the recent history of their guests' home country.

Remember that your guests are no more representatives of their country's government than you are of yours. Remind others of this, particularly at forums where your guests will be asked questions. There's nothing more embarrassing than having a zealot in the audience criticize your Indian guest for the caste system or demand justification for Pearl Harbor from your speaker from Japan.

It can be tough to strike a balance between addressing crucial issues and shielding your guests from confrontations. Ask your guests what kind of interaction they are comfortable having and try to guide discussion in that direction when you are facilitating an event or hosting a dinner. Remind participants in roundtable discussions or "Q and A" periods that diplomacy is key and your guests have graciously given their time to the group. Watch body language: If a guest is clearly becoming uncomfortable, go to people who you know will be asking "safe" questions or cut the session short.

After your guests have returned home, try to orchestrate some follow-up projects or events that "cement" the visit in your community's memory. Have students, particularly younger ones, write thank-you letters. Think about what kinds of things could be built upon the visit: an aid program to your guests' rural school in Africa, a pen pal project, or another exchange that involves "the other side" from a region in conflict.

Establishing Long-term Relationships

Another exciting way to bring the world into your community is by establishing a long-term relationship with a town or city in another country. This kind of program, called a "twinning" or "sister city" project, involves a serious and long-term commitment of time and energy. If you're thinking about creating a twinning project, contact Sister Cities International near Washington, D.C., and ask for a copy of their book *Your City and the World: A Sister City Handbook.* SCI specifically asks that groups thinking about twinning contact them at the outset to avoid overlap with existing sister cities projects, and because they maintain files on foreign cities that are actively looking for U.S. "twins."

Sister cities projects can lead in many exciting directions. There are opportunities for school-to-school exchange, professional contact, cultural and artistic programs, and even pen pal projects. You can exchange e-mail and videos with your "twins," local physicians can host the other communities' medical students, or you can organize a reciprocal sports or theatrical exchange. Anything—from environmental projects to ham radio—can be made even more fun and exciting by coordinating them with your foreign counterparts.

The idea of sister cities is based on a program of international town affiliations begun after World War II by President Dwight Eisenhower. Hundreds of cities are involved, and some—like Santa Barbara, California—have sister cities in several countries. The projects are meant to foster international understanding through people-to-people exchanges and by focusing on the issues and problems specific to urban areas.

City twinning programs are not generally student-run projects. They require the official involvement of the mayors and city councils of both cities, and they focus on developing reciprocal contacts among a variety of groups—professionals like doctors and lawyers, trade organizations, and ethnic associations, as well as students and teachers. *Your City and the World* is full of ideas and resources to develop these contacts. Somebody just has to get the ball rolling. A talented, energetic group of students can rally the support and put in the time needed to develop the intercity relationship.

More than anything, developing a sister cities project means coalition building within your community. You need the support of a variety of organizations—industrial, ethnic, religious, and more—demonstrating genuine enthusiasm for the chance to interact with a foreign city. Once the relationship is established, these groups will have to put in the time and energy to develop it.

The project will ultimately be developed under the auspices of the municipality, with official contact between the cities overseen by a committee made up of people representing community organizations. It will involve some kinds of financial backing that you may not be used to in your other projects: "public funds" from municipal and state government. (Hmm . . . maybe this is the entrée into politics that you've been looking for!)

One of the challenges in developing a program of this type is staying power. It's not fair to your foreign twin to be "a flash in the pan," to start off with a lot of enthusiasm but then let the relationship deteriorate. Part of developing a sister cities project is to plan for sustainability. You can do this by how you structure the committee, by making sure there's an enthusiastic group of up-and-coming students to fill your shoes, and by beginning with a long-term plan—say, three years—of projects spread out to help the community gain and keep its momentum.

Voices of Experience

In addition to the handful of large organizations that have their own exchange programs, there are plenty of groups out there that have done this before. These include your local Rotary Club (through its affiliation with Rotary International), Peace Child International, and global youth camps such as Legacy International. Your state's department of education should have some resources available from programs it has worked with. Consult with these groups and see how you can make use of their experience, contacts, funding, and materials in creating your program. If you're so inclined, just approach them with your interest and let them run with it. But think first: Will they really create the kind of exchange that you want to have? And even if they do, what makes it your project?

Even without bringing foreign citizens to your community, there is a great deal you can contribute to your school or community's sensitivity to international issues. Compared to the rest of the world, we Americans know woefully little about other countries. Seek out resources at the library or through organizations such as the Center for Teaching International Relations. Work with your school's social studies or geography department to improve the international education curriculum. Approach cultural organizations in your community, particularly those representing immigrant communities or those with strong ties to "the old country," and organize a cultural fair on the grounds of your school or place of worship. Even bring in their leaders for a classroom presentation. There are so many unexplored ways to learn about different cultures, languages, and nations.

There's nothing like the experiences of learning and sharing that grow out of international exchange and educational projects. It's ambitious stuff—especially for a young activist—but entirely possible. In this small and shrinking world, where even within our own country we are experiencing ever more cultural diversity, we each have a responsibility to reach out, to build bridges and help ourselves and others understand the world beyond our shores. There are remarkable things waiting for you just over the horizon.

25

The Good Fight: Human Rights Advocacy

JENNIE E. BURNET

Jennie E. Burnet, twenty-four, founded an Amnesty International chapter in her Texas high school eight years ago. She held several leadership positions in the organization while in college and is now the youngest member of the board of directors of AI-USA.

> Human rights—two words that refer to a broad range of issues, rooted in the belief that all humans, regardless of their nationality, race, gender, religion, political beliefs, economic status, or any other innate or cultural attribute, should enjoy certain inalienable rights.

Unfortunately, human rights violations are not a new thing in this world, but with the onset of the information age, we can now know about wrongs being perpetrated around the world. That access gives us a responsibility to act on behalf of those who become victims of corrupt and repressive regimes. As Nobel Peace Laureate Elie Wiesel said at the dedication of the Holocaust Memorial Museum in Washington, D.C.: "[from the Holocaust] we have learned that though every human being has the right to be different, none has the right to be indifferent to suffering." To know about an injustice and not to act is to be complicit.

Human rights activism springs from a moral imperative. It asks us to learn what is happening beyond our doorstep and to do whatever we can to pressure U.S. and foreign officials to end the violation of universal rights to personal safety and self-expression. My lesson to you, I hope, will be that whoever and wherever you are, you can have an effect on the lives of people you don't even know.

Human rights advocacy can take many forms: protesting the imprisonment of peaceful political activists, fighting for equitable treatment of refugees, calling for divestment from countries that exhibit a blatant disregard for these rights, opposing discrimination against gays and lesbians, demanding the dismantling of all vestiges of the apartheid system in South Africa, boycotting companies that remove natural resources from regions of the world without compensating the indigenous population. All this and more falls into the category of human rights activism.

No Justice, No Peace

Since its beginning, the human rights movement has been intimately linked to the movement for world peace. The majority of peace activists around the world believe that without human rights, a just and lasting peace is impossible. A worldwide upsurge in the movement for human rights took place at the end of World War II when the full extent of the atrocities perpetrated in Nazi Germany came to light. In the years following the war, world leaders created the United Nations and issued a call for a treaty protecting human rights. The Universal Declaration of Human Rights, ratified in one of the first acts of the U.N. General Assembly, set international standards for human rights.

There are dozens of organizations around the world involved in the human rights cause. Some—such as Amnesty International, Human Rights Watch, the International Committee of the Red Cross, and Physicians for Human Rights—have an international focus. Others—the American Civil Liberties Union, the Anti-Defamation League, and the National Coalition to Abolish the Death Penalty, and others—concern themselves with domestic human rights issues.

One of the first organizations to champion the cause of human rights was begun in 1961 when British lawyer Peter Benenson read about two Portuguese students who had been sentenced to seven years' imprisonment. Their crime: raising their glasses in a toast to freedom. Benenson tried to think of ways to persuade Portugal and other oppressive governments around the world to release victims of injustice, and he settled on the idea of bombarding such regimes with letters of protest. In an appeal published in newspapers around the world, Benenson called for peaceful protest of human rights abuses based on an impartial analysis of the facts. Within months, thousands of letters poured in, and Benenson's idea grew into an organization, Amnesty International.

Amnesty's growth reflects the global sentiment for human rights, and its philosophy remains an important one to the movement: gathering and analysis of information without consideration for political motives. Amnesty's reputation for accuracy and impartiality is its greatest strength; the fact that it is independent of all world governments, political factions, ideologies, economic interests, and religious affiliations has made its voice a potent moral force.

Know Where Your Information Is Coming From

The key to effective human rights advocacy is accurate and up-to-date information. There are many sources of information out there, including the United Nations Human Rights Commission, Amnesty International, Human Rights Watch, the U.S. government, and organizations focusing on specific human rights issues (women's rights, gay rights, environmental issues, and so forth) or on specific countries. Human rights issues are often tied up in politically volatile situations, and all parties have their own interests to "protect." Be aware of where your information is coming from and how it was gathered. There is nothing inherently wrong with having a certain political agenda, but be aware that the appearance of taking sides may affect your ability to advocate effectively. Avoid this by using information only from reputable and impartial organizations.

One example of how human rights information can be manipulated was an ad run in *The New York Times* by the government of Nigeria. The ad defended the execution of environmental activist Ken Saro-Wiwa and eight others by using lies and half-truths. It pointed out that Amnesty and Greenpeace sent observers to the trial but did not acknowledge that those observers were not allowed to enter the courtroom or that these organizations and a host of world governments decried the proceedings as unfair. And on "our side" there is always the risk that an opposition group will exaggerate or even fabricate certain human rights abuses by the government it is attempting to overthrow. Be skeptical of information whose sources are unclear or that just doesn't seem logical in context.

What Are Your Limits?

Because human rights apply to everyone—children and adults, peace activists, opposition leaders, murderers and terrorists—there are some questions you should ask yourself when preparing to work for human rights. We all have our own limits on what we consider "legitimate" advocacy. Will you appeal for the release of peaceful activists? Are you willing to seek justice for violent political activists? Will you go so far as to call for the release of those who advocate violence? Will you oppose the death penalty for murderers? The answers to these questions will bear heavily on how many people you are able to involve in your project. The more potentially objectionable your stance, the harder it will be to rally a large group behind your efforts.

When thinking about these issues, I divide cases into three categories: "Prisoners of Conscience," "Political Prisoners," and "Criminals."

Prisoners of conscience, a term coined by Peter Benenson, applies to those imprisoned for their beliefs, ethnicity, language, or religion, provided they have neither used nor advocated violence. One example is 1991 Nobel Peace Prize winner Aung San Suu Kyi, whose opposition to the military regime in Myanmar (formerly Burma) earned her six years of house arrest before and after the annulment of an election which her party, the National League for Democracy, won in 1990. Ms. Kyi's actions involved only peaceful appeals for an end to military dictatorship and political oppression.

Virtually no one will dispute work on behalf of prisoners of conscience. They are innocent of any violent crime, and cases like theirs are a strong rallying point for human rights organizing.

The choice of who you are willing to support becomes more difficult when considering *political prisoners* and opposition groups. Around the world people are standing up against repressive political regimes, and some choose to resort to violence. In response, many governments ignore the standards of due process or imprison people for a long time without trial. When considering this kind of work, think about whether or not you believe violence is justified in opposition to an oppressive government. The answer is not always clear-cut, especially in cases where the abuses are longstanding and the government itself has also used violence against its people.

A famous example of a political prisoner is Nelson Mandela, now president of South Africa. He was imprisoned for more than two decades by the apartheid government for his violent opposition to the system. In the debate on the legitimacy of violence in that situation, people found their own place. Some advocated Mandela's release, others ignored the case entirely. Amnesty International refused to appeal for Mandela's release because of his use of violence but did pressure South Africa to try him quickly and fairly. Amnesty suffered a great deal of criticism for its position, even from some of its allies.

Criminal cases introduce another tough issue for human rights advocates: opposition to torture and the death penalty. Article Five of the Universal Declaration of Human Rights reads, "No one shall be subjected to torture or to cruel, inhuman, or degrading treatment or punishment." Many will argue that individuals who commit crimes and who receive a fair trial forfeit certain rights. Many nations use torture and cruel treatment as forms of punishment: lashing in Singapore, rape of women by Pakistani police, amputations ordered by Saudi Arabian courts, systematic torture of Palestinians in Israeli prisons, and paddling in American public schools. Where do you stand?

SUCCESS STORY

Voices Raised for a Voice Silenced

Iqbal Masih didn't go to school. Instead, sold into slavery to pay for an older brother's wedding, he spent most of his life chained to a carpet loom in Pakistan. When he escaped this bondage, he worked with child rights advocates in Pakistan to bring the issue of Third World child labor to light. At twelve he traveled across the United States, speaking at schools full of carefree American children who had never seen a loom or Pakistan. For his work he won the Reebok Human Rights Award in 1994.

But this is not Iqbal Masih's story. Iqbal was gunned down just four months after his visit to the United States. This is the story of those he touched.

After his visit to their school, students at Broad Meadows Middle School in Quincy, Massachusetts, started a letter campaign protesting the use of child labor in Pakistan. Shocked by the news of his death, the group moved quickly to carry on his legacy. They began with a petition demanding an independent investigation into Iqbal's death, and they vowed to establish a school in Pakistan named for their young hero.

Because Iqbal had been sold for $12 and was killed at the age of twelve, the Broad Meadows students decided to seek $12 donations toward the school. They set up a World Wide Web site (http://www.digitalrag.com/mirror/iqbal.html) and sent e-mail to schools across the United States. The group received endorsements from the likes of Aerosmith, R.E.M.'s Michael Stipe, and U.S. Senator Edward Kennedy, and even Prime Minister Benazir Bhutto of Pakistan.

In December, 1995 *they* won the Reebok Human Rights Award. With their initial goal of $30,000 raised, the group announced plans to continue fund-raising until the anniversary of Iqbal's death, then work with Pakistani partners to build the school.

In the United States today we are hearing increasingly vocal calls for the reinstatement of chain gangs, the use of whippings as punishment, and more executions. Opposition to the death penalty and torture is not easy in the current "tough on crime" political climate. Many human rights groups that oppose the death penalty or torture find that some people are turned away by their position. Sometimes it's best to steer clear of these difficult issues, especially when you're just starting out. Even if you yourself aren't sure where you stand in the death penalty or corporal punishment debates, there are plenty of human rights issues that need your attention. (Of course, you also have a responsibility to look beyond your family and society to educate yourself on the tough issues and eventually make a personal decision on where you stand.)

Getting Involved

Okay, so we've talked about the issues you'll face. Now let's get down to the nitty-gritty—making your voice heard. The centerpiece of human rights activism is the letter-writing campaign. Letters are written to foreign regimes to protest certain actions or express concern for victims of human rights abuses, to the president and Congress to ask for support of human rights in foreign policy and disbursements of foreign aid, and to multinational corporations requesting that they bring their influence to bear on human rights situations wherever they do business.

Experience has shown that the impact of your letter, combined with others' from around the world, can have a huge influence on human rights policy. The account of a released prisoner of conscience in the Dominican Republic is instructive here: "When the first two hundred letters came, the guards gave me back my clothes. Then the next two hundred letters came, and the prison director came to see me. When the next pile of letters arrived, the director got in touch with his superior. The letters kept coming and coming: three thousand of them. The president was informed. The letters still kept arriving, and the president called the prison and told them to let me go."

Get yourself involved in a network that can let you know when to write. Amnesty, for example, issues Urgent Action Appeals on a regular basis; with members around the world informed, thousands of letters can be directed to a human rights crisis in a matter of days. Many domestic organizations will let you know when relevant legislation is being considered in Congress. Look in the Resource Directory of this book and make some calls to get started.

Working with a group allows you to motivate more letters each time. Meet regularly to write letters and plan events. If your organization demonstrates staying power, think about adopting a case that your group can stay with until the issue is resolved. Amnesty calls these "Action Files" and assigns them to well-established member groups. If the Action File is a prisoner of conscience, the group will work for that person's unconditional release and will continue to do so until the prisoner is freed. If it's a case of "disappearance"—a neologism referring to the faked disappearance (kidnapping, really) of an individual whether by the government or an opposition group—the group will put pressure on the foreign government until the whereabouts of the individual is confirmed or the remains are returned to the family.

Another alternative is to have your group campaign for a certain human rights issue or in a region of the world for an intensive period. The East Timor Action Network (ETAN), for example, works for self-determination and an end to oppression in the Indonesian-occupied island nation of East Timor. With annual commemorations of a November 1991 massacre, educational materials, and an active network of activists, ETAN has exerted influence on Indonesia, the U.S. Congress, and the United Nations for changes in policy. Campaigning allows your group to develop a good knowledge base for action through intensive study of the issue or region.

Use your campaign or major actions as a springboard for getting even more people involved. Organize a write-a-thon in your school or community and combine it with other activities to attract more people. Use the inspiring quotes like those of Elie Wiesel, Martin Luther King Jr., and Mahatma Gandhi to motivate otherwise skeptical individuals to give letter writing a try. Sponsor a "coffeehouse" some evening with live music and snacks for letter writers. Or hold a Human Rights Fair with "countries" set up around the room and a "border guard" at each to explain the situation in that country and instruct people on letter writing. Decorate creatively. Print up a "passport" that participants can get stamped at each country and give donated prizes for the most prolific letter writers.

Boycotts, Divestment, and Encouraging Socially Responsible Business

One strategy that was especially effective in the fight against the apartheid system in South Africa was boycotts and divestment. By demanding that their schools and the companies they supported get rid of their investments in South Africa or face a boycott, thousands of Americans brought their economic power to bear on a human rights situation.

Boycotts should not be undertaken lightly. A great deal of knowledge of the country and the situation is necessary before making the decision to boycott. Each case should be evaluated on an individual basis to form a cohesive strategy with a specific goal. In other words, tell them—the companies and the foreign governments—what you're doing, why you're doing it, and what it will take to end the boycott. There's more to a boycott than just not using a certain company's products. Update them periodically on your decision and tell them whether the boycott is continuing. For students it may be easier to focus on local corporations. Unless you're part of a national effort such as César Chavez's well-known grape boycott, you may not wield the economic power to change company policy.

Choose your boycotts carefully and on a limited basis. With corporate America becoming dominated by a few companies, it's easy to become paralyzed if you choose to boycott too much at once. For example, I have been boycotting Pepsico for the past two years because of their involvement in the terrible human rights situation in the Republic of Myanmar. Keeping my commitment is not easy. Because Pepsico is a corporate giant, I have to avoid Pepsi, Slice, Mountain Dew, the fast-food chains Pizza Hut, Kentucky

Fried Chicken, Taco Bell, and California Pizza Kitchen, all Frito-Lay snack products, and small-size Ocean Spray drinks. Several times a day I have to make a conscious decision *not* to use a Pepsico product.

Spread the Word

Although the concept of human rights has existed formally for at least forty years, many people in the United States still aren't clear on what they are and why they're important. Human rights education can be a good way for a well-organized group to move beyond direct advocacy. The Amnesty chapter at Virginia Tech, for example, conducts periodic human rights lessons in area grade schools. Their curriculum combines lessons from several disciplines, including geography, writing, and politics, and gives students the chance to take some human rights–related action as part of each lesson.

Panel discussions and conferences, or even just inviting a speaker to your school, are also important aspects of human rights education. They can offer the opportunity to bring other organizations into your work too. The largest Amnesty International event in the United States each year is the Amnesty Activism Day in Boston. More than five hundred activists, mostly students, come together for a day of training workshops, keynote speakers, educational workshops, and collective action. Several other regional groups hold similar events. Find out if there's one in your neck of the woods, and if there's not, then create one.

Making the Connection

One of the biggest challenges in human rights work is to show people the connection between local action and global policies. Many of the things we're working on seem pretty obscure to the average American. Add that to the "what can one letter really do" attitude, and you're facing a pretty significant challenge. Here are some strategies I've found useful in "making the connection."

Take advantage of local visits by foreign dignitaries, U.S. government officials, and other international figures. For example, in August 1995, His Holiness the Dalai Lama toured the United States. Amnesty used his visit as an opportunity to speak out about the pattern of human rights abuses perpetrated in Tibet by the Chinese government. Prior to his Boston appearance, our organization held several events and attended events held by other organizations. Not only were we reinvigorated by His Holiness's visit, but we also tapped into an entire community bound by a common interest in the region and the issues.

Make sure when piggybacking your work on this kind of occasion that your message is heard distinctly and clearly from those competing with it. During His Holiness's visit, not only was most of the media attention focused on the Dalai Lama himself but there was also a number of other organizations competing with us for attention. Students for a Free Tibet, for example, was speaking out against China's occupation of sovereign Tibet. Because Amnesty does not take a position on whether or not China should leave Tibet, we had to take care always to present Amnesty's concerns distinctly in order to uphold our standards of impartiality.

Another technique I've found effective is picking up "hot issues" in the news. In early 1994 many Americans heard the names Rwanda and Burundi for the first time thanks to news reports of the genocide and refugee crisis there. Local human rights organizations were able to use this opportunity to get additional media attention for events and vigils focusing on that crisis. At these events the groups were able to distribute membership information and get some air time for other human rights concerns.

The major pitfall of the hot-issue technique is that most human rights crises are never addressed by the media. Indeed, most of our media work involves just getting some coverage for those who are suffering out of the world's sight. When we buy into the hot-topic approach, we tacitly accept American ignorance of ongoing violations in Sierra Leone, Liberia, Sri Lanka, Colombia, Peru, and Indonesia, and dozens of other countries around the world.

Analogies are another tool you can use to "make the connection." For people not familiar with the field, human rights information sounds like a morbid numbers game: 20,000 killed in Hama, 250 in Dili, 8 in Nigeria. Creating an analogy—some "local" comparison for your facts and figures—gives your audience a chance to internalize the facts and empathize with the victims. Analogies humanize abuses, making them somehow more real.

At Woodstock '94 I was a coordinator for Oxfam America's Light a Candle for Rwanda project. We had to recruit volunteers to sell 100,000 candles to festival goers to heighten awareness and raise money for Oxfam's work in Rwanda. Recruiting, I had to explain the need for assistance quickly and passionately to compel people to help. I pointed out that the festival crowd—just over 400,000—was slightly lower than the estimated number of people killed in Rwanda. Hearing this, people already stunned by the teeming masses were shocked: To imagine every single person around them dead was almost impossible.

Analogy can also personalize abuses by showing a "reality." One technique you can try is "guerrilla theater"—staging an arrest or "disappearance" in a public place to demonstrate what happens on a daily basis in some countries. After the drama, give an additional informational presentation and allow people an opportunity to take action. Another example of personalizing tragedy is the way the Museum of Tolerance in Los Angeles gives each child who visits a card with the photograph and biography of a Jewish child who died in the Holocaust. Seeing the photo and feeling that affinity for a single individual brings out the human tragedy better than any figures could. Be creative but stay accurate.

The Rights Fight

As human rights activists we deal with many issues that are an easy sell, like the case of the two Portuguese students imprisoned for toasting freedom or the plight of Aung San Suu Kyi. But just as often we address issues that fall into a moral "gray area"—the torture of people who have themselves used violence, violations carried out by a U.S. ally, or the always volatile topic of capital punishment in America. Get as involved as you comfortably can. There are more than enough clear-cut cases to keep us all busy. But as you learn more and develop a commitment to the cause, educate yourself and come to some decisions about what you support. If you truly believe in the *universality* of human rights, you'll find that there's plenty more you can do. Challenge yourself and others to turn lip service into concrete action on behalf of those who don't have the good fortune of your freedom.

Part Three

Resource Directory

Resource Directory

There are vast wellsprings of experience and advice out there that you should tap to make yourself more effective. Any directory of active organizations is limited, including this one. We don't have the space to list the local and regional organizations that will be most helpful to you, but we've listed a cross-section of organizations and publications in the United States and abroad that can help point you in the right direction and provide you with a great deal of information.

It isn't fair to these organizations to put them in categories, especially the broad ones used below. As you peruse this list, remember that many of the organizations could fit in more than one place. The Sierra Student Coalition, for example, could also be in the environmental justice category because of its work on lead poisoning in urban communities. There's plenty of crossover between the anti-bias resources and the social and environmental justice groups. Look through the descriptions and contact the organizations you think can help; the worst thing that can happen is they won't have what you're looking for.

Spend time perusing appropriate sections of your local library or bookstore for the most up-to-date books and periodicals on the issues that matter to you. Do this frequently; there's always new knowledge out there, and publications quickly become dated.

If you're wondering where to start, look at the biographies of the people who wrote chapters in this book. The organizations they work with—the SSC, EnviroLink, CityKids, the Center for

Third World Organizing, NARAL, and others—are some of the most effective and some of the most receptive to young people's queries and input. That's not to say that the other organizations are any less interested, promising, and useful, of course. There's a heck of a lot more enthusiasm out there than even this book could hold.

On The Internet...

The Net is growing and expanding at such a rate that many things written here will be out of date by the time this book hits the shelves. Since parts of the Internet link to other parts, however, I can give you some idea of good "on-ramps," and you can explore from there.

For access to just about anything that's on the net, the best place to start is the Yahoo index (http://www.yahoo.com/), which is the closest thing the Internet has to a yellow pages directory. Browse through Yahoo's categories or use their search page to find key words related to your area of interest.

Environmental activists will want to head straight for the EnviroLink Network (http://www.envirolink.org/), which was created five years ago by students at the University of Pittsburgh and has now become one of the most popular environmental sites on the net.

The Institute for Global Communications supports a variety of progressive causes on the Internet. If you spot someone whose address ends in <@igc.apc.org>, you've probably located a new ally. The hub of IGC's web site can be found at http://www.igc.apc.org/. From there you can reach any of IGC's more specific (and self-explanatory) sites: ConflictNet, EcoNet, LaborNet, PeaceNet, WomensNet.

Electronic Activist, an e-mail directory of state legislators and media outlets, can be found at http://www.berkshire.net/~ifas/activist.

More issue-specific sites on the Internet are provided in the listings below.

As you learn your way around the Internet, you may find the following resources useful:

The Internet for Dummies by John R. Levine and Carol Baroudi (IDQ Books, 1995). Part of the popular "for Dummies" series, this book offers the basics of navigating the Internet in accessible lay terminology. It's the book, not the CD-ROM package, that you're after.

Navigating the Internet by Mark Gibbs (Macmillan Computers, 1993). This includes strategies and technical guidelines for accessing and using the diverse resources to be found on the Internet.

The Definitive Guide to HTML by Dave Raggett (Addison-Wesley, 1996). A primer on programming and designing World Wide Web pages in HTML, the computer language of the Internet.

Remember, it's the people you talk to who are going to help you. Learn their names and establish a rapport. Developing an ongoing relationship with organizations on this list can lead in many exciting directions. Make best use of their resources in your own efforts and seize opportunities—conferences, summer internships, and the like—that come your way in the process.

Happy networking.

ANTI-PREJUDICE

American Arab Anti-Discrimination Committee
4201 Connecticut Avenue, N.W., Suite 500
Washington, DC 20008
(202) 244-2990
Fax (202) 244-3196
An independent organization defending the rights of and promoting the heritage of Arab Americans.

American Institute for Managing Diversity
Morehouse College
830 Western Drive, Suite 315
Atlanta, GA 30304
(404) 524-7316
A research institute offering educational materials on fostering understanding in America's increasingly diverse workforce and communities.

Anti-Defamation League of B'nai B'rith
823 United Nations Plaza
New York, NY 10017
(212) 490-2525
A Jewish organization fighting bias, particularly anti-Semitism, in the United States. Has educational resources and reports on white supremacist movements. B'nai B'rith Canada can be reached at (416) 630-2159; fax (416) 633-6224.

Asian Americans United
801 Arch Street
Philadelphia, PA 19107
(215) 925-1538
Fax (215) 925-1539
asianau@libertynet.org
William Kishi, Resource Center Manager
A highly successful advocacy group for Asian Americans in the Philadelphia area. AAU offers information and materials on anti-Asian violence, advocacy for immigrants and young people in limited English proficiency programs, and support for youth initiatives in the field.

Canadian Ministry of Citizenship, Ontario Anti-Racism Secretariat
77 Bloor Street West, 16th Floor
Toronto, Ontario M7A 2R9
Canada
(416) 326-9202
Fax (416) 326-9725
Offers extensive resources, including films (see below), for anti-racism workshops and other programs.

City Kids Foundation
57 Leonard Street
New York, NY 10013
(212) 925-3320
Brings together young people of diverse backgrounds to talk about issues that matter to them and increase their understanding of others. Offers dialogue groups, leadership training, school and

community outreach programs, performing arts, video, and other creative outlets.

Facing History and Ourselves
16 Hurd Street
Brookline, MA 02146
(617) 232-1595
Fax (617) 232-0281
Educational organization offering information, including a resource center of books, videos, and other research, on the Holocaust and other manifestations of prejudice and anti-Semitism. Curricula, speakers, and materials available.

Highlander Research Education Center
1959 Highlander Way
New Market, TN 37820
(423) 933-3443
Fax (423) 933-3424
Offers leadership training workshops for grassroots organizations in the Southeast, mostly on weekends. Attempts to foster a multiregional, multi-issue, multinational approach to social change though Global Youth Economic Gatherings, environmental justice programs. Also maintains an extensive library of books, videos, tapes, and CDs on environmental, civil rights, and economic issues.

National Conference
71 Fifth Avenue, Suite 1100
New York, NY 10003
(212) 206-0006
Formerly called the National Conference of Christians and Jews, NC offers anti-prejudice programs and materials, including the well-known "Anytown" workshop program. It has regional and state offices across the country, which are more useful to contact than the national office.

Refuse and Resist
305 Madison Avenue, Suite 1166
New York, NY 10165

(212) 713-5657
refuse@calyx.com
Grassroots organization sponsoring conferences, direct action, and lobbying against all forms of bias and oppression. A few regional chapters exist.

Teaching Tolerance
400 Washington Avenue
Montgomery, AL 36104
(334) 264-0286
Offers educational materials on prejudice reduction and civil rights for sale to schools and organizations, plus a semiannual journal for teachers.

Toronto Coalition Against Racism
P. O. Box 133
339A College Street
Toronto, Ontario M5S 1S2
Canada
(416) 978-8201
au694@torfree.net
Sponsors conferences and "strategy meetings" on community struggles against racism. Encourages networking with the goal of building a large coalition to fight racism in the workplace, neighborhoods, schools, and social and political arenas. Resources and advice available for student activists just getting started.

Publications

"Actions Speak Louder: A Brotherhood/Sisterhood Curriculum" (National Conference, 1995). This brochure is a collection of prejudice-reduction workshop and activity ideas, and curricula for various age levels written for Brotherhood/Sisterhood Week 1995.

Bigotry, Prejudice and Hatred: Definitions, Cases and Solutions by Robert M. Baird and Stuart E. Rosenbaum, eds. (Prometheus Books, 1992). This series of articles by various authors addresses the phenomenon of hatred and prejudice.

Encyclopedia of Multiculturalism by Susan Auerbach, ed. (Marshall Cavendish, 1994). A six-volume encyclopedia on issues and history of just about any kind of bias or cultural issue you can think of—from anti-Semitism to the "Zoot-suit riots" of the early twentieth century.

"Mirrors and Windows: Seeing the Human Community" (National Conference, 1995). A bibliography of books and other resources appropriate for various age groups, plus a list of other useful bibliographies.

Open Minds to Equality by Nancy Schniedewind (Prentice-Hall, 1983). A sourcebook of educational activities on a variety of bias issues, including race, sex, class, and age equity.

Respecting Our Differences: A Guide to Getting Along in a Changing World by Lynn Duvall (Free Spirit Publishing, 1994). Offers thoughts on personal attitude change, stereotypes, and "the ups and downs of diversity," plus information on skinhead and other racist groups and an extensive bibliography of other resources.

Skipping Stones: A Multi-Cultural Children's Quarterly (P. O. Box 309, Eugene, OR 97403; (503) 342-4956). A magazine for kids that encourages "celebration of cultural and linguistic diversity." Includes a parents' and teachers' guide in each issue.

Spinning Tales, Weaving Hope by Teaching Tolerance (New Society Publishers, 1994). A collection of stories for children that encourages discussion of stereotypes and racial and ethnic differences. Includes guides for follow-up activities.

Stereotyping and Prejudice: Changing Conceptions by Daniel Bar-Tal (Springer-Verlag, 1989). Looks at the formation of stereotypes and prejudice, the structure and meaning of stereotypes and prejudice, and how change occurs.

Videos

"Colours of Racism," "For Angela," and "Listening Through the Walls" are recent films addressing racism and diversity issues for a middle school and high school audience. They include accompanying study guides published by the Canadian government. They are available from the Ministry of Education for the cost of shipping but can usually be found more easily through your local library system.

"It's Not Easy" is a video produced by teens that uses the story of a young interracial couple to address racial bias issues. Used by New York City public schools as part of their prejudice-reduction programs. Available from Teaching Tolerance.

"Valuing Diversity: Multicultural Communication" distributed in Canada by McIntyre Media. This film is a study of prejudice that encourages viewers to decrease their discomfort in communicating with people from different cultures, social classes, age groups, or physical disabilities and relate to them as people. Designed for middle school to adult audiences, it comes with a discussion handbook.

On the Internet

Multi-Cultural Pavillion Discussion Group moderated by Paul Gorski, <PCG9R@virginia.edu>.
A mailing list of concerned individuals discussing issues and reviewing literature on racism, sexism, ageism, and other forms of bias. A good information resource that also holds annual conferences on questions of multiculturalism. Sponsored by Dr. Robert Covert, Professor of Education, Evaluation, and Multicultural Education at the University of Virginia.

ENVIRONMENT

American Solar Energy Society
2400 Central Avenue, Suite G-1
Boulder, CO 80301
(303) 443-3130
Advocates use of solar energy through educational outreach campaigns.

Antarctica Project
P. O. Box 76920
Washington, DC 20013
(202) 544-0236
Fax (202) 544-8483
antarctica@igc.org
Charles Webb, Communications Coordinator
Nongovernmental organization dedicated solely to the protection of the environmental and scientific value of the Antarctic. Newsletter, tours, and other information.

Center for Environmental Education
881 Alma Real Drive, Suite 300
Pacific Palisades, CA 90272
(310) 454-4585
Fax (310) 454-9925
<mle@earthspirit.org>
Mary Edie, Outreach Director
A resource library offering books, videos and curricula for teachers and students on current environmental issues.

Chesapeake Bay Foundation
162 Prince George Street
Annapolis, MD 21401
(410) 268-8816
Fax (410) 268-6687
Works on environmental problems in the Chesapeake Bay by employing lawyers, scientists, and activists as advocates for the bay on Capitol Hill. Also sponsors regular environmental expeditions.

Concern, Inc.
1794 Columbia Road, N.W.
Washington, DC 20009
(202) 328-8160
Fax (202) 387-3378
Promotes environmental literacy and action by providing individuals and organizations with information on a broad range of issues including recycling, pollution prevention, safe pest management, water resource protection, and energy efficiency.

Conservation International
1015 18th Street, N.W., Suite 1000
Washington, DC 20036
(202) 429-5660
Fax (202) 887-5188
http://www.conservation.org/
Jill McLaughlin, Communications Assistant
A non-profit, private organization dedicated to saving endangered rain forests and other ecosystems worldwide. Focuses on program development, working with indigenous peoples living in endangered ecosystems. Publications and videos available.

Co-op America
2100 M Street, N.W., Suite 403
Washington, DC 20063
(202) 874-5307
Fax (202) 223-5821
Educational programs, publications, and grassroots organization focusing on the issue of consumer accountability—how we can get our consumption in line with our environmental goals. Also publishes the green consumer's bible, *Shopping for a Better World,* and a quarterly newsletter.

Earth Foundation
5151 Mitchelldale Road, #B-11
Houston, TX 77092
(800) 5-MONKEY

Provides education programs and products to educators and students. Sells T-shirts and offers free curricula and other community-based environmental ideas.

EnviroLink Network
4618 Henry Street
Pittsburgh, PA 15213
(412) 268-7187
Fax (412) 268-7035
admin@envirolink.org
http://www.envirolink.org/
World's largest online environmental information service, designed and run primarily by students. Sponsors an environmental online library, environmental chat area, links to other online environmental resources, and other projects.

Environmental Action Coalition
625 Broadway, 2nd Floor
New York, NY 10012
(212) 677-1601
Fax (212) 505-8613
Blair Baker, Environmental Education Program Director
Acts as a liaison between neighborhoods and institutions to help solve environmental problems, organize neighborhood improvement projects, and conduct research. Main program areas are waste management, environmental education, and community liaison and technical assistance.

Environmental Defense Fund
257 Park Avenue South
New York, NY 10010
(212) 505-2100
Fax (212) 505-2375
Addresses major environmental issues such as global warming through a combination of public education, policy recommendations, and scientific research to develop creative new ways of dealing with the problems confronting the planet. Newsletter.

Farm Animal Reform Movement (FARM)
P. O. Box 30654
Bethesda, MD 20824
(301) 530-1737
Fax (301) 530-5747
Educates and agitates against factory farming, with an ultimate vision of a vegan world in which people would live in harmony with animals. Provides "Vegetarian Information Service" and materials for protesting abuse of farm animals.

Free The Planet!
218 D Street, S.E.
Washington, DC 20003
(202) 547-3656
Fax (202) 546-2461
freetheplanet@essential.org
Rick Taketa, Campaign Director
A national network of student environmental and community action groups. Coordinates a national environmental campaign through direct action and letter-writing initiatives. Also offers technical and informational assistance to student groups organizing on environmental issues.

Friends of the Earth
1025 Vermont Avenue, N.W., 3rd Floor
Washington, DC 20005
(202) 783-7400
Fax (202) 783-0444
foedc@igc.apc.org
http://www.xs4all.nl/~foeint/
A network of environmental organizations with offices in fifty-two countries. Coordinates campaigns on global environmental issues, focusing on international policy. National organizations also carry out their own educational, direct action, and policy campaigns. Web site offers texts of international environmental treaties, updates on international negotiations and UN meetings, and links to member group sites.

Greenpeace
1436 U Street, N.W.
Washington, DC 20009
(202)462-1177
Fax (202) 462-4507
Sanjay Mishra, Public Information Manager
http://www.greenpeace.org/
High-profile organization lobbying to strengthen environmental protection. Focuses on public action to bring attention to environmental threats worldwide.

INFORM, Inc.
381 Park Avenue South
New York, NY 10016-8806
(212) 689-4040
Fax (212) 447-0689
Non-profit environmental research organization that examines business and municipal practices threatening the environment and public health. Publications include information on reducing industrial and municipal waste.

Kids For A Clean Environment (Kids F.A.C.E.)
P. O. Box 158254
Nashville, TN 32715
(615) 331-7381
Membership organization designed to provide children with information and support for protecting nature in their communities. Offers membership book, bimonthly newsletter, hands-on project ideas, and other environmental information.

League of Conservation Voters
1707 L Street, N.W., Suite 750
Washington, DC 20036
(202) 785-8683
Fax (202) 835-0491
http://www.lcv.org/
A political action group with national environmental priorities, the League publishes *The National Environmental Scorecard,* an

annual report on how Congress votes on the environment—useful information for any would-be eco-lobbyist at the national level.

National Audubon Society
Headquarters for Regional and Governmental Affairs
666 Pennsylvania Avenue, S.E.
Washington, DC 20003
(202) 547-9009
A well-established, scholarly society advocating conservation and restoration of natural ecosystems, focusing on birds and other wildlife for the human benefits of nature. Publishes magazines, leads educational programs manages sanctuaries, and runs an activist network.

National Healthy Air License Exchange (INHALE)
P. O. Box 14148
Cleveland, OH 44114
(216) 523-1111
Not-for-profit organization that tries to reduce pollution by purchasing and "retiring" marketable pollution rights. Provides information about and access to pollution markets as well as information on personal pollution prevention.

National Wildlife Federation
1400 16th Street
Washington, DC 20036
(202) 797-6800
Fax (202) 797-6646
http://www.nwf.org/nwf/
Nick Keller, Director of Campus Ecology Department
The nation's oldest and largest conservation and education organization offering educational programs for all ages. Publishes magazines for pre-kindergarten to adult levels, disseminates information, and holds camps, summits, and conferences on conservation issues.

Natural Guard
142 Howard Avenue
New Haven, CT 06519

(203) 787-0229
Fax (203) 787-0229
Environmental and social justice organization for youth that encourages members to become informed about the environmental status of their communities. Offers advice for initiating hands-on problem solving.

Organization for Economic Cooperation and Development (OECD)
2001 L Street, N.W., Suite 700
Washington, DC 20036-4910
(202) 785-6323
Fax (202) 785-0350
The largest source of comparative data on the industrial economies of the world. The OECD produces a wide range of publications including economic surveys, statistics, analyses, and policy recommendations. The aims are to achieve the highest sustainable economic growth and employment in its member countries.

Pacific Whale Foundation
101 North Kihei Road, Suite 21
Kihei, Maui, HI 96753-8833
(808) 879-8860
Fax (808) 879-2615
A center for marine research, conservation, and education. Has developed marine education programs for the public and conservation policy proposals for endangered marine life.

People for the Ethical Treatment of Animals (PETA)
P. O. Box 42516
Washington, DC 42516-0516
(301) 770-PETA (7382)
An animal protection organization "dedicated to defending the rights of all species" through public education, research and investigations, legislation, and direct action. Offers products and information about the treatment of animals, including videos and an action handbook.

Sea Shepherd Conservation Society
3107A Washington Boulevard
Marina Del Rey, CA 90292
(310) 301-SEAL (7325)
http://www.envirolink.org/elib/orgs/seashep/seashep.html
A non-profit organization involved with the investigation and documentation of violations of international regulations and treaties protecting marine wildlife. Sea Shepherd's confrontational strategies include intervening directly between, for example, whaling vessels and whales. Quarterly newsletter.

Sierra Student Coalition (SSC)
223 Thayer Street, #2
Providence, RI 02906-1237
(401) 861-6012
Fax (401) 861-6241
sierra.student.coalition@sierraclub.org
http://www.ssc.org/ssc/
The student-run arm of the Sierra Club runs nationwide lobbying and direct-action campaigns and sponsors summer retreats for environmental activists. An excellent informational and advisory resource with access to America's largest environmental organization. Newsletter.

Student Environmental Action Coalition (SEAC)
P. O. Box 1168
Chapel Hill, NC 27514-1168
(919) 967-4600
Fax (919) 967-4698
SEAC@igc.apc.org
http://www.seac.org/
A national coalition of over two thousand high school and college environmental groups that coordinates national and regional projects to challenge and change current environmental laws. Its information clearinghouse offers books, fact sheets, and other materials as resources to members. Organizes training programs on current environmental issues.

Worldwatch Institute
1776 Massachusetts Avenue, N.W.
Washington, DC 20036
(202) 452-1999
Fax (202) 296-7365
worldwatch@igc.apc.org
Reah Kauffman, Executive Assistant
A public-interest research institute focusing on the global environment and related issues. Offers publications on global economic, social, and environmental conditions, including the excellent annual *State of the World* report.

Youth for Environmental Sanity (YES!)
706 Frederick Street
Santa Cruz, CA 95062
(408) 459-9344
Fax (408) 458-0253
yes@cruzio.com
Youth-created and youth-run, the YES! tour brings a multimedia stage show to schools around the United States each year, designed to motivate environmental action. YES! also sponsors summer camps and other action-oriented workshops for student organizers across the country and advises members on local organizing efforts. Newsletter.

Zero Population Growth
1400 16th Street, N.W., Suite 320
Washington, DC 20036
(202) 332-2200
Fax (202) 332-2302
zpg@igc.apc.org
Educational clearinghouse and lobbying organization that encourages creative solutions to the problem of global overpopulation.

SUCCESS STORY

Getting Students to say "YES!"

In 1990, Ocean Robbins and Ryan Eliason didn't like what they saw: growing environmental destruction and a generation of bright young people following the path of apathy and despair. Working under the auspices of EarthSave, a non-profit organization that promotes vegetarianism and other environmental lifestyle changes, they organized the Creating Our Future Tour, a short theatrical production about the environment that reached 30,000 students in three states and one Canadian province.

That was the first year.

Since then, the one-time project has grown into an organization—Youth for Environmental Sanity, or YES!—that has performed 1,380 assemblies for 306,000 students in 38 states and organized workshops and summer camps for hundreds of aspiring young environmentalists. Each year at least four YES! tour members are on the road, working with a growing network of young volunteers who make all the arrangements for their shows and accommodations while on the road. Performers have also opened shows for the late Jerry Garcia and spoken at the United Nations. The tour credits itself with encouraging thousands of young people to become vegetarian, register to vote, use less packaging, and avoid environmentally destructive companies like Mitsubishi in favor of firms (and YES! tour supporters) like Aveda and Esprit.

In 1994, YES! launched the Green Schools Program, designed to engage students in changing their own schools' environmental policies. Cosponsored by Friends of the Earth, the Green Schools Program has the tough task of convincing schools to *save* $150,000 per year through a no-risk switchover to fluorescent lighting. Ocean Robbins and fellow YES! founder Sol Solomon wrote a book for young people called *Choices for Our Future* in 1995, which outlines their personal philosophy of informed personal decisions and environmental responsibility.

With an annual budget of less than a million dollars, YES! has reached fully two percent of American high school students. And each year, with the help and enthusiasm of volunteers across the country, the show goes on.

Publications

Choices for Our Future by Ocean Robbins and Sol Solomon (Book Publishing Company, 1995). The founders of YES! (Youth for Environmental Sanity) pull no punches in their analysis of what's wrong, how we can fix it, and why we care. Informative and inspiring like few other books out there. Available from YES!

E The Environmental Magazine published quarterly by the Earth Action Network. Interviews with politicians, actors, and other prominent public figures about the current state of the world. Also has consumer news, food and health tips, and in-depth coverage of new environmental projects.

Earth Child by Kathryn Sheehan and Mary Waidner (Council Oak Books, 1991). A resource book of games, stories, activities, experiments, and ideas about "living lightly on planet Earth" for children of all ages.

Earth First Journal published eight times a year by Earth First!. A forum for the no-compromise environmental movement. The journal acts as a line of communication among activists so they can keep one another informed on tactics and strategy. For more information write Earth First Journal, P. O. Box 1415, Eugene, OR 97440.

Ecodefense: A Field Guide to Monkey Wrenching by Dave Foreman (Earth First!, 1985). A "how-to" guide offering tips on environmentally inspired vandalism like spiking trees and sabotaging logging equipment—acts that, by the way, are illegal and can often endanger your safety or that of others.

Education for the Earth: The College Guide for Careers in the Environment from Peterson's Guides (Princeton University Press, 1995). The typical college guide with a twist—this one looks at schools' environmental studies programs and campus resources for the environmentally concerned high school senior.

Embracing the Earth: Choices for Environmentally Sound Living by D. Mark Harris (The Noble Press, 1990). A concise, well-organized, illustrated sourcebook on the specific things we can do every day to lessen our burden on the Earth. Includes several directories on environmental service organizations and political resources.

Environment published ten times a year by Heldref Publications. A more scholarly journal, *Environment* offers analyses of current environmental problems, book reviews, and other data. Telephone (202) 296-6267 for more information.

Environmental Action Magazine published quarterly by the Environmental Action Foundation. Provides in-depth features on current trends and threats to the environment, "econotes," book reviews, action reports, and activist alerts. Telephone (202) 745-4870 for more information.

The Environmental Sourcebook by Edith C. Stein (Lyons & Burford Publishers, 1992). Brings together a variety of pertinent information on most environmental issues. Explains what is happening, which issues are most important, who is taking action, and where to go amid books, periodicals, and magazines for further information.

EPA Journal published bimonthly by the U.S. Environmental Protection Agency. Inexpensive to subscribe to but not always easy to find in the library, *EPA Journal* covers the activities of the EPA, environmental legislation, and issues of current interest. Telephone (202) 783-3238 for more information.

50 Simple Things You Can Do to Save the Earth by The Earthworks Group (Earthworks Press, 1989). Maybe the first "best-seller" of environmental guides for the lay reader. There are several more titles in the 50 Simple Things series, such as *50 Simple Things Kids Can Do to Save the Earth.*

The Green Consumer by Joel Makower (Penguin Books, 1988). A book that explains how to buy products that don't hurt the earth. Divided into three parts covering the effect of everyday purchases on the state of the environment; a guide to environmentally sound product choices, including brand names and addresses; and a section for people interest in becoming more involved in environmental issues.

The Green Encyclopedia by Irene Franck and David Brownstone (Prentice Hall General Reference, 1992). An A-to-Z sourcebook (literally!) of environmental concerns and solutions designed to provide fast, accurate information on a range of environmental concerns. The cross-reference system provides easy access to topics.

The Green PC: Practical Choices That Make a Difference by Steven Anzovin (Windcrest/McGraw Hill Publishing, 1994). A source of information on practical, low-cost ways to lower your computer's energy consumption, reduce pollution, and protect personal health. Includes information on EPA programs, green bulletin boards, environmental software, and hundreds of enviro-aware computing resources.

How On Earth! published four times a year by Vegetarian Education Network. For and by young people, *HOE!* advocates compassionate, ecologically sound living. Everything from information on vegetarian and vegan diets to artwork, poetry, and features on young activists.

Information Please® Environmental Almanac compiled annually by World Resources Institute (Houghton Mifflin Company). Information, tips, and other resources regarding water supplies, toxics, energy, and air pollution worldwide. Includes information on the history behind many of today's environmental problems.

The Kids' Environment Books: What's Awry and Why by Anne Pederson (John Muir Publications, 1991). Provides a clear, balanced, and positive discussion of the environmental problems we face today and are likely to face tomorrow. Examines the relationship between human beings and the earth, explains how all aspects of our environment are related to one another, and suggests actions that anyone can take.

Let the Mountains Talk, Let the Rivers Run by David Brower (HarperCollins, 1995). Brower, conservationist and climber, advises environmental organizations on how they might more effectively work to restore both the natural world and the hope of its peoples.

National Green Pages published annually by Co-op America. A directory of products and services, including food, clothing, and co-op organizations nationwide, for people concerned about their impact on the planet. Also includes articles on environmental businesses, earth-saving tips, and consumer reports.

Rescue Mission: Planet Earth by Peace Child International (Kingfisher Publications, 1994). Written and compiled by teens from around the world, *Rescue Mission* summarizes the U.N.'s Agenda 21—the 1992 "Rio Summit" agreements—in an understandable way and offers suggestions on how young people can help put them into effect.

Save the Animals! 101 Easy Things You Can Do by Ingrid Newkirk (Times Warner Books, 1990). The director of PETA offers advice on ways to educate and agitate on issues of animal rights—from encouraging alternatives to dissecting animals in biology class to avoiding products tested on animals, and more.

Save the Earth: An Action Handbook for Kids by Betty Miles (Alfred A. Knopf, 1991). An illustrated environmental-action guide for children. Includes sections on land, atmosphere, and energy; stories about kids who have taken action in their communities; projects and checklists of activities kids can do; and a how-to section with a resource list of environmental organizations.

Shopping for a Better World by Benjamin Hollister et al. (Council on Economic Priorities, 1994). A good guide to "walking your talk" in what you buy and what companies you patronize. Grades products and firms based on a variety of issues—environment, equal opportunity, labor relations, and more. Its companion volume, *Students Shopping for a Better World,* gives the same treatment to products for students.

Sierra published bimonthly by the Sierra Club. Includes information on endangered species and profiles of specific areas and problems. Conveys the current news of the Sierra Club and lists upcoming Sierra Club outings. Subscribe by joining the Sierra Club.

Silent Spring by Rachel Carson (Houghton Mifflin, 1962). One of the founding documents of the modern environmental movement, it was vital to the banning of DDT. A moving, eloquent narrative on the harms done to nature and to human life by chemical toxins. Carson's works also include *The Sea Around Us* (Penguin Books, 1950) and *The Edge of the Sea* (Houghton Mifflin, 1955).

State of the World: A Worldwatch Institute Report on Progress Toward a Sustainable Society by Lester R. Brown (W.W. Norton, 1995). An annual overview of current trends and research on developments toward (and away from) a just and environmentally sustainable society, addressing technological, economic, and diplomatic issues relating to the environment and the human condition. An excellent and well-respected source with good analysis of current problems, available from the Worldwatch Institute.

The Student Environmental Action Guide by the Student Environmental Action Coalition (SEAC) (Earth Works Press, 1991). Designed to show students what they can do to protect the planet, the guide offers examples of "simple things" that anybody can do on campus or in their community.

Voices for the Earth: Vital Ideas from America's Best Environmental Books by Daniel D. Chiras (Johnson Books, 1995). Explores the current landscape of contemporary environmental ideas by prominent environmental authors who wrote summaries of their own books to showcase their main insights and ideas. Includes writings about global citizenship, earth education, lessons from nature, and ecological literacy.

On the Internet

EcoNet
http://www.igc.apc.org/econet

EnviroLink
info@envirolink.org
http://www.envirolink.org/
For EnviroChat, telnet to envirolink.org2000
The most comprehensive environmental resource on the Internet right now, with links to hundreds of other sites around the world. Student run, too.

EnviroNews mailing list
Send mail to listproc@envirolink.org with a body reading: subscribe environews firstname lastname.

Environmental Information Center
http://www.igc.apc.org/eic

Sierra Club
http://www.sierraclub.orb/
Home page for America's largest environmental organization.

State-by-state environmental quality information
http://www.ewg.org/

FUND-RAISING

Blooms Across America
P. O. Box 12926-I
Pittsburgh, PA 15241
(412) 279-7993
Fax (412) 563-0665
blooms@telerama.lm.com
http://www.ibp.com/pit/blooms/index.html

Offers Blooming Action Kits of "patriotic seeds"—red, white, and blue flowers—for resale as a fund-raiser. Provides community outreach materials.

Creative Marketing
2734 Fountain View Circle
Naples, FL 33942
(800) 591-6347 or (813) 591-2042
Fax (813) 591-8735
Janie Levin, President
A company marketing and distributing water-saving devices and other environmentally designed products. Provides information on products and assists inventors and manufacturers in product distribution. Can arrange to work with individual student organizations to market products in their school and community, enabling the organization to retain a portion of the profits.

The Foundation Center
79 Fifth Avenue
New York, NY 10013-3076
(800) 424-9836 or (212) 620-4230
Fax (212) 807-3677
http://fdncenter.org/aboutfc/about.html
Offers a comprehensive library of information on grant-making foundations and corporate giving programs. Knowledgeable librarians can offer advice on grant-seeking. The Center has four regional offices; the Washington, D.C., location offers national information as well, while the rest have information only on grantmakers in their region. Phone numbers for these locations are (202) 331-1400 for Washington; (415) 397-0902 for San Francisco; (404) 880-0095 for Atlanta; and (216) 861-1933 for Cleveland.

Human-i-Tees, Inc.
19 Marble Avenue
Pleasantville, NY 10570
(800) 275-2638; (914) 741-1509 or 741-2424
Fax (914) 741-2386
"The Environmental T-Shirt Company" works with organizations

to sell environmentally themed T-shirts. Provides marketing advice and access to other environmental resources and allows organizations to keep a portion of the proceeds for their use.

Publications

Dynamic Fund-Raising Projects by Rick Arledge with David Friedman (Precept Press, 1994). Offers suggestions for planning and carrying out fund-raising events in your community.

Foundation Directory published annually by The Foundation Center. A comprehensive directory of grant-making organizations and corporate giving programs, available in the reference section of most libraries.

Program Planning and Proposal Writing by Norton Kiritz and Jerry Mundel (The Gransmanship Center, 1988). An excellent guide to writing well-structured proposals for corporate and foundation fund-raising.

GENDER AND SEXUALITY ISSUES

Association of Reproductive Health Professionals
(800) 584-9119
Offers a national hotline for women who have questions on the morning-after pill and other forms of emergency contraception.

Global Fund for Women
2480 Sand Hill Road, Suite 100
Menlo Park, CA 94025-6941
(415) 854-0420
Fax (415) 854-8050
gfw@igc.apc.org
http://www.igc.apc.org/gfw/
A grant-making organization that focuses on "female human rights," supporting women's groups based outside the United States that are working on such issues as literacy, domestic vio-

lence, economic autonomy, and the international trafficking of women.

National Abortion and Reproductive Rights Action League (NARAL)
462 Broadway, Suite 540
New York, NY 10013
(212) 343-0114 or (202) 971-3000 (Washington, DC)
Fax (212) 343-0119
naralny@aol.com
Annie Keating, Student/Youth Training Initiatives
A pro-choice abortion rights association with affiliates in every state. Runs a high school student network to train leaders to organize in high schools and colleges and offers publications on abortion rights and pro-choice organizations, including clinic booklets and shopping guides listing companies supporting anti-choice and pro-choice initiatives. Distributes general information and encourages local networking.

National Coalition Against Domestic Violence
P. O. Box 18749
Denver, CO 80218-0749
(303) 839-1852
National information and referral center for the public, the media, battered women, and their children. Provides assistance and works to improve public policy and legislation that affect battered women and their children.

National Gay and Lesbian Task Force
2320 17th Street, N.W.
Washington, DC 20009-2702
(202) 332-6483
Fax (202) 332-0207
ngltf@ngltf.org
http://www.ngltf.org/ngltf
One of America's high-profile gay and lesbian organizations, NGLTF is a policy institute that also operates as a resource center for organizations and activists. It is involved in lobbying and educating on current national legislation. Offers publications and

provides resources for legal defense and listings of other organizations around the country where people can get involved in the gay and lesbian community.

National Organization for Women (NOW)
1000 16th Street, N.W., Suite 700
Washington, DC 20036
(202) 331-0066
Fax (202) 788-8576
now@now.org
The premier women's rights organization in the United States, NOW offers information and publications on woman's rights, organizes crowds for protests on issues such as violence against women and abortion rights, acts as advocates for survivors of rape, sexual harassment, and sexual discrimination, and sponsors conferences, demonstrations, and other efforts. The national office can put you in touch with affiliates in your community.

Parents and Friends of Lesbians and Gays (P-FLAG)
1012 14th Street, N.W., Suite 700
Washington, DC 20005
(202) 638-4200
Through more than three hundred chapters across the United States, P-FLAG offers advice to people trying to figure out how to come out to their parents. It sponsors support groups for parents who are wrestling with the news that their child is gay and participates in lobbying and organizing on gay rights issues. Offers a newsletter, reading list, and speakers bureau.

Planned Parenthood Federation of America, Inc.
810 Seventh Avenue
New York, NY 10019
(212) 541-7800
Fax (212) 765-4711
http://ppfa.org/ppfa/
Promotes full access to reproductive health information, availability of contraception, and reproductive choice through educational materials, lobbying, and direct action. Has an excellent

library of books, reports, and educational resources on reproductive rights and sex education. Telephone (800) 431-PLAN to be connected to the Planned Parenthood clinic in your community.

San Francisco Sex Information Service
(415) 989-7374
Provides the only independent phone service in the country dedicated to sexuality education. Available from 3:00 P.M. to 9:00 P.M. Pacific time.

Sexuality Education and Information Council of the U.S. (SEICUS)
130 West 42nd Street, Suite 350
New York, NY 10036
(212) 819-9770
Fax (212) 819-9776
One of the best sources for information on sex education in the United States, including recommended curricula for all levels.

Women's Health Action Mobilization (WHAM!)
P. O. Box 733
New York, NY 10009
(212) 560-7177
http://www.echonyc.com/~wham/
A direct action group committed to demanding, securing, and defending "absolute" reproductive freedom and access to quality health care for all women, regardless of age, socioeconomic status, sexual orientation, race, or ethnicity.

Womankind Worldwide
122 Whitechapel High Street
London E1 7PT
United Kingdom
(44 171) 247-9431 or 247-6931
Fax (44 171) 247-3436
Conducts educational programs and direct assistance to reduce the number of women who die during pregnancy and childbirth because of inadequate information or lack of access to clean birth environments, primarily in the Third World.

Publications

The ACT UP/NEW YORK Women, AIDS & Activism Handbook by the ACT UP/New York Book Working Group (South End Press, 1989). One of the top publications on women and HIV/AIDS out there. Concise and well written with contributions from both activists and medical professionals, it also makes the link between HIV/AIDS and reproductive rights.

AIDS: The Facts by John Langone (Little, Brown, 1988). A somewhat dated analysis of what is known about AIDS, how the virus works, symptoms, treatment methods, precautions against AIDS, and research.

Backlash: The Undeclared War Against Women by Susan Faludi (Anchor Books, 1991). Thoughtful and thoroughly researched account of the current backlash against the gains women have made economically, socially, and politically since the late 1960s.

Feminist Theory: From Margin to Center by bell hooks (South End Press, 1984). A leading black feminist author and thinker, hooks urges us to make the feminist movement build upon the diversity and complexity of the female experience.

From Abortion to Reproductive Freedom: Transforming a Movement edited by Marlene Gerber Fried (South End Press, 1990). An anthology of different voices involved in the reproductive freedom movement. An excellent introduction to thoughts and debates from a variety of perspectives, including grassroots organizing, legal aspects, women of color, socioeconomic questions, and lesbian and gay issues.

Listen Up: Voices From the Next Feminist Generation by Barbara Findlen, ed. (Seal Press, 1995). Collection of firsthand stories from young women on the front lines of the feminist movement today. Candid personal accounts deal with a range of issues that are pertinent to today's movement, including sexuality, body image, race and ethnicity, working in a collective, abortion, and single motherhood.

Ms. Magazine published bimonthly by Lang Communications. A feminist/activist magazine that features extraordinary women, news about women's conferences and activists, book reviews, and health reports, all geared toward active, educated women.

Our Bodies, Our Selves by the Boston Women's Health Collective (Touchstone/Simon & Schuster, 1992). A huge tome offering a little of everything about women and the women's movement—from information on reproductive rights and women's health to the political and social history of the women's movement in America. Considered a cornerstone of feminist know-how.

A Room of One's Own by Virginia Woolf (Harcourt, Brace, 1929). Radical in her time and still pertinent in ours, Woolf walks women through the process of creating their own space and explains the need to have one's own "space"—income, privacy, and other aspects of personhood—to be free from oppression.

Words of Fire: An Anthology of African-American Feminist Thought by Beverly Guy-Sheftall, ed. (The New Press, 1995). An excellent collection that chronicles the dual oppression—racial and sexual—that African-American women have faced, viewed through writings from the 1830s to the present.

On the Internet

Activists for Choice on the Internet
http://www.choice.org/
Offers an excellent online library of articles, statistics, and links to other resources dealing with a variety of reproductive rights issues, clinic violence, contraception, women's health, and current events.

California Catholics for a Free Choice
http://www.stasek.com:80/ccffc/
Pro-choice information site maintained by the California chapter

of a national organization of Catholics supporting reproductive choice.

Office of Population Research at Princeton University
http://opr.princeton.edu/ec/contrac.html
Offers accurate information about contraception—including emergency contraception and help finding clinicians in your area who are willing to provide it—as well as links to other informative sites and a bibliography of current research on contraception.

Queer Resources Directory
http://www.qrd.org/QRD/
Links to online resources on most major issues facing the queer community—families, HIV/AIDS, religion, media, political and legal rights issues—and organizations worldwide.

Virtual Sisterhood
Send mail to majordomo@igc.apc.org with only "subscribe vs-online-strat" in your message.
A conference encouraging online communication among and support for activists on a variety of women's issues. A web site is also in development. For information, e-mail <vsister@igc.apc.org>.

WomensNet
http://www.igc.apc.org/womensnet/
A site offering information on current events and debates on women's issues. WomensNet also tries to help women activists use the Internet to network by offering e-mail accounts and technical assistance. Their e-mail address is <womensnet@igc.apc.org>.

Youth Action Online
Offers online resources for gay, lesbian, bisexual, and questioning youth, including links to advice and resources and to the Usenet newsgroup *soc.support.youth.gay-lesbian-bi,* which offers a safe discussion space and support for young people. To contact the group's moderators, mail to glb-youth-request@ucsd.edu.

GOVERNMENT

Closeup Foundation
Community Outreach Department
44 Canal Center Plaza
Alexandria, VA 22314-1592
(800) CLOSEUP
Fax (703) 706-0001
Non-profit, non-partisan foundation that organizes study visits, workshops, seminars, and other activities in Washington, D.C., for students and educators. Also conducts community-based government education programs and offers books and videotapes for sale.

Democratic National Committee
430 S. Capitol Street, S.E.
Washington, DC 20003
(202) 863-8000
webmaster@democrats.org
http://www.democrats.org/
Offers information on the Democratic Party and national races. Can also provide information for local affiliate offices.

League of Women Voters
1730 M Street, N.W., Suite 1000
Washington, DC 20036
(202) 429-1965
Fax (202) 429-0854
LOWV encourages informed political action by citizens on a variety of major public policy issues through education and advocacy. Operates on local, state, and national levels and has community organizations throughout the United States. Projects include voter registration, environmental advocacy, and support for violence prevention. The League also offers leadership training for youth. Members receive leadership, networking, and public speaking opportunities, subscription to *National Voter* magazine and local and state newsletters, and discounts on the League's extensive line of publications.

Project Vote Smart
129 N.W. Fourth Street, #240
Corvallis, OR 97330
(800) 622-SMART (76278) or (503) 754-2746
pvs@neu.edu
http://www.oclc.org/VoteSmart/
Provides voting records on a variety of issues for most members of Congress, based on information gathered by a national network of volunteers. Also offers analysis from across the political spectrum on voting records and patterns.

Republican National Committee
310 1st Street, S.E.
Washington, DC 20003
(202) 863-8500
http://www.rnc.org/
Offers information on the Republican Party and national races. Can also provide information for local affiliate offices.

20/20 Vision
1828 Jefferson Place, N.W.
Washington, DC 20036
(202) 833-2020
Fax (202) 833-5307
vision@igc.apc.org
One of the most respected and effective national grassroots lobbying organizations. Provides subscribers with background information and suggestions for letter-writing action on national legislation relating to environmental and peace issues. Monthly mailings. Membership costs $20 a year.

United States Government
The following are the general addresses at which you can reach the president and vice president, your representatives, and your senators. A congressional directory, listing members' contact information, committee assignments, staff lists, general information about the U.S. Congress, and how to contact other government offices, is available from the Superintendent of Documents at the U.S. Government Printing Office.

The President of the United States
The White House
1600 Pennsylvania Avenue
Washington, DC 20500
(202) 456-1414 (White House switchboard)

(Your Senator)
United States Senate
Washington, DC 20510
(202) 224-3121 (Capitol switchboard)

(Your Representative in Congress)
U.S. House of Representatives
Washington, DC 20515
(202) 224-3121 (Capitol switchboard)

U.S. Government Printing Office
P. O. Box 371954
Pittsburgh, PA 15250-7954
(202) 512-1800

Publications

Almanac of American Politics by Michael Barone and Grant Ujifusa with Richard E. Cohen, eds., published annually by National Journal.
Offers contact information, biographies, and other data on members of Congress and other offices in the U.S. government.

On the Internet

Act Now
http://way.net/actnow.html
Links to e-mail directories for members of Congress and the executive branch, plus the ability to send your message directly from this site if you have a form-capable browser.

Capitol Web
http://www.policy.net/capweb
Information about the U.S. government and the city it is in. In-

formation on members of Congress, committees, and state government data. Links to campaign sites, government sites, and the Library of Congress.

Library of Congress
http://lcweb.loc.gov/homepage/lchp.html
Online resources, including documents and information on state and national governments and access to some government documents.

Thomas: Legislative Information on the Internet
http://thomas.loc.gov
"In the spirit of Thomas Jefferson, a service of the U.S. Congress through its Library" offering texts of current legislation, indexed text of the Congressional Record, information on how laws are made, and links to related sites.

Toby Scott's Political Gopher
gopher://toby.scott.nwu.edu
Offers biographical and professional information on current members of Congress, plus some information on state governments.

U.S. House of Representatives
http://www.house.gov

U.S. Senate
http://www.senate.gov

White House
http://www.whitehouse.gov

HUMAN RIGHTS

Amnesty International U.S.A.
1118 22nd Street, N.W.
Washington, DC 20037

(202) 775-5161
Fax (202) 775-5992
http://organic.com/non.profits/amnesty/
http://www.amnesty.org/
A worldwide human rights organization working for the release of prisoners of conscience. Amnesty campaigns against torture and executions, and encourages political asylum for refugees. The National Student Program provides training materials for student chapters on high school and college campuses.

Cultural Survival
53-A Church Street
Cambridge, MA 02138
(617) 441-5400
Fax (617) 441-5417
csinc@cs.org
http://www.cs.org/
Research center and advocacy group for the rights and needs of indigenous peoples around the world. Backs academic studies and supports programs in the United States and abroad that assist indigenous people in retaining their culture and environment while also making a living.

Human Rights Resource Center, Inc.
615 B Street
San Rafael, CA 94901
(415) 453-0404
Fax (415) 453-1026
Maintains an informational database on a variety of human rights issues and provides clients with a bimonthly newsletter on national human rights issues.

Human Rights Watch
485 Fifth Avenue
New York, NY 10017
(212) 972-8400
Fax (212) 972-0905
hrwnyc@hrw.org

gopher://gopher.humanrights.org:5000
Robert Kinzey, Publications Director
A human rights advocacy group using urgent action letter-writing and phone campaigns to put pressure on governments committing human rights abuses. The Publications Department offers reports and other materials on individual cases, trouble spots, and related issues such as censorship and arms control.

International League for Human Rights
432 Park Avenue South, 11th Floor
New York, NY 10016
(212) 684-1221
Fax (212)684-1696
ilhr@undp.org
ILHR focuses its efforts on The Children of War project, the Religious Freedom Project, the Eastern European Gender Discrimination project, and the Human Rights and Business project. Students can join the ILHR affiliate network of grassroots human rights advocacy groups to exchange information, strategy, and insights, and to bring local human rights issues into international forums. Publications focus on global human rights issues, including specific information on women's and refugee rights.

On the Internet

Amnesty International On-Line
http://www.amnesty.org/
Information on current campaigns, links to Amnesty chapters in twenty countries, urgent action updates, and AI Country Reports detailing human rights abuses worldwide.

Human Rights Watch mailing list
Send mail to majordomo@igc.apc.org with body of message reading "subscribe hrw-news."

Human Rights Web
http://www.traveller.com/~hrweb/
A good place to start for access to human rights information from

a variety of international sources, including major human rights organizations, the U.S. State Department, and the United Nations. Offers a "getting started" primer for new human rights activists.

INTERNATIONAL

The International section is a sort of "catch-all," first for organizations abroad addressing a variety of issues, and also for domestic organizations whose primary focus is on foreign countries or which coordinates international programs.

Adam Institute for Democracy and Peace
P. O. Box 3353, Jerusalem Forest
Jerusalem 91033
Israel
(972 2) 752-933
Fax (972 2) 752-932
Ruth Ostrin
Creates educational programs for diverse groups of students on issues of human rights and democracy, and publishes a newsletter.

African-American Institute
833 United Nations Plaza
New York, NY 10017
(212) 949-5666
Fax (212) 682-6174
An institute whose mission is to foster development in Africa by strengthening human resources development, encouraging democratization, and expanding multiethnic relationships between Africans and Americans.

AFS International Intercultural Program, Inc.
313 East 43rd Street
New York, NY 10017
(212) 949-4242

American Field Service is one of the oldest organizations coordinating international high school student exchange programs for Americans wishing to study or live abroad and for those who wish to host international visitors.

Americans for Peace Now
27 West 20th Street, 9th Floor
New York, NY 10011
(212) 645-6262
Fax (212) 645-7355
The U.S. partner of Israel's Peace Now movement, supporting the Middle East peace process. Offers educational programs, grassroots activities, and meetings with decision makers and government officials.

Center for Global Education
Augsburg College
2211 Riverside Avenue
Minneapolis, MN 55454
(800) 299-8889
Fax (612) 230-1695
globaled@augsburg.edu
http://www.augsburg.edu/global/
Don Christensen
Offers semester-long and short-term (one to three weeks) study-abroad programs for students and young adults. Participants travel to developing countries where CGE has permanent field sites to study local issues by interacting with indigenous peoples.

Center for Teaching International Relations
University of Denver
Denver, CO 80208
(303) 871-3106
Fax (303) 871-2906
Peter Downing
Regional organization that maintains a resource center of materials on teaching international issues and a speakers bureau of Denver-area graduate students available to speak about international issues.

Housemans Peace Diary and World Peace Directory
5 Caledonian Road
London NI 9DX
United Kingdom
(44 171) 837 4473
Directory containing almost two thousand peace, environment, and human rights organizations in over 140 countries. It costs money, but the profits go toward worldwide movements for peace and social justice.

International Fellowship of Reconciliation (IFOR)
Spoorstraat 38
1815 BK Alkmaar
The Netherlands
(31 72) 123 014
Fax (31 72) 151 102
ifor@gn.apc.org
Like its U.S. counterpart, IFOR focuses on the power of nonviolence as a tool for social change. Advocates peace, an end to crimes against humanity, and solidarity with people struggling for human rights.

Kids Meeting Kids
380 Riverside Drive, Box 8H
New York, NY 10025
(212) 662-2327
Fax (212) 222-1416
A youth-run organization of young people, ages five to nineteen, from around the world working together on issues of peace and children's rights.

Legacy International
Route 4, Box 265
Bedford, VA 24523
(703) 297-5982
Fax (703) 297-1860
legacy@igc.apc.org
Mary Helmig
A camp in rural Virginia offering summer gatherings of young

people from around the world that address peace and environmental issues. Travel programs also available.

National Council for International Visitors
Meridian House
1623 Belmont Street, N.W.
Washington, DC 20009
(202) 842-1414; Fax (202) 289-4625
Encourages international exchange, particularly the welcoming of foreign guests to the United States. Offers instructional materials for people thinking of hosting an international visitor.

Peace Child International
The White House
Buntingford, Herts SG9 9AH
United Kingdom
(44 176) 327 4459
Fax (44 176) 327 4460
Sponsors conferences and productions of the youth-written musical play "Peace Child" to increase the voice of youth in world affairs. Publishes a newsletter and books for children, including a children's version of the 1992 Rio Summit agreements.

Sacred Earth Network
267 East Street
Petersham, MA 01366
(508) 724-3443
Fax (508) 724-3436
sacredearth@igc.org
Assists environmental activists in the former U.S.S.R. to network via computer, providing hardware and technical assistance.

Sister Cities International
120 South Payne Street
Alexandria, VA 22314
(703) 836-3535
Organizes international municipal twinning programs and publishes *Your City and the World: A Sister City Handbook,* which gives or-

ganizing suggestions and guidelines for establishing formal ties with a town or city overseas.

United Nations Association of the U.S.A. (UNA/USA)
1010 Vermont Avenue, N.W., Suite 904
Washington, DC 20005
(202) 347-5004
Focuses on education and advocacy, teaching American citizens about the work of the United Nations and encouraging their involvement in U.N. affairs. Chapters sponsor "United Nations Day" each year.

United Nations Publications
Two United Nations Plaza, DC2-853
New York, NY 10017
(800) 253-9646 or (212) 963-8298
Fax (212) 963-3489
Christopher Woodthorpe, Sales Officer
A source for global news and research on fields of U.N. interest—including environment, development, and other U.N. agency projects—and how U.N. agencies are addressing these issues worldwide. Publications available include academic reports, periodicals, and educational resources.

Witness for Peace
2201 P Street, N.W., Room 109
Washington, DC 20037
(202) 797-1160
Fax (202)797-1164
"Faith-based" movement dedicated to changing U.S. political and economic policies toward Central America. Sends volunteers to three program sites for eighteen- to twenty-four-month terms to work in rural communities, assemble information, and work with the media.

World Federalist Association
418 Seventh Street, S.E.
Washington, DC 20003-2796

(202) 546-3950
Fax (202) 546-3749
Advocates "world federalism," a central, democratic, international authority based on the United Nations and capable of ensuring peace, economic progress, and environmental protection.

World Game Institute
3215 Race Street
Philadelphia, PA 19107-2597
(215) 387-3009
Administers Buckminster Fuller's "World Game," a day-long interactive project for students of all ages. Interacting on a basketball-court size map of the world, World Game participants learn about challenges of environmental degradation, resource allocation, and diplomacy by representing individual countries. An excellent, award-winning way to teach about international issues.

Publications

Your City and the World: A Sister City Handbook published by the Town Affiliation Association, Washington, D.C. A guide to the process of forming a sister-cities relationship with a community abroad.

On the Internet

United Nations Gopher
gopher://nywork1.undp.org:70/1
Current information on the United Nations and its agencies, background papers, and other documents.

ORGANIZING

Campus Outreach Opportunity League (COOL)
1511 K Street, N.W., Suite 307
Washington, DC 20005
(202) 637-7004
homeoffice@cool2serve.org
http://www.cool2serve.org/homeofc/home.html
A national organization helping college students start, maintain and expand service organizations on campus. Holds an annual conference that attracts more than 2,000 students from across the U.S. COOL staff visits college campuses, giving workshops on skills and issues relating to community service.

National Coalition Building Institute
1835 K Street, N.W., Suite 715
Washington, DC 20006
(202) 785-9400
Fax (202) 785-3385
ncbiinc@aol.com
Offers training for community organizers, particularly in the fields of conflict resolution and anti-prejudice activism. Curricula available.

National Youth Leadership Council
1910 West County Road
St. Paul, MN 55113-1337
(612) 631-3672
Works to develop leadership and service among young people through their involvement in environmental, international, and prejudice-reduction projects.

Political Research Associates
678 Massachusetts Avenue, Suite 205
Cambridge, MA 02139-3355
(617) 661-9313
A research institute on right-wing organizations and activities nationwide, including those on campuses. PRA has extensive written materials, bibliographies, speakers, and classes.

University Conversion Project
Center for Campus Organizing
P.O. Box 748
Cambridge, MA 02142
(617) 354-9363
ucp@igc.apc.org
Assists college students to organize on student rights and other progressive issues. Publications available.

Youth Action
1001 Yale Boulevard, S.E., Suite E
Albuquerque, NM 87106
(505) 248-1796
Fax (505) 248-1587
youthaction@igc.apc.org
Offers educational and "skills-training" resources to organizations that work with young people.

Youth Action Network
100 Adelaide Street West, Suite 906
Toronto, Ontario M5H 1S3
Canada
(416) 368-2277 or (800) 718-LINK
Fax (416) 368-8354
yan@web.apc.org
A youth-directed non-profit organization that works with student organizers to confront important issues of our time, from environment to human rights. Their Resource Action Centre is an information and referral service providing contact information to access resources, media, and government officials in Canada.

Youth Service America
National Service Affiliates Program
1101 15th Street, N.W., Suite 200
Washington, DC 20005-5002
(202) 296-2992
Fax (202) 296-4030
ysnl@aol.com
A strong advocate of youth service and "service learning"—inte-

grating service into the school curriculum. YSA offers service programs and networking information nationwide and program and funding guidelines, topical publications, access (including an online network) to a listing of media contacts and community service professionals across the country; it also lobbies on national-service legislation.

Publications

The Guide to Uncovering the Right on Campus by Dayla Massachi and Rich Cowan, eds. (University Conversion Project, 1994). The collected wisdom of progressive college organizers on dealing with conservative groups, and a list of helpful organizations. For more information, contact the University Conversion Project.

Making a Difference College Guide by Miriam Weinstein (Sage Press, 1994). A college guide for students who want to use their education to build a better world. Includes information on colleges offering programs in peace, environmental, women's, developmental, and educational studies.

National Youth Service: Answer the Call (A Resource Guide) (Youth Service America, 1994). Includes information on national service and service learning, with a fairly comprehensive list of organizations in YSA's four streams of service: K-12 service learning, college, youth corps, and national service programs.

150 Ways Teens Can Make a Difference by Marian Salzman and Teresa Reisgies (Peterson's Guides, 1991). A handbook for volunteer action on various issues. Includes the names, addresses, and telephone numbers of hundreds of organizations looking for teenage volunteers.

Rules for Radicals by Saul Alinsky (Vintage Books, 1971). Alinsky, one of the most prominent radical thinkers and activists in the early part of this century, offers counsel to radicals on how to effect social change. Contains chapters on organizing, communicating, and activist tactics. Alinsky's *Reveille for Radicals* offers more of his political philosophy and radical organizing.

WhoCares A quarterly magazine for young adults who are committed to volunteering and activism. WhoCares offers nonpartisan coverage of service-related issues and profiles of successful activists and crucial issues, and advocates innovative ways of fixing old problems. Available on the Web at http://www.whocares.org/, along with their own resource directory and information on upcoming events in activism.

Youth Action Forum, published monthly by the Youth Action Network. A newsletter offering organizing guidelines, networking information, and stories from successful student organizers around the world.

On the Internet

Campus Activists' NETwork (CANET)
canet-info@pencil.cs.missouri.edu
CANET sponsors a series of mailing lists on progressive topics such as economic conversion, combatting conservatives on campus, anti-racism, and educational rights.

National Service Learning Clearinghouse
gopher://nicsl.coled.umn.edu/
Part of a three-year federal grant from the Corporation for National Service, the National Information Center gopher provides access to online searching of resources, programs, and organizations in the service learning field.

PEACE AND CONFLICT RESOLUTION

Campaign for Peace and Democracy
P. O. Box 1640, Cathedral Station
New York, NY 10025
(212) 666-5924
Fax (212) 668-5892
camppeacedem@igc.apc.org
Organizes activists in the peace movement and environmentalists, trade unionists, feminists, and gay and minority rights activists to bring about social change. Coordinates conferences, rallies, letter-

writing campaigns, and protests to help build support for movements throughout the world that challenge oppressive institutions and promote popular power.

Center for Defense Information (CDI)
1500 Massachusetts Avenue, N.W.
Washington, DC 20005
(202) 862-0700
Fax (202) 864-0708
Jeffrey Mason, Research Librarian
Originally founded as an independent monitor of the military, today the CDI is the foremost research organization in the country analyzing military spending, policies, and weapons systems. CDI makes its military analyses available to Congress, the media, and the public through a variety of services and publications.

Coalition to Stop Gun Violence
100 Maryland Avenue, N.E.
Washington, DC 20002
(202) 544-7190
Fax (202) 544-7213
Lobbies Congress to ban the import, manufacture, sale, and use of handguns and assault weapons by the general public.

Conflict Resolution Center International, Inc.
2205 East Carson Street
Pittsburgh, PA 15203-2107
(412) 481-5559
Fax (412) 481-5601
crcii@igc.apc.org
Offers resources for conflict resolution within communities, including a library of materials and information on mediators, arbitrators, and conflict resolution trainers who can help.

Conflict Resolution Unlimited
845 106th Avenue N.E., Suite 109
Bellevue, WA 98004
(800) 922-1988 or (206) 451-4015

Fax (206) 451-1477
cru@conflictnet.org
http://www.conflictnet.org/cru/
Provides peer mediation training programs and materials for elementary to high school students and faculty.

Council for a Liveable World
110 Maryland Avenue, N.E.
Washington, DC 20002
(202) 453-4100
Fax (202) 453-6297
Political action committee lobbying for arms control and supporting the campaigns of sympathetic members of Congress. Educational material available.

Fellowship of Reconciliation
P. O. Box 271
Nyack, NY 10960
(914) 358-4601
Fax (914) 358-4924
fornatl@igc.apc.org
http://www.nonviolence.org/~nvweb/for
An interfaith organization offering educational programs on peace and conflict resolution at a variety of levels, from community racial and economic justice to nuclear disarmament. FOR's Peacemaker Training Institute offers training programs across the country each year.

Program for Young Negotiators (PYN)
131 Mt. Auburn Street
Cambridge, MA 02138
(617) 492-7474
Fax (617) 492-1919
Phyllis Emigh, Co-Director
A resource center promoting the teaching of nonviolent methods for dealing with conflict. Offers middle school curricula for small group discussions on social and political issues and "how-to" information on addressing issues such as race relations, violence, and the death penalty. Newsletter.

Rural Southern Voice for Peace (RSVP)
1898 Hannah Branch Road
Burnsville, NC 28714
(704) 675-5933
Fax (704) 675-9335
David Grant, Director
Offers organizing assistance, networking, and training in the rural communities and small cities of the southern United States. RSVP programs are designed to focus on "our common humanity and . . . our environment" by resolving conflict through communication between opposing groups.

War Resisters League
339 Lafayette Street
New York, NY 10012
(212) 228-0450
Fax (212) 228-6193
A section of War Resisters International. WRL advocates Gandhian nonviolence as the method for creating a democratic society free of war, sexism, and human exploitation. Offers literature on peace and justice organizing.

Publications

Required reading for anyone who thinks and works seriously on issues of peace and justice are the works of this century's two foremost nonviolent activists, Mohandas (Mahatma) Gandhi and the Rev. Dr. Martin Luther King, Jr. There are more titles than can be listed here; check them out in your library.

The Chomsky Reader by Noam Chomsky (Pantheon Books, 1987). Essays and thoughts from one of the United States' foremost modern philosophers and theorists. Chomsky addresses questions of war and peace, global crises, and human intelligence and creativity. Also by Chomsky are *Necessary Illusions* (South End Press, 1989) and *Deterring Democracy* (Hill and Wang, 1991).

Getting to Yes: Negotiating Agreement Without Giving In by Roger Fisher (Houghton Mifflin, 1981; and Penguin Books, 1983). Designed for businesspeople, this thin book is a "how-to" guide to negotiating and conflict resolution based on the resources of the Harvard Negotiation Project.

Handbook for Nonviolent Action by the War Resisters League (Donnelly & Company, 1989). Offers extensive advice on nonviolent civil disobedience. Discusses goals and strategies as well as other things like legal help and bail money that nonviolent resisters sometimes have to deal with. Available from the War Resisters League.

The Peace Book by Bernard Benson (Bantam Books, 1982). Conveys the insanity of the international arms race in a nutshell, through the eyes of a child. More a work of art than a book, *The Peace Book* integrates vibrant, childlike drawings to convey a strong message about the simplicity of peace. Other Benson titles, including the environmental *Tashi,* are available outside the United States.

The Politics of Nonviolent Action by Gene Sharp (Sargent, 1973). A handbook of strategies for nonviolent protest, including noncooperation and nonviolent intervention.

On the Internet

ConflictNet
http://www.igc.apc.org/conflictnet/
Offers current information on conflict resolution, including facilitated topical discussions on critical issues in the field, current legislation, and conference and training activity.

PeaceNet
http://www.igc.apc.org/peacenet/
Offers issue analysis and resources within the broad field of "peace and justice," including international conflict, human rights, and anti-racism. PeaceNet offers other services available to members only; information on membership can be received via e-mail by sending a blank message to <peacenet-info@peacenet.apc.org>.

PEER COUNSELING

A Place to Talk
The Johns Hopkins University Counseling Center
Merryman Hall
3400 N. Charles Street
Baltimore, MD 21218
Clare King, Ph.D.
Offers a wide range of support for students who want to start a peer counseling program. The Johns Hopkins program conducts trainings and has copious resources and ideas on how to develop a successful program.

Peer Resources
4452 Houlihan Court
Victoria, British Columbia V8N 6C6
Canada
(604) 721-2209
Rey A. Carr
A clearinghouse offering extensive resources and training information for peer counseling programs.

Publications

Helping Ourselves: Organizing a Peer Support Centre (Authority of Minister of National Health and Welfare, 1988).Offers guidance for designing a peer counseling and support center on campus, including training resources for students.

Peer Counseling: Skills and Perspectives by Vincent D'Andrea and Peter Salovey (Science and Behavior Books, 1983). Basic techniques for training students and residential advisors to counsel their colleagues. Special chapters on counseling regarding issues of race, gender, and sexuality. Includes detailed accounts of skills, questions, and examples, information on listening skills, crisis counseling, ethnic peer counseling, and extensive references and curricula for further information.

Peer Counseling Starter Kit by Rey A. Carr and Gregory A. K. Saunders (Peer Resources, 1980). A peer counseling training manual that focuses on building a peer training program within your school.

Peer Power, Books One and Two by Judith A. Tindall, Ph.D. (Accelerated Development, 1989). *Peer Power One* presents the application of skills and awareness of peer helper skills. *Peer Power Two* helps peer counselors to learn more about themselves and others, and helps them apply the skills learned from *Peer Power One.*

SOCIAL AND ENVIRONMENTAL JUSTICE

Center for Immigration Rights, Inc.
48 St. Marks Place
New York, NY 10003
(212) 505-6890
Fax (212) 995-5876
Ursula Levelt, Director of Education
Defends immigration rights through congressional lobbying, community education, and workshop programs, a newsletter, and a hotline—(212) 505-6890, extension 129—and participates in coalitions that monitor immigration rights.

Center for Third World Organizing (CTWO)
1218 East 21st Street
Oakland, CA 94606
(510) 533-7583
Fax (510) 533-0919
ctwo@igc.apc.org
Offers organizer training and leadership development programs in communities of color and organizes direct action and public education campaigns on issues affecting communities of color. Also publishes a bimonthly magazine documenting current actions and issues in Third World communities.

Environmental Action
6930 Carroll Avenue, Suite 600
Takoma Park, MD 20912

(301) 891-1100
Fax (301) 891-2218
National political lobbying and education organization working to unite environmental and social justice concerns through reform of government policy.

Habitat for Humanity International
Campus Chapters Department
121 Habitat Street
Americus, GA 31709
(912) 924-6935
Fax (912) 928-4167
ccint@habitat.org
Works with poor communities to build homes for those in need. The Campus Chapters Department performs three main functions: participating in the construction of Habitat homes, educating communities about Habitat, and raising funds for the work of Habitat.

Indian Law Resource Center
601 E Street, S.E.
Washington, DC 20003
(202) 547-2800
Fax (202) 547-2803
Stephen Tullberg, Director
Provides legal defense to Native American nations and tribes on issues of human rights, environmental rights, rights to self-government, and the protection of land and cultures. Can also provide information on past legal cases and referrals to individuals needing legal defense.

National Student Campaign Against Hunger and Homelessness
29 Temple Street
Boston, MA 02111
(800) NO-HUNGR (664-8647)
Fax (617) 292-8057
Part of the Fund for Public Interest Research, NSCAHH coordinates campaigns and advises student organizers throughout the United States on how to organize around issues of hunger and homelessness.

New York City Environmental Justice Alliance
271 West 125th Street, Suite 303
New York, NY 10027
(212) 866-4120
Fax (212) 866-4511
nyceja@undp.org
Michelle DePass, Director
An alliance linking grassroots organizations concerned with the right of communities of color and low-income communities to a clean and safe environment. Supports organizations in New York City by providing technical assistance and resources to communities of color and organizes a city-wide transportation and environmental justice campaign.

Project Vote
739 8th Street, S.E., Suite 202
Washington, DC 20003
(202) 546-3492
Fax (202) 546-2483
A non-profit, nonpartisan organization that registers low-income and minority citizens to vote.

Refugee Voices
3041 4th Street, N.E.
Washington, DC 20017-1102
(202) 832-0020
Fax (202) 832-5616
refvoices@igc.apc.org
http://www.crosslink.net/~rvi
Promotes public awareness and understanding of refugees in the United States and encourages citizens to get involved in refugee assistance in their own communities. Offers job skills training and references for refugees across the country.

Seventh Generation Fund
P. O. Box 4569
Arcata, CA 95518
(707) 825-7640

Fax (707) 825-7639
The only Native American advocacy and grant-making organization of its kind, the Seventh Generation Fund offers small grants, technical assistance, leadership training, and administrative support to selected grassroots Native American advocacy programs and organizations. Advocates Native American autonomy and self-reliance.

Southern Organizing Committee for Economic and Social Justice (SOC)
P. O. Box 10518
Atlanta, GA 30310
(404) 755-2855
Fax (404) 755-0575
socejp@igc.apc.org
Connie Tucker, Executive Director
A direct action group working toward economic, social, and environmental justice. Distributes information about issues and helps organize direct action initiatives in the South. Students can call for information packets and activist tips and strategies.

Southwest Network for Environmental and Economic Justice (SNEEJ)
P. O. Box 7399
Albuquerque, NM 87194
(505) 292-0476
Fax (505) 242-5609
sneej@igc.org
A coalition of grassroots organizations including Native, labor, and student groups in the southwestern and western United States and Mexico confronting issues of environmental and economic justice. Programs include youth leadership and development, border justice, and environmental justice issues.

On the Internet

HandsNet
hninfo@handsnet.org
An online service connecting members to thousands of human-service organizations across the United States, particularly on is-

sues of poverty, economic development, and substance abuse. Provides venues for discussion and coordination of projects via e-mail. For "off-line" information, write 20195 Stevens Creek Boulevard, Suite 120, Cupertino, CA 95014, or call (408) 257-4500.

LaborNet
http://www.igc.apc.org/labornet/

YOUTH RIGHTS

American Bar Association
Special Committee on Youth Education for Citizenship
541 N. Fairbanks Court
Chicago, IL 60611-3314
(312) 988-5735
Fax (312) 988-5032
pnessel@attmail.com
http://www.abanet.org/publiced
Paula Nessel, Project Coordinator
Publishes *Update on Law-Related Education,* a magazine addressing legal issues affecting students. Offers free referrals to *pro bono* legal defense across the United States; the special referral number is (312) 988-5522. Provides updates on Supreme Court cases involving civil rights, as well as information on constitutional law, jury trials, first amendment cases, and environmental law.

Child Welfare League of America
440 First Street, N.W., Suite 310
Washington, DC 20001-2085
(202) 638-2952
Fax (202) 638-4004
Susan J. Brite, Director of Publications
An association dedicated to the welfare and well-being of children. Its Publication Department offers videos, books, and magazines on topics ranging from adoption and proper foster care to adolescent pregnancies.

Children Now
Communications Department
926 J Street, Suite 1400
Sacramento, CA 95814
(916) 441-2444
Fax (916) 441-2463
cnow@tweety.sna.com
http://www.dnai.com/~children
An advocacy organization for children focusing on policy development, mass communications, and community outreach programs. Offers publications and action guides about the media and kids, kids and guns, and "how to help America's children," as well as policy reports documenting the status of children's legislation nationally and locally.

Children's Defense Fund
25 E Street, N.W.
Washington, DC 20001
(202) 628-8787
cdf@tmn.com
http://www.tmn.com/cdf/index.html
A prominent advocacy group for children in America, particularly the poor and minorities. Lobbies and educates to encourage "preventive investment" in the health, education, and welfare of young people. Offers extensive publications and educational materials.

Constitutional Rights Foundation
601 S. Kingsley Drive
Los Angeles, CA 90005
(213) 487-5590
Fax (213) 386-0459
crfcitizen@aol.com
Kathleen Kirby, Education Director
National "Community Action" outreach programs offer education on legal issues. CRF can also put you in touch with legal support and other information.

End Violence Against the Next Generation, Inc. (EVAN-G)
977 Keeler Avenue
Berkeley, CA 94708-1498
(510) 527-0454
A society of physicians and educators working to end domestic violence in homes and in schools, especially against children. Newsletter.

National Association of Independent Colleges and Universities
1025 Connecticut Avenue, N.W., Suite 700
Washington, DC 20036-5405
(202) 785-8866
Fax (202) 835-0003
mike@naicu.edu
http://student-aid.nche.edu/
Mike Combs
An association of private colleges in the United States, NAICU has useful resources for campus organizing against cuts in student aid.

National Crime Prevention Council
1700 K Street, N.W., Second Floor
Washington, DC 20006-3817
(202) 466-6272
Fax (202) 296-1356
Nonpartisan educational organization seeking to make communities safer for children. Publications available.

National Clearinghouse on Child Abuse and Neglect Information
P. O. Box 1182
Washington, DC 20013-1182
(800) FYI-3366 or (703) 385-7565
Fax (703) 385-3206
A resource for professionals and others interested in the prevention, identification, and treatment of child abuse and neglect. Collects, stores, organizes, and disseminates information on the issue.

National Child Rights Alliance
Box 61125
Durham, NC 27705

(919) 682-5509 or (914) 647-3670
jimsenter@delphi.com,
72673.2030@CompuServe.com
Jim Senter or Jeanne Lenzer
Network of students and youth rights activists across the United States that sponsors annual meetings to discuss a variety of issues affecting young people around the world—from child abuse and AIDS to war and poverty.

Publications

The Child Abuse Handbook is published annually by the Frontenac County Board of Education (Kingston, Ontario, Canada). This handbook is designed to provide concise information to help education staff respond to suspected child abuse and to disclosures by the victims. A short version of the book is available online at http://www.fcbe.edu.on.ca/www/welcome.html.

On the Internet

Alliance to Save Student Aid
http://student-aid.niche.edu/
Part of a national campaign to fight federal cuts of financial aid programs.

National Data Archive on Child Abuse and Neglect
gopher://ndacan.cornell.edu/
Archive of current data on child abuse and neglect provided by the Family Life Development Center at Cornell University.

Index

About the Editor

John W. Bartlett, 24, is a 1995 graduate of Brown University and an alumnus of the Raoul Wallenberg Scholarship program at the Hebrew University in Jerusalem.

In 1991, he was one of four students honored at the White House for their achievements in publicizing Soviet brutality in the Baltic States; a video on the subject, created from smuggled footage by the students, was shown at more than two dozen colleges across the United States and Canada. The following year, he worked with the East Timor Action Network of Rhode Island, which spearheaded a successful nation-wide campaign to cut U.S. military training aid to Indonesia.

In the summer of 1992, John organized a five-city student exchange tour in Bulgaria for Peace Child International. He remains active in a variety of environmental and human rights campaigns around the world. This is his first book.

John can be reached by mail care of Henry Holt and Company and by e-mail at jwb@igc.org.